Adrian Gramps
The Fiction of Occasion in Hellenistic and Roman Poetry

Trends in Classics –
Supplementary Volumes

Edited by
Franco Montanari and Antonios Rengakos

Associate Editors
Stavros Frangoulidis · Fausto Montana · Lara Pagani
Serena Perrone · Evina Sistakou · Christos Tsagalis

Scientific Committee
Alberto Bernabé · Margarethe Billerbeck
Claude Calame · Jonas Grethlein · Philip R. Hardie
Stephen J. Harrison · Stephen Hinds · Richard Hunter
Christina Kraus · Giuseppe Mastromarco
Gregory Nagy · Theodore D. Papanghelis
Giusto Picone · Alessandro Schiesaro
Tim Whitmarsh · Bernhard Zimmermann

Volume 118

Adrian Gramps

The Fiction of Occasion in Hellenistic and Roman Poetry

DE GRUYTER

ISBN 978-3-11-127064-7
e-ISBN (PDF) 978-3-11-073160-6
e-ISBN (EPUB) 978-3-11-073164-4
ISSN 1868-4785

Library of Congress Control Number: 2021936228

Bibliographic information published by the Deutsche Nationalbibliothek
The Deutsche Nationalbibliothek lists this publication in the Deutsche Nationalbibliografie;
detailed bibliographic data are available on the Internet at http://dnb.dnb.de.

© 2023 Walter de Gruyter GmbH, Berlin/Boston
This volume is text- and page-identical with the hardback published in 2021.
Editorial Office: Alessia Ferreccio and Katerina Zianna
Logo: Christopher Schneider, Laufen
Printing and binding: CPI books GmbH, Leck

www.degruyter.com

Foreword

The aim of this book is to devise a method for approaching the problem of presence in Hellenistic and Roman poetry. The problem of presence, as defined here, is the problem of the availability or accessibility to the reader of the fictional worlds disclosed by poetry. Responding to the problem of presence, it is argued, is an integral part of the experience of reading Hellenistic and Roman poetry, and theorising this problem is essential if we are to approach an understanding of the experience of poetic reading (and yet the act of theorising cannot ultimately be dissociated from the poetic experience itself). 'The fiction of occasion' is proposed as a new conceptual tool for approaching the problem of presence in a more immediate and positive way than is possible with the methods and frameworks currently prevalent in the field. Its purpose is to elucidate how poetry can produce aesthetic effects of presence without relying on narrativity.

The introduction offers an exposition *in medias res* of the problem of presence by way of Catullus *c.* 4, which features a boat inexplicably endowed with the power of speech and delivering a discourse in a radically underdetermined context. This prompts the question of how a reader can possibly imagine herself in relation to this anomalous act of speech, which in turn serves as a preface to the problem of presence.

Chapter 1, 'Rethinking mimetic poetry and Callimachus' *Hymn to Apollo*', interrogates the theory of 'mimetic poetry' as applied to its central exemplar, Callimachus' *Hymn to Apollo*. This serves as an occasion to survey the current status of the problem of presence in the study of Hellenistic and Roman poetry and to thereby chart the conceptual territory which the idea of the fiction of occasion is meant to occupy. The discussion concludes by advocating a move away from certain narratological precepts as well as from the dichotomy of orality and literacy, and a turn towards a new appreciation of the structural role of epiphany in this and similar poems.

Chapter 2, 'Figuring occasion in Propertius 4.6 and Bion's *Adonis*', takes the two poems named in its title as examples of how the fiction of occasion works through sustained formal devices, or 'figures'. Propertius 4.6 uses the figure of the path of song to guide the reader through the experience of mentally surveying the monumental space of the bay of Actium. Bion's *Lament for Adonis*, on the other hand, employs refrain-like repetitions and plaintive apostrophes to coax the reader into a kind of sympathetic communion with the bereaved Aphrodite at the moment of her lover Adonis' death.

Chapter 3, 'Occasion and presence in Horace, *Odes* I', takes a focussed look at a single poet, using poems 9, 12, and 20 of the first book of *Odes* to elucidate

Horace's specifically lyric approach to the fiction of occasion. The key argument here is that Horace finds a way to articulate the problem of presence dialectically, so that competing modes of presence can be felt within the frame of a single poem.

Chapter 4, 'Occasioning the choral in Horace, *Odes* IV', turns from the first to the last book of Horatian lyric, which is preoccupied at a number of key junctures with the idea of choral song or other forms of collective voicing. This chapter feeds this often-noted peculiarity of the final book of *Odes* directly into the fiction of occasion, arguing through readings of odes 1, 2, 5, 6, and 15 that what these poems are really concerned with is the fantasy of the collective voice as a privileged node of lyric presence.

Finally, the conclusion offers a recap of some of the central goals which unify each of the discussions, followed by a prospectus of possible futures to which the ideas pursued in this book may potentially lead.

Contents

Foreword —— V
Introduction —— IX

1	**Rethinking Mimetic Poetry and Callimachus'** *Hymn to Apollo* —— **1**	
1.1	Introduction —— 1	
1.2	The *Hymn to Apollo* and 'mimetic poetry' —— 2	
1.3	Discourse and events —— 5	
1.4	The space of inclusion —— 8	
1.5	*Mimesis* and *diegesis*: from modes of presentation to experiential frames —— 13	
1.6	Fictionality and epiphany —— 20	
1.7	*Mimesis* and the oral —— 24	
1.8	The 'epiphanic effect' and the fiction of occasion —— 28	
1.9	Conclusion —— 32	
2	**Figuring Occasion in Propertius 4.6 and Bion's** *Adonis* —— **35**	
2.1	Introduction —— 35	
2.2	The path of song in Propertius 4.6 —— 36	
2.3	Leading songs to Caesar —— 41	
2.4	Actium as monumental space —— 45	
2.5	*Inauguratio* and Augustus —— 49	
2.6	The path of Apollo —— 53	
2.7	Recall and refrain in Bion's *Lament for Adonis* —— 57	
2.8	Measureless measures: the Adonis-cry and refrain —— 58	
2.9	Sensing Adonis, (ad)dressing Aphrodite —— 64	
2.10	Bion *bucolicus* and resonant space —— 71	
2.11	Conclusion —— 74	
3	**Occasion and Presence in Horace,** *Odes* **I —— 76**	
3.1	Introduction —— 76	
3.2	*c.* 1.20: The merry echo —— 78	
3.3	Seeing Soracte: *c.* 1.9 —— 85	
3.4	The Soracte ode as dramatic monologue —— 91	
3.5	Setting limits —— 94	
3.6	The power of now —— 99	
3.7	Situation and response —— 104	
3.8	*c.* 1.12: Following Orpheus —— 108	

4	**Occasioning the Choral in Horace, *Odes* IV** —— 125
4.1	Introduction —— 125
4.2	Fantasising the choral —— 129
4.3	Choral presence and the future tense —— 134
4.4	Rhythm and repetition: *c.* 4.1 —— 142
4.5	*c.* 4.5: Return and recognition —— 162
4.6	*c.* 4.2: Imitation and identification —— 168
4.7	The name of Icarus —— 175

5	**Conclusion** —— 187

Bibliography —— 193
Index Rerum et Nominum —— 203
Index Locorum —— 205

Introduction

One of Catullus' best-known poems (*Carmen* 4) begins like this:

> Phaselus ille, quem uidetis, hospites,
> ait fuisse nauium celerrimus...
>
> That boat which you are looking at, strangers, says that it was once the fastest of ships...

Three elements leap out at the reader at once: there is a boat endowed with the power of speech, a group of 'strangers' (or 'guests') who are viewing the boat, and someone who addresses the strangers, delivering the 'speech' of the boat through indirect discourse. The rest of the poem comprises an account of the boat's 'biography', from its origin as a tree through its many nautical adventures and up to its final resting place, the shore of the 'limpid lake' (*limpidum lacum*, 24) at which the strangers now find it moored.

The point in space occupied by the docked vessel has a special status in this poem: it is not only the place where the boat happens to be, but a shared space in which the strangers' act of viewing, the boat's act of 'speaking' (whatever we take this to mean), and the address to the strangers converge. The narrative which emerges out of the reported speech of the boat employs this shared space as both starting point and endpoint, concluding as it does with the account that the boat made its way here to the lake-shore at the end of its long travels to dedicate itself to Castor and Pollux (22–27). The physical presence of the boat in the here and now of its moorage is thus both the initial prompt which gives rise to the narrative and the setting of its final act.

Catullus conjures up this presence through deixis, one of the most basic and most powerful tools of language.[1] The deictic pronoun *ille* ('that', 1) works like a pointed finger gesturing linguistically towards the boat, a gesture which implies a shared field of vision between speaker and addressee. Deixis returns to centre the field of vision towards the end of the poem with the pronoun *hunc* ('this', 24), which informs us that the lake where the boat made its final stop is the same one which the strangers see now in front of them. This final *hunc* marks the point at which the narrated past of the boat's youthful adventures comes full circle to

---

[1] The best general introduction to deixis is Levinson 1983: 54–96. For the cognitive-linguistic 'deictic shift theory', see Galbraith 1995 and Stockwell 2002: 41–57. See also the essays collected in the special 2004 edition of *Arethusa* (37.3), titled 'The poetics of deixis in Alcman, Pindar, and other lyric'.

https://doi.org/10.1515/9783110731606-204

meet the lived present of the strangers' viewing of it on the lake-shore. This second deictic signal thus bespeaks not only a shared visual field but the shared knowledge of the boat's history which our storyteller imparts to the strangers in a gesture of hospitality.

Up to a certain point, it is unproblematic to claim that the experience of the strangers named in the first line of this poem resembles our experience as its readers. We begin the poem ignorant of the boat's past journeys, and we learn about them at the same time and in the same way as the strangers do. But while we share in their journey from ignorance to knowledge, it is less easy to claim that we share in the field of vision which they purportedly share with the storyteller. The strangers are given an opportunity which is not extended to us, the opportunity to refer the story they have just heard back to a physical presence which lies before them. Feeney remarks that 'the mimetically vivid invitation to "see" the boat which is being pointed out simultaneously reminds readers that we cannot see it even as it teases us to imagine that we can.'[2] Following on this suggestion, we could say that behind this overt invitation to 'see' the boat lies a tacit invitation, issued directly to the reader, to produce a substitute for the boat's missing presence.[3]

One way to produce substitute presences is through narrative. Current theories of narrative advance the view that readers understand narratives, whether factual or fictional, by situating themselves imaginatively within the world of the story.[4] This account privileges the role of the body and embodied cognition in the experience of narrative worlds. In order to make sense of a story, this account holds, we have to be there with the characters, navigating their environment and inhabiting their world as if it were our own, using many of the same cognitive tools we use when undergoing similar experiences in the real world.

Readers of Catullus' poem find such an opportunity in the reported story of the boat. Its anthropomorphic characterisation permits us to understand the history of this object in accordance with the patterns of human experience. Rather than being built by human hands to be the instrument of human endeavours, this boat was born and went on adventures of its own, with each of its destinations representing a milestone in an ongoing life story. Making the boat relatable in this way grants it a kind of presence to the reader which could be said to compensate for the absence of the bodily nearness enjoyed by the *hospites*. Before being brought to life as a humanlike figure, the boat is just a 'that' (*ille*) whose very

---

[2] Feeney 2012: 31–32.
[3] Davis 2002: 118 discusses how the reader is 'included' in the *hospites*' act of viewing.
[4] See e.g. Caracciolo 2011, Galbraith 1995, Fludernik 1996.

'thatness' is utterly unreal to the reader, unable as she is to relate even to the perspective of someone for whom the boat is a 'that'. Once transformed into the hero of its own story, however, the boat becomes narratively *knowable* irrespective of its situation within (or in relation to) the factual world. The bond of shared knowledge and experience we form with the boat while reading its story substitutes for the direct visual contact with which the poem 'teases' us.

This even modifies the status of the deictic pronoun *hunc* (24) which indicates the lake that serves as the backdrop for the strangers' encounter with the boat. Outside of the context of the story, the deixis here only foregrounds the epistemic gap between the audience of *hospites* and the readers of the poem, a gap which has long exercised scholars concerned to pinpoint Catullus' lake on a map.[5] Within the story, however, the 'here' of the lake-shore represents the last stop in the boat's lifetime of sea-voyages, and consequently the meeting point between the past time of the narrative and the present of its telling. The sequential temporality fundamental to narrative discourse renders the otherwise empty shifters *ille* and *hunc*, 'that there' and 'this here', pregnant with meaning.

Immediately following the reference to 'this lake' is another form of the same deictic pronoun, *haec*, which refers by way of conclusion to the events just related in the story:

> sed **haec** prius fuere: nunc recondita   25
> senet quiete seque dedicat tibi,
> gemelle Castor et gemelle Castoris.

> But **this** was before: now he grows old in peaceful seclusion and dedicates himself to you, twin Castor and Castor's twin.

Referring to the events of the story as 'this' (lit. 'these things') implies that they are present to the addressee just as referring to 'this lake' implies the presence of a lake, but in the case of *haec*, there is no longer any epistemic gap dividing the reader from the *hospites*; both parties become acquainted with the boat's past life only through the medium of the story. It was noted above that, for the *hospites*, the conjunction of *hunc* and *haec* marks the point at which the past reality of the story comes full circle to meet the present reality of their act of viewing the boat. For the reader, however, the 'thisness' of the story and of the boat itself are of the same order; both are presences made present by the poem, experienced in the act of reading.

---

5 See e.g. Putnam 1962.

The term *enargeia* is sometimes used to describe the faculty of language to make absent things present.[6] In ancient rhetorical theory, this was typically considered an element of style essential for crafting an engaging story or a vivid description. Modern narrative theory, as we have seen, elevates *enargeia* to a fundamental principle of narrative comprehension; summoning things into what Elaine Scarry calls 'imaginary vivacity' is not just something that skilled writers know how to do well, rather it is something we have to do in order to make sense of narratives.[7] What is it that is brought into imaginary vivacity, into presence, in Catullus *c.* 4? The obvious answer is: the boat, as a preternaturally animated object. But where exactly does this calling into presence happen?

I suggested above a conceptual link between the boat's animation and its possession of narrative agency. Imagining the boat as humanlike is the enabling conceit which makes possible its weaving into story. But the most conspicuous feature of the boat's animacy is its power of speech, its capacity not only to be the hero of a story but to tell that story in its own words. This consideration adds another dimension to the question of presence raised above. What is made present by the poem — what is revealed to the eyes of the *hospites* and to the imagination of the reader — is not only the content of the story delivered by the boat, but also the phenomenon of the boat's speech itself. The speech of the boat is announced in v. 2 as if in answer to an implicit question posed by the strangers' act of viewing. The *content* of the boat's speech satisfies their questioning gaze by providing them (and us) with an origin story or aetiological myth, but the speech *itself* satisfies a different desire, the desire to be in the auditory (as well as the visual) presence of the boat.

Feeney emphasises how many layers of mediation separate us as readers from the direct perceptual experience of the boat's speech, noting, '[the] poem does not straightforwardly represent a boat, nor does it represent a boat speaking [...] it represents the speaker presenting the boat speaking, i.e. presenting the self-presentation of the boat.'[8] This is apt if we are concerned above all with the epistemic dimension of storytelling; each additional layer of representation separates us one step further from the ultimate 'truth' which the story purports to relate. If taken too far, however, this approach risks misrecognising the poem as a (quasi-)historical document, a collection of true or false facts about a real or fictional boat.

---

6 Webb 2016: 87–106.
7 Scarry 1999: 3–9.
8 Feeney 2012: 31–32.

As a factual statement, the fiction of the boat's voice has no value whatsoever; but for the poem, this fiction is foundational. If we were 'really there' with the *hospites* viewing the boat, we would immediately discover the truth: the boat cannot of course 'really' speak. While the content of the story can be rightly thought of as mediated through multiple channels, the act of speech performed by the boat is not mediated at all; it exists only for the poem and only within the poem. Only by means of the poem's language, through its texture, form, and style, can we hope to enjoy the aural presence of the boat's voice. The boat's speech, moreover, provides direct evidence of the lifelikeness to which its biography only indirectly attests. We might say, then, that the poem does not make the boat speak just so that it can tell its story; equally, it gives it a story to tell so that we can hear it speak.

My initial argument here is that the fiction of the boat's act of speech takes priority over the narrative as a device for making absent things present. Unlike the fiction of our being able to 'see' the boat, which threatens to violate the boundaries of textual representation, the fiction of the boat as a speaking object is inextricably bound up with the linguistic nature of the text. We can take this further by saying that the fiction of the boat's speech is also the fiction of the production of the poem as a piece of language. The fiction of the boat as speaker grants the story determinacy in space and time; the fiction of the audience of *hospites* then makes this act of speaking into a particular event. As readers, I suggest, we are obliged as part of our experience of the poem to imagine ourselves in some way as participants in this localised event. But this event, crucially, is not just something represented by the poem and therefore separable from it; it includes within itself the originating event of the act of language which is the poem, in this case, the 'speech' of the boat. The event of the boat relaying its story through its spokesperson before the *hospites* is therefore what I propose to call the poem's *occasion*.

The term occasion has been used in the study of classical literature in a few different ways without ever graduating to the status of a technical term. Citroni uses the word in its most traditional sense, referring to an interpersonal situation or sociopolitical state of affairs which prompts the writing of a given poem.[9] 'Occasion' by this definition points to something more specific than 'historical context'; it also implies a communicative context in which the poem presents itself as participating, such as when Catullus or Horace addresses a poem to a named

---

9 Citroni 1995; 2009. The other common use of the word is as shorthand for 'occasion of performance'; significant publications using the term in this way are Harder 1992, Nagy 1994–5, Barchiesi 2009, Depew 2000, and Lowrie 2009a.

individual and presents this address itself as an act of social cohesion. In order to speak of the 'occasion' of Catullus *c.* 4 in this sense, we would have to consider the boat as an artefact with a history bound up with the genesis of the poem in which it appears. To this end we can try to piece together a historical narrative that fits the details of the boat's itinerary, supplies the identity of the boat's unspecified 'master' (*erum*, 19), and matches the 'limpid lake' to a point on a map.[10] In doing so, we can imbue the boat with a substantiality it did not have before, and thus partially compensate for its missing presence.

But no matter how detailed a picture we end up with, our reconstructed scenario must necessarily exclude the most important fact of the poem, the boat's power of speech.[11] In order to come into contact with the boat's historical reality, we have to persuade ourselves of the unreality of its voice, which we can do by suspending our disbelief and writing off its voicedness, its animacy, as a mere 'device'.[12] We might have come closer to standing in the presence of our hypothetical historical boat, but in the process we risk losing sight of that which engendered the desire for this presence in the first place. Any attempt to look beneath or behind the poem to find something underpinning it is also necessarily an engagement with the poem, and belongs no less to aesthetic experience.

'The poem is the cry of its occasion, | Part of the res itself and not about it', cries Wallace Stevens metapoetically.[13] 'Occasion' means: the time for something; something which needs time to be set aside for it, an event; or, the enabling circumstance of something. Talking of a poem as having an occasion thus grants it eventhood, the sense of being or belonging to a happening.[14] If we accept that this sense of eventhood or occasionality is a product of the poem and of reading, we ought to ask what there is in Catullus' poem that produces it. Leaving aside appeals to vague impressions of authenticity or sincerity — which only lead us back around to the role of the text in fostering those impressions — the best candidate, I would argue, is the poem's use of sense-perception.

The relative clause *quem uidetis*, 'which you are looking at', immediately follows the introduction of the boat itself into the text in the first line, as *phaselus ille*, 'that boat'. In terms of pragmatics, this relative clause can be thought of as

---

10 See e.g. the very different approaches of Putnam 1962; Williams 1968: 192–93; Courtney 1997; and Davis 2002.
11 I discuss the boat's power of speech in greater detail in Gramps forthcoming.
12 See Fitzgerald 1995: 107–8.
13 'An ordinary evening in New Haven', stanza XII (Stevens 2006: 414).
14 See further Gadamer 2013: 144–48.

an attempt to persuade the addressee that the boat is a relevant topic of discourse, meriting the attention of listeners.¹⁵ The viewing of the boat is thus made into the occasion of the act of speech which comprises the poem. From the perspective of the *hospites*, that is, the boat's story is told to them because they are already there with it at the lake-shore, looking at it and perhaps wondering about its past.

From the reader's perspective, the causality of looking and telling is reversed; for her, the boat comes into being only once the word *phaselus* is read, and she can only come to 'see' the boat after the text's powers of description have worked on her. The *hospites*, as spectators of the boat and audience of its story, mirror the reader and model for her the imaginative act of perception she is invited to perform, but they invert the logical order of the experience so that the perception comes first, prior to the mediation of language. Language as such is introduced into this world in the second line, with the fantastic event of the boat's animated testimony. Rather than language mediating visual perception (*enargeia*), visual perception is made into the background of ordinary experience against which an extraordinary event of language comes to pass. Identifying with the perspective of the *hospites* thus allows the reader to experience the speech of the boat as a dynamic presence, an event, which is disclosed to her by the poem.

My name for what happens between poem and reader to produce this effect is the fiction of occasion. The phrase is borrowed from Benjamin Acosta-Hughes, who uses it in passing (his topic is Callimachus' *Iambi*) to refer to the habit of framing poems with invented scenarioes.¹⁶ In my usage, the term 'fiction' is not meant to indicate feigning or falsehood, but rather a creative engagement of the imagination. It is also meant to suggest both a connexion with and a departure from 'fiction' considered as a category or property of narrative. The argument behind this is that poems like Catullus *c*. 4 produce effects which belong to the realm of fiction and fictionality, but which cannot be properly understood in terms of a dichotomy of truth and falsehood and equally cannot be considered as subfunctions of narrative discourse.

The aim of this book is to formulate and develop the concept of the fiction of occasion and explore its possibilities through readings of a small selection of poems written in Latin and Greek between the 3rd century BCE and the 1st century CE. The central texts for discussion are Callimachus, *Hymn to Apollo* (chapter 1); Bion, *Lament for Adonis* and Propertius 4.6 (chapter 2); and a series of poems from

---

15 On pragmatics and relevance, see Levinson 1983; Sperber and Wilson 1995; Walsh 2007: 13–37.
16 Acosta-Hughes 2002: 266.

books 1 and 4 of Horace's *Odes* (chapters 3 and 4). I selected these poems above all because of the problems they pose: each of them follows Catullus *c.* 4 in affecting to involve the reader intimately while also building a world which is manifestly not her own.[17]

This book aims to address this problem — the problem of involvement or presence — from two perspectives which may at first seem to conflict. The first perspective is informed by the scholarly discourse in the study of Hellenistic and Roman poetry, and takes its cue from the ongoing debate about 'performance' and the relationship between oral and written language, a debate which I will argue needs rethinking. Within this perspective, the problem of presence is a problem for literary theory, and bears directly on overtly academic questions such as genre and periodisation. But the experience of literature also belongs to literary theory, and the problem of presence is something we experience in the act of reading as well as an intellectual puzzle. Rather than try to draw an arbitrary line between literary theory and the experience of reading, I propose to use the fiction of occasion to address the problem of presence in a way that involves both of these perspectives equally.

This means that the 'reader' whom I invoke for the purposes of my argument is intended to stand in for a wide range of different actual readers belonging to different reading communities across time and space, for whom 'reading' certainly means different things. The most pressing of these differences is the gap between ancient and modern, between the contemporary reception of texts and their curation by philologists. Throughout this book I will be talking about texts in terms of the experience of reading, and I will not draw hard distinctions between ancient and modern experiences, or those of any other group.[18] This is not based on a conviction that the two can be reconciled under the banner of universal human experience, but rather on the recognition that they cannot be separated. Philology is a form of reading, and trying to see ancient texts through the eyes of ancient people is one of the tasks of philology. The best work in the field embraces the recursive nature of its practices rather than distancing itself from it.

The term 'presence' as I use it here is meant to keep this recursivity prominently in view. This usage derives from the work of Hans Gumbrecht, who argues that aesthetic experience cannot be reduced to a search for meaning, but is also

---

17 As McCarthy puts it in a related context, each of these poems as we read it appears as both 'for-us' and 'not-for-us' (McCarthy 2019: 4).
18 See Grethlein 2015 for ancient and modern perspectives on aesthetic experience.

driven by the desire to simply be in the presence of the things of the world.[19] Gumbrecht uses 'presence' to designate the bare materiality of the encounter with the aesthetic, which he sees as prior to and separable from 'meaning', the dimension of interpretation. These two dimensions of aesthetic experience, he argues, express themselves through 'presence effects' and 'meaning effects', which manifest themselves in an oscillation which itself produces aesthetic tension.[20]

When brought to bear on literature, this approach allows us to see a text for its surface as well as for its depths.[21] What we take away from reading a work of literature — worldly insight, social awareness, technical appreciation, emotional resonance, etc. — only accounts for part of what we do when we read; we also read in order to *be reading*, to be in contact with texts.[22] For Gumbrecht, philology is in service of what is fundamentally the same impulse, 'the desire to make the past present again by embodying it.'[23] This book is an attempt to re-evaluate its small corpus of Hellenistic and Roman poems in a way that leaves room for the working of presence effects, in the hope that this will allow them to be something more than receptacles of meaning which challenge readers to draw out their hidden contents.

The first chapter will offer an introductory discussion of Callimachus' *Hymn to Apollo*. Firstly I will make a case for rejecting the label of 'mimetic poetry' for this poem and, by extension, for other poems that are grouped under this heading. Next, I will challenge narratological approaches which attempt to solve the poem's enunciative ambiguities by attributing sections of text to various fictional speakers; I argue that the question we need to be asking is not 'who is speaking?' but rather 'what kind of experience are we presented with?' I will offer the following answer: the poem ties the *hic et nunc* of its performance to a 'space of inclusion' which is also the space in which an epiphany of Apollo is about to occur, and in this way the poem presents *itself* as an epiphanic experience.

Chapter 2 will expand on the claim that the fiction of occasion makes possible a spatial or spatialised experience which goes beyond the mimetic. In order to do this, I will look at two poems which bear a noticeable debt to the *Hymn to Apollo* and exhibit some of the same features: Propertius 4.6 and Bion's *Lament for Adonis*. The first section of this chapter will focus on Propertius 4.6 and how that

---

19 Gumbrecht 2004.
20 Gumbrecht 2004: 2, 104–11.
21 See Best and Marcus 2009 (with Purves 2016) on 'surface reading' as opposed to 'symptomatic reading'.
22 Cf. Fitzgerald 1995: 1–4 on 'aesthetic positionality' in Catullus, i.e. the aesthetics of the reader's positioning in relation to the text.
23 Gumbrecht 2003: 99.

poem uses the metaphor of the 'path of song' as an experiential schema to guide the reader through the poem. The next section will turn to Bion's *Lament for Adonis* and its employment of the verbal gestures of address and refrain to construct a resonant space of sympathetic communion with the mourning Aphrodite. Both of these poems will serve as examples of how poetic occasion takes its shape from poetic figures and from effects of rhythmic pacing and metre, a conclusion which allows us to cut through the dichotomy of text and performance space.

The third chapter will move on to Horace's *Odes* and will consider the problem of presence more directly than the previous two. Through a reading of *cc.* 1.9, 1.12, and 1.20, I will explore how Horace not only produces the fiction of occasion but also actively negotiates the occasionality of his poetry by way of the philosophical themes and ideas raised therein. In so doing, I argue, Horace works out a dialectic between two competing modes of poetic presence, the metaphysical and the material, in which the latter wins out over the former.

The final chapter is concerned with a more specific topic in Horace's *Odes*, namely the new predominance of the choral voice in the fourth and final book. Here, I will draw on Steven Connor's essay 'Choralities' to explore how Horace creates fantasy visions of choral song in poems 1, 2, 5, 6, and 15. In imagining the choral mode of poetry, I will argue, Horace takes the ideas of poetic presence and occasion to their furthest limits. This chapter is written so as to stand on the borderline between the current project, on the fiction of occasion, and future trajectories for the project which lead into new territories.

1 Rethinking Mimetic Poetry and Callimachus' *Hymn to Apollo*

1.1 Introduction

In this first chapter, I would like to take a detailed look at a single poem, Callimachus' *Hymn to Apollo*. This poem will serve as a useful starting point for the readings to follow, primarily due to its close association in the contemporary scholarly conversation with the category of 'mimetic poetry'.[1] The idea of the 'mimetic' or 'mimeticism' in poetry, which will be explored in depth below, was formulated in response to the same questions from which I began in my introduction, questions about reader involvement and presence in the face of the intricate play of fictions we encounter in poems like this one. My initial goal in this chapter will be to show that the approach of labelling such poems 'mimetic' is inadequate, and secondarily to open the way for a new framework for thinking about the same set of problems.

My argument will be structured as follows. Firstly I will make a case for rejecting the label of 'mimetic poetry' for this poem (and, by extension, for other poems that are grouped under this heading) by demonstrating the term's theoretical flimsiness and lack of explanatory power. Next I will challenge narratological approaches which attempt to solve the poem's enunciative ambiguities by attributing sections of text to various fictional speakers; I argue that the question we need to be asking is not 'who is speaking?' but rather 'what kind of experience are we presented with?'.

My thesis is that what shifts in the poem is not the identity of the speaker, but the modality of the hymnic discourse. I argue, following Fludernik's proposals on the experiential structures underlying narrative discourse,[2] that we need to see in the poem an oscillation between two *experiential frames*, which I will call 'experience-report' and 'performed speech'. This conclusion is founded on the premiss that what is referred to in the poem as the 'song of Apollo' (Ἀπόλλωνος ἀοιδῇ, 17) can be conceived as a multimodal, multisensory experience which functions as a *mise-en-abyme* of Callimachus' own *Hymn to Apollo*. The ultimate goal of this revisionist approach is to change what kinds of questions we ask of the *Hymn to Apollo*: not how to *identify* the performance occasion and the voices that speak

---

[1] Vestrheim 2012; Calame 2005; Bulloch 2010; Bing 1993; Depew 1993; Stephens 2015a: 72–73. On mimetic poetry as a whole see esp. Albert 1988.
[2] Fludernik 1996.

therein (a question which leads to aporia and circular reasoning), but how a reader or audience might contextualise them within a communicative frame.

1.2 The *Hymn to Apollo* and 'mimetic poetry'

Since Reitzenstein coined it in 1906,[3] the term 'mimetic poem' or 'mimetic poetry' has been adopted by many scholars as a means of explicating some of the interpretive problems raised by certain of the *Hymns* of Callimachus. While this term has been criticised on various accounts, and has not won wide acceptance in itself as a subcategory of Greek or other poetry, it nevertheless remains common practice to refer to *Hymns* 2, 5, and 6 (and occasionally 4) as the 'mimetic hymns' (as opposed to the other 'rhapsodic hymns') and to place this 'mimetic' quality at the centre of critical treatments of the poems.[4] Albert provides the standard definition of the term:

> Ein mimetisches Gedicht besteht in einer poetisch gestalteten zusammenhängenden Rede, die eine als Sprecher auftretende Person in einer Szenerie äußert und in der sie auf Vorgänge oder Geschehnisse Bezug nimmt, die sich während des Sprechens in der Szenerie ereignen und eine Szenerieveränderung bewirken.[5]
>
> A mimetic poem consists of a poetically constructed, cohesive discourse which is enunciated in a setting by a person appearing as the speaker and in which this person refers to processes or events which occur in the setting in the course of the speaking and which bring about a change of setting.

In Callimachus' *Hymn to Apollo*, this *Szenerie* is specified at the outset of the poem as a shrine (μέλαθρον, 2) in which a number of portents (Albert's *Geschehnisse*) herald the imminent arrival of the god himself, and 'the speaker'[6] alternates between describing these portents in simultaneous narration (1–5), commanding a

---

[3] Reitzenstein 1906: 157–60. The closest thing he offers to a definition of 'mimetisches Gedicht' is in the negative, as he is concerned to argue that there is no such thing in Tibullus: 'es gibt keine bestimme Situation, in der das Lied gewissermaßen mimisch vorgetragen sein könnte, wie manche bukolische Lieder (157).'
[4] See e.g. Attridge 2019: 76–82; Payne 2007: 53–60; Both Reitzenstein (1906: 160) and Albert (1988: 15) use Callimachus' *Hymns* 2, 5, and 6 to illustrate the category of the mimetic poem.
[5] Albert 1988: 24, and cf. p. 15, where he sets forth this definition with specific reference to Callimachus' *Hymns* 2, 5, and 6.
[6] I borrow the term 'the speaker' here and below only as a heuristic, in the interest of engaging more closely with the theoretical inclinations of Albert and others. Nothing is gained by the attempt represented by this term to remove the enunciating self of poetry from the equation.

group of onlookers to maintain ritual silence and for sinners to depart (2) and urging a chorus of boys to begin singing and dancing in the god's honour (8-16), after which, according to Albert, a *Szenerieveränderung* takes place — viz. the choral song and dance actually begins (17);[7] we will return to this later.

Interpretive comment on the poem has tended to cluster around the opening lines which introduce this setting, which it is worth quoting in full:

> οἷον ὁ τὠπόλλωνος ἐσείσατο δάφνινος ὅρπηξ,
> οἷα δ' ὅλον τὸ μέλαθρον· ἑκάς, ἑκὰς ὅστις ἀλιτρός.
> καὶ δή που τὰ θύρετρα καλῷ ποδὶ Φοῖβος ἀράσσει·
> οὐχ ὁράᾳς; ἐπένευσεν ὁ Δήλιος ἡδύ τι φοῖνιξ
> ἐξαπίνης, ὁ δὲ κύκνος ἐν ἠέρι καλὸν ἀείδει.
> αὐτοὶ νῦν κατοχῆες ἀνακλίνεσθε πυλάων,
> αὐταὶ δὲ κληῖδες· ὁ γὰρ θεὸς οὐκέτι μακρήν. (1–7)

> How the laurel shoot of Apollo trembled, and the whole shrine as well! Begone, begone, whosoever is unworthy! Surely that is Phoebus knocking on the doors with his beautiful foot — don't you see? The Delian palm nodded sweetly of its own accord, and the swan is singing a beautiful song in the air. Open yourselves now, gate-bars, open yourselves, bolts, for the god is not far off now!

Commentators concerned to highlight the 'mimetic' quality of the poem usually point to these lines, and often all that the epithet indicates is that an imaginary situation is being evoked,[8] one which is divorced from any conceivable performance setting and is thus best seen as wholly fictional.[9] The sudden apostrophe to an unspecified observer in v. 4 — οὐχ ὁράᾳς; — has received particular attention in this respect: Reitzenstein observes that the phrase turns the reader into a witness to the imagined scene,[10] and Bing sees the phrase as pulling the reader into the drama, inviting her to imagine herself as one of the worshippers.[11] These poems will then be the hymnic equivalent to the ecphrastic epigram, the artistry of which consists in its *enargeia* in evoking an entirely unreal situation:[12] in Friedländer's words, 'The act of perception is accentuated precisely because, broadly speaking, no such act takes place'.[13]

---

7 Albert 1988: 69–70.
8 e.g. Stephens 2015a: 11, 72; Vamvouri Ruffy 2004: 60–1, 177–8.
9 So, most recently, Bulloch 2010: 173.
10 Reitzenstein 1906: 160.
11 Bing 1993: 184; cf. Hunter 1992: 13: '"do you (sing.) not see?" asks the poetic voice (v. 2, 4), and we are compelled to answer "well, no".'
12 See e.g. Gutzwiller 2002: 91 and 110.
13 Friedländer 1931: 36 (my translation), quoted in Bulloch 1985: 5.

The tendency to interpret the hymn as a 'literary drama' has led to a focus on the ambiguity of voice in the poem, which Calame most fully outlines as oscillating between the implied author, a *choregos* or 'master of ceremonies' who directs the singing of a hymn, and the chorus of boys who follow him.[14] Following on this line of argument, Depew sees in the poem a deliberate 'scrambling' of the 'ambiguities of deictic reference' which highlights the 'essential textuality' of Callimachus' work;[15] likewise Falivene states that the purpose of the mimetic hymns is 'to imitate an oral performance in writing', and draws an analogy with the Platonic dialogues, which present themselves as written transcripts of conversations.[16] Bing goes even further, seeing in the *Hymn* the primal encounter of the Alexandrian scholar with the written poetic text, suggesting to him a new kind of 'play' which could not have been conceived by his predecessors.[17] Calame, considering the element of polyphony and enunciative ambiguity in the poem, affirms this thesis of 'essential textuality' when he concludes:

> the constant interplay among persons occupying in succession enunciative stances that are usually kept distinct gives the strong impression that this 'mimetic' effect is operating on the level of literary fiction [...] [T]he 'mimesis' is in fact hermetic: its construction is such that it is probably self-referential and intradiscursive and does not refer to any action outside the poem itself (unlike what we find in archaic melic poetry, where singers refer to the external ritual actions in which they are involved). From this point of view, it is particularly significant that the poet has so much more to say on the (fabricated) performance context of his poem than the *Homeric Hymns* or the archaic melic poets do.[18]

Calame's formulation makes clear that the label of 'literary fiction' as applied to the *Hymn to Apollo* does not only pertain to its truth-value but also to the mode it which it communicates. Where archaic poets index performance occasions to reinforce the connexion between text and context, Calame suggests, the perfor-

---

[14] Calame 2005: 80–2. Cf. Morrison 2007: 128–32, Vamvouri Ruffy 2004: 219, and Fantuzzi 2011: 437, who speaks of a 'strategic fragment of the authorial voice.' Hopkinson 1984: 3–4 argues that the narrating voice of the *Hymn to Demeter* is similarly ambiguous ('this nebulous and uncharacterised voice is above and outside the ceremony', 3).
[15] Depew 1993: 59. See also Bing 1993: 190, who comes to a similar conclusion.
[16] Falivene 1990: 108 (my translation). See also Fantuzzi-Hunter 2004: 31 and n. 121 for a summary statement of this view.
[17] Bing 1993: 194. The interpretations of Morrison 2007: 128–33 and Fantuzzi-Hunter 2004: 364 are along the same lines.
[18] Calame 2005: 82.

mance occasion in the *Hymn to Apollo* is folded inside it as the object of its *mimesis*.[19] According to this schema, 'fictionality' amounts to a pragmatic frame whereby the hymn is transformed from a first-degree speech act (the hymnic performance) into a represented action, and reader engagement with this represented action is conceived as an activity of reconstructing the fictional situation built up by the text.

This conception of the hymn as representing a fictional occasion to the reader is closely bound up with the question of the status and identity of the poem's 'speaker', who is often said to be a fictional character.[20] Morrison even considers 'mimetic' to be a property of the 'narrator' (his blanket term for the primary speaker in any genre of poetry), and states that the term 'is used [...] to describe a narrator who does not stand in the conventional relationship of narrator to audience in a hymn, but appears as a fictional character who addresses himself or other fictional characters, rather than the audience of the hymn'.[21] According to the standard account, then, the distinguishing elements of Callimachus' *Hymn to Apollo*, and of 'mimetic poetry' in general, are fictionality and enunciative ambiguity as functions (or symptoms) of an 'essential textuality'.[22] In order to provide a critique of this account, we must return to Albert's much more precise definition of the term.

1.3 Discourse and events

Albert draws attention to something in his definition which is crucial, but not adequately accounted for in any of the treatments mentioned above. According to him, the 'mimetic' effect is produced by the seemingly paradoxical running together of two elements, namely the time of the speaker's discourse and the time of the events that are occurring; the events and the 'change of setting' that they effect go on seemingly under the narrator's nose, rather than subject to his exposition.[23] His definition does not, however, offer an explanation for this running

---

[19] Cf. Depew 2000, who sees the 'mimetic' hymns as the final stage in a historical process whereby Greek hymns increasingly 'self-contextualise'.
[20] Harder 1992: 385; Payne 2007: 53.
[21] Morrison 2007: 109.
[22] See Vestrheim 2012: 62: 'What distinguishes Callimachus' mimetic hymns from previous poetry is the way they describe a series of actions via a voice that appears to be taking part in them, but which on closer inspection, turns out not to be identifiable with any imaginable participant.'
[23] 'Der vorherrschende Eindruck [...] ist der, daß es in ihnen Handlung gibt, die gleichzeitig mit den Worten der redenden Person vor sich geht (Albert 1988: 1).'

together of discourse and events. In failing to elucidate the correlation between the two, Albert's definition fails to significantly set apart 'mimetic poems' from such commonplace literary devices as simultaneous narration and dramatic exposition. The real crux of the problem rather seems to me to lie in the *relation* between the speaker's discourse and the 'events' to which he refers.

The key to discovering this relation lies in considering the 'setting' in which, in Albert's formulation, both discourse and events occur. We can note at the outset that, in the case of this poem, the setting is not simply any setting, but rather the occasion of the hymn. 'Occasion' denotes not simply a setting in place and time, but rather the state of affairs which originates the discourse; the hymn itself is presented as arising of necessity out of the ceremony to which it answers. The poem itself makes this clear: the speaker urges the boys to begin the dance *because* Apollo is almost here, and he must be greeted with song and dance:

> οἱ δὲ νέοι μολπήν τε καὶ ἐς χορὸν ἐντύνεσθε.
> ὡπόλλων οὐ παντὶ φαείνεται, ἀλλ' ὅ τις ἐσθλός·
> ὅς μιν ἴδῃ, μέγας οὗτος, ὃς οὐκ ἴδε, λιτὸς ἐκεῖνος.
> ὀψόμεθ', ὦ Ἑκάεργε, καὶ ἐσσόμεθ' οὔποτε λιτοί.
> μήτε σιωπηλὴν κίθαριν μήτ' ἄψοφον ἴχνος
> τοῦ Φοίβου τοὺς παῖδας ἔχειν ἐπιδημήσαντος,
> εἰ τελέειν μέλλουσι γάμον πολιήν τε κερεῖσθαι,
> ἑστήξειν δὲ τὸ τεῖχος ἐπ' ἀρχαίοισι θεμέθλοις. (8–15)

> Boys, prepare yourselves for merriment and for the dance. Apollo does not appear to everyone, but to him who is worthy: whoever should see him, this is a great man; who does not see him, that is a base man. We shall see you, O Far-Worker, and we shall be not at all base. Let not the boys keep the cithara silent or their steps noiseless while Phoebus is among us, if they are to accomplish marriage and to cut their hair when it is gray, and if the wall is to stand on its ancestral foundations.

This already sets up a *causal* relation between the song to be performed and the setting in which this performance takes place. At this point we see the first clear instance of Albertian 'change of setting', when the speaker reacts (in the singular!) to the apparent fulfilment of his command to begin the song:

> ἠγασάμην τοὺς παῖδας, ἐπεὶ χέλυς οὐκέτ' ἀεργός. (16)

> I marvel at the boys, for the tortoise-shell is no longer idle.

Here the speaker remarks that the song has apparently begun, independently of his own discourse. The action of beginning the song is treated as a spontaneous occurrence, much like the θαύματα of the trembling temple, the waving palm-branch and the singing swan, to which the speaker can only react.

The speaker's reaction is thus a distancing gesture, by which the hymn to be sung is notionally detached from his own discourse and thus from the hymn with which the audience is presented, namely Callimachus' *Hymn to Apollo*. This effect continues in the next line, when the speaker refers to the 'song of Apollo' as an event which is currently in progress:

εὐφημεῖτ᾿ ἀίοντες ἐπ᾿ Ἀπόλλωνος ἀοιδῇ.
εὐφημεῖ καὶ πόντος, ὅτε κλείουσιν ἀοιδοὶ
ἢ κίθαριν ἢ τόξα, Λυκωρέος ἔντεα Φοίβου.
οὐδὲ Θέτις Ἀχιλῆα κινύρεται αἴλινα μήτηρ,
ὁππόθ᾿ ἰὴ παιῆον ἰὴ παιῆον ἀκούσῃ. (17–21)

Keep reverent silence as you listen to the song of Apollo. Even the sea is silent when singers celebrate the gear of Phoebus Lycoreus, whether his cithara or his bow and arrows, and Thetis no longer mournfully laments her son Achilles whenever she hears '*hie Paiêon, hie Paiêon*'.

The command in v. 17 reinforces the divide between the singers and their silent audience without making it at all clear on what side of the divide the speaker himself stands; will he be silent or take part in the song? Is the present sentence part of the song or more 'prologue'? The *choregos'* commands to the chorus of boys to sing (8–10) are punctured by a response in the first person plural which would seem to refer collectively to all in attendance:[24]

ὀψόμεθ᾿, ὦ Ἑκάεργε, καὶ ἐσσόμεθ᾿ οὔποτε λιτοί. (11)

We shall see you, Far-worker, and we shall be not at all base.

And what about the following vv. 18–24, where the speaker offers mythological exempla for the reverent silence that Apollo inspires? The question is, what role is the primary speaker playing; is he simply reporting the discourse or taking part in it?

Such questions have led commentators to divide the poem into two broad sections, namely the 'hymn proper', notionally sung by the chorus of boys, and the 'mimetic frame' in which the *choregos* takes over, narrating the events occurring around him. There is some consensus for delineating the former at vv. 32–96, with the surrounding vv. 1–31 and 97–113 relegated to the 'mimetic frame'.[25]

---

24 Fantuzzi 2011: 434–35.
25 Harder 2012: 86; Erbse 1955: 422; Wilamowitz 1924: 78, 83, 85; Williams 1978: 3 and *ad* 32–96. Albert argues that 'der eigentliche Lobgesang auf Apollon mit V. 32 anhebt', and that vv. 17–31 are 'eine Art Vorgesang', also sung by the chorus and *choregos* (Albert 1988: 68–70).

For example, Callimachus closely imitates the hymnic transitions of the *Homeric Hymns* in vv. 28–31, which may be taken to suggest that a new hymn starts after this point:

> τὸν χόρον ὡπόλλων, ὅ τι οἱ κατὰ θυμὸν ἀείδει,
> τιμήσει· δύναται γάρ, ἐπεὶ Διὶ δεξιὸς ἧσται.
> οὐδ' ὁ χόρος τὸν Φοῖβον ἐφ' ἓν μόνον ἦμαρ ἀείσει,
> ἔστι γὰρ εὔυμνος· τίς ἂν οὐ ῥέα Φοῖβον ἀείδοι; (28–31)

> Apollo will honour the chorus because it sings after his heart: he has the power, for he sits at the right hand of Zeus. Nor will the chorus hymn Phoebus for one day only, so suitable for song is he; who would not readily hymn Phoebus?

The similarity of this passage to prooemial utterances in the *Homeric Hymns* such as πῶς τ' ἄρ σ' ὑμνήσω πάντως εὔυμνον ἐόντα; (*H.H.* 3.19, 207)[26] might encourage us to read the following vv. 32–96 as spoken by the chorus, or alternatively as the song of the chorus as 'quoted' by the *choregos*.[27] However, there are problems with such a neat division, and some critics have rejected it. Bing emphasises the difficulty in setting clear boundaries between the frame and the framed, concluding that 'We cannot find the seam; perhaps we were never meant to';[28] similarly Vestrheim argues that the ambiguity of voice in the poem renders any such division impossible.[29]

It seems clear from these discussions that the text offers us no unambiguous signals partitioning poet, chorus-leader, and chorus. The first person singular and plural alternate in such a way that at any point any of these may conceivably be said to be included; the second person singular and plural, moreover, can conceivably be identified with the chorus and an audience outside the chorus (to whom, for example, the chorus-leader addresses remarks about the chorus).

1.4 The space of inclusion

Among all these oscillating persons there is a sliver of continuity, however. Falivene identifies in the poem a '*persona* of the collectivity' and a '*persona* of exclusion', in line with Bassi's observations on the theme of exclusion in the

---

26 On this and other techniques of 'prooimial apology', see Bundy 1972.
27 See e.g. Rawles 2019: 71.
28 Bing 1988: 186–88.
29 Vestrheim 2012: 33; cf. Stephens 2015b: 63.

poem.³⁰ It is rather counter-intuitive, however, to apply the title *persona* to an entity which can apparently be referred to in the first, second, or third person and in the singular or plural. I suggest therefore that we take into account the spatially orienting function of person deixis³¹ and identify rather two *spaces* opened up in the poem: a space of inclusion and a space of exclusion. In this I am expanding on Harder's suggestion that the banishment of Envy in v. 113 and of 'sinners' in v. 2 together make up an 'outer space' which is defined in opposition to Apollo and his devotees.³² But there is one more aspect of these spaces to which I want to draw attention. Let us take another look at these lines:

ὡπόλλων οὐ παντὶ φαείνεται, ἀλλ' ὅ τις ἐσθλός·
ὅς μιν ἴδῃ, μέγας οὗτος, ὅς οὐκ ἴδε, λιτὸς ἐκεῖνος.
ὀψόμεθ', ὦ Ἑκάεργε, καὶ ἐσσόμεθ' οὔποτε λιτοί. (8–10)

Apollo does not appear to everyone, but to him who is worthy: whoever should see him, this is a great man; whoever does not see him, that is a base man. We shall see you, O Far-Worker, and we shall be not at all base.

Here, inclusion in the group of ἐσθλοί (8) is represented as contingent upon an act of visual perception, *seeing* Apollo. In v. 9, deictic pronouns further demarcate the spaces of inclusion and exclusion: the 'great man' who sees Apollo is indicated by the proximal deictic οὗτος, while the 'base man' who fails to see him is indicated by the distal deictic ἐκεῖνος. The group of those who will see Apollo is then indicated in the following verse with the first person plural. The group is therefore defined by a shared field of vision as well as a shared interpretation of what they see. The focus then shifts to auditory perception, as the chorus is urged to answer sight with sound:

μήτε σιωπηλὴν κίθαριν μήτ' ἄψοφον ἴχνος
τοῦ Φοίβου τοὺς παῖδας ἔχειν ἐπιδημήσαντος (12–3)

Let not the boys keep the cithara silent or their steps noiseless while Phoebus is among us.
Thereafter, the song which the boys had just been urged to begin becomes itself an object of perception as Apollo himself is transferred from the recipient of song to its source and originator:

---

30 Falivene 1990: 115; Bassi 1989.
31 See Bühler 1934.
32 Harder 2012: 87.

εὐφημεῖτ' ἀίοντες ἐπ' Ἀπόλλωνος ἀοιδῇ. (17)

Keep sacred silence, you who hear, for the song of Apollo.

The imperative εὐφημεῖτε is a command to form a group, to unite in ritual silence, and the participle ἀίοντες stipulates a shared auditory experience as a further criterion of the group's cohesion. The space of inclusion, then, is the space in which Apollo, his epiphany, and his song are all aurally and visually manifest to the occupants.[33]

The audiovisual manifestness of the 'song of Apollo' is thematised throughout the hymn, particularly in the echoes of the *paean*-refrain scattered throughout.

εὐφημεῖτ' ἀίοντες ἐπ' Ἀπόλλωνος ἀοιδῇ.
εὐφημεῖ καὶ πόντος, ὅτε κλείουσιν ἀοιδοὶ
ἢ κίθαριν ἢ τόξα, Λυκωρέος ἔντεα Φοίβου.
οὐδὲ Θέτις Ἀχιλῆα κινύρεται αἴλινα μήτηρ,
ὁππόθ' ἰὴ παιῆον ἰὴ παιῆον ἀκούσῃ. (17–21)

Keep reverent silence, you who hear, for the song of Apollo. Even the sea is silent when singers celebrate the gear of Phoebus Lycoreus, whether his cithara or his bow and arrows, and Thetis no longer mournfully laments her son Achilles whenever she hears '*hie Paiêon, hie Paiêon*'.

ἰὴ ἰὴ φθέγγεσθε· κακὸν μακάρεσσιν ἐρίζειν. (25)

Cry '*hie! hie!*': it is wrong to strive with the immortals.

ἰὴ ἰὴ Καρνεῖε πολύλλιτε (80)

Hie hie, much-beseeched Carneius!

   ἐπηύτησε δὲ λαός,
'ἰὴ ἰὴ παιῆον, ἵει βέλος.' (102–3)

And the people cried out, '*hie hie Paiêon*, shoot an arrow!'

Whereas the mention of the 'song of Apollo' which urges its hearers into sacred silence (εὐφημεῖτ' ἀίοντες ἐπ' Ἀπόλλωνος ἀοιδῇ, 17) seems to refer only to the present song, the following lines (18–21) generalise the effect of hearing the song

---

[33] Cf. Call. fr. 227.1 Pf., where Apollo's presence and the audibility of lyre music are represented as practically coextensive: ἔνεστ' Ἀπόλλων τῷ χορῷ· τῆς λύρης ἀκούω ('Apollo is in the chorus; I hear the lyre').

to any praise-song of Apollo, so that the immediate present shades into the iterative. At 20–1, the *paean*-refrain is mentioned as the equivalent to the 'song of Apollo'; whenever Thetis hears it, she ceases her mourning for Achilles. From this point onward the refrain-fragment ἰὴ ἰὴ is echoed with striking variations of modality. Whereas for Thetis the refrain is something to be heard, at v. 25 it becomes something to be cried out (ἰὴ ἰὴ φθέγγεσθε); then, at v. 80, the speaker utters it directly as a self-conscious affirmation of his native allegiance to Apollo Carneius (ἰὴ ἰὴ Καρνεῖε πολύλλιτε). The climax of this series comes at vv. 97–105, where the speaker offers an αἴτιον for the refrain (ἐφύμνιον) itself:

ἰὴ ἰὴ παιῆον ἀκούομεν, οὕνεκα τοῦτο
Δελφός τοι πρώτιστον ἐφύμνιον εὕρετο λαός,
ἦμος ἐκηβολίην χρυσέων ἐπεδείκνυσο τόξων.
Πυθώ τοι κατιόντι συνήντετο δαιμόνιος θήρ,
αἰνὸς ὄφις. τὸν μὲν σὺ κατήναρες ἄλλον ἐπ' ἄλλῳ
βάλλων ὠκὺν ὀιστόν, ἐπηύτησε δὲ λαός,
'ἰὴ ἰὴ παιῆον, ἵει βέλος.' εὐθύ σε μήτηρ
γείνατ' ἀοσσητῆρα, τὸ δ' ἐξέτι κεῖθεν ἀείδῃ. (97–105)

'*hie hie Paiêon*' — we hear this because the people of Delphi first invented it as a refrain for you, when you showed them your far-shooting bow of golden arrows. When you came there, the terrible beast Pytho, a dire serpent, confronted you. You slew him, firing one swift dart after another, and the people cried out, '*hie hie Paiêon*, shoot an arrow!' Your mother bore you to be a helper from the first, and ever since then you are sung of in this way.[34]

The present aural experience (ἀκούομεν, 97) is aetiologically traced to a primeval act of 'showing' (ἐπεδείκνυσο, 99) — an archetype of the presently anticipated epiphany — which was reciprocated[35] by the inaugural utterance of the refrain (πρώτιστον, 98),[36] reported in yet another modality, that of quoted speech: ἐπηύτησε δὲ λαός, | 'ἰὴ ἰὴ παιῆον, ἵει βέλος (103–4).' The spontaneity of the invention of the refrain — reputedly proceeding from a 'natural' utterance, 'ἵει, παῖ,

---

34 Cf. 47ff.: Φοῖβον καὶ Νόμιον κικλήσκομεν **ἐξέτι** κείνου κτλ.
35 The μέν...δέ construction of vv. 95–6 emphasises the reciprocity of the god's deed and the people's praise.
36 The superlative πρώτιστον (98) is interesting here. Race notes that Callimachus' use of τὰ πρώτιστα at v. 30 of the *Hymn to Delos* 'finally marks the very beginning of the narrative (in contrast to the previous uses of πρῶτος in 4, 6, 16, and 22)', following Hesiod's marked use of the superlative at *Theogony* vv. 24, 116 (Race 1992: 36). In the present *Hymn*, the superlative is consistent with Callimachus' representation of this paean-refrain as the mythical archetype of the paean being sung at present.

ἰόν' — recalls the spontaneous, epiphanic quality of the 'song of Apollo' and, by extension, Callimachus' *Hymn to Apollo* itself.

Calame interprets this interplay of narrated and narrating voices as proceeding from a fundamental 'ambiguity' in the 'enunciative structure' of the hymn.[37] However, taking into account my suggestion that the hymn is represented as a shared audiovisual experience which is manifest to those admitted into the space of inclusion, I would argue that 'enunciative ambiguity' does not adequately capture how Callimachus employs these multimodal echoes of his own hymnic utterance. By offering his αἴτιον in 97–105 not only as a detached, objective explanation for the refrain, but as an origin-story of *what we now hear* (ἀκούομεν, 97), Callimachus draws a line of continuity between this and other past iterations of the refrain (cf. esp. vv. 17–21), subsuming these past analogues and their narrative presentation into the space of inclusion containing the present performance. The effect, then, is less a paradoxical synthesis of voices than a pulling together of multiple instantiations of the hymnic utterance in varying modalities into a composite experience centred on the mutual manifestness of worshipper and god, of *laudator* and *laudandus*.[38]

The experience of the 'song of Apollo', however, is not a unilateral one, since Apollo will reciprocate with his blessings:

> τὸν χορὸν ὡπόλλων, ὅ τι οἱ κατὰ θυμὸν ἀείδει,
> τιμήσει· δύναται γάρ, ἐπεὶ Διὶ δεξιὸς ἧσται.
> οὐδ' ὁ χορὸς τὸν Φοῖβον ἐφ' ἓν μόνον ἦμαρ ἀείσει,
> ἔστι γὰρ εὔυμνος· τίς ἂν οὐ ῥέα Φοῖβον ἀείδοι; (28–31)

> Apollo will honour the chorus because it sings after his heart: he has the power, for he sits at the right hand of Zeus. Nor will the chorus hymn Phoebus for one day only, so suitable for song is he; who would not readily hymn Phoebus?

The space of inclusion is therefore also the space in which Apollo hears and approves of the hymn being offered to him. To take this further, we may say that, in a sense, the creation of the space of inclusion by means of this audiovisual reciprocity between chorus and god *is* the epiphany of Apollo. It is appropriate in this regard that when Envy intervenes at the close of the poem to criticise the hymn,

---

37 Calame 2005: 79–82.
38 Cf. Morgan's observations about Pindar's similarly multimodal employment of the κῶμος as analogue and *mise-en-abyme* for his epinician odes, which has the effect of transforming his poetry into 'a self-sufficient and totalizing poetic discourse that throws the excellence of his song into relief by subsuming all aspects of the present revel, the poetry of the past, and the performative context of the future (Morgan 1993: 15)'.

he is explicitly described as invading the god's field of aural perception by 'whispering in his ears' (105), thus interrupting the desired audiovisual reciprocation between chorus and god and trying to create a smaller space of inclusion occupied only by himself and Apollo.

This leads us to another observation. If the space of inclusion is the very space in which the 'song of Apollo' is heard, and the 'song of Apollo' can at least notionally be identified with the present poem, viz. the *Hymn to Apollo* of Callimachus, then there is a convergence of the medium of representation and the represented object, and we can hardly avoid the conclusion that the hymn is engaged in presenting the experience of *itself*.[39] Thus the exposition of the 'song of Apollo', and the whole performance of which it is a part, is an instance of what Dällenbach calls the '*mise-en-abyme* of the enunciation', that is, a narrative reproduction within the *Hymn to Apollo* of the process of its own enunciation, or performance.[40] This brings us back to the problem with which we started: the relation, flagged by Albert, between the poem's discourse (the enunciation of the *Hymn to Apollo*) and the events it portrays (the 'song of Apollo'). We are now prepared to approach the concept of mimetic poetry more directly.

1.5 *Mimesis* and *diegesis*: from modes of presentation to experiential frames

Harder understands the *Hymns* of Callimachus in general as oscillating between mimetic and diegetic modes of narrative presentation, modelling her *mimesis-*

---

[39] Cf. Calame 2005: 77, on the narrative of the foundation of Cyrene: 'there is a kind of coincidence (in the strong sense of the term) created between the present poem's enunciative form, a hymn, and the content of what is uttered - the description of a ritual musical performance.'

[40] Dällenbach defines the '*mise-en-abyme* of the enunciation' as '(i) the "making present" in the diegesis of the producer or receiver of the narrative; (ii) the revelation of the production or reception *per se*; or (iii) the explicitation of the context that determines (or has determined) this production/reception (Dällenbach 1989: 75).' All three are relevant to the present poem. Vamvouri Ruffy 2004: 149–55 offers a useful discussion of a similar type of *mise-en-abyme* in the *Homeric Hymns*, based on passages in *Hymns* 19 (to Pan), 21 (to Apollo), and 4 (to Hermes) in which 'le chant du locuteur-aède trouve sa configuration dans le chant divin (149).' Her observations on the uses and effects of this '*configuration*' are limited, however, to the realm of metapoetic posturing: e.g., 'Le locuteur-aède fournit ici aussi une représentation narrative des qualités de sa composition (153)'; 'La relation d'Hermès avec Apollon peut être utilisée comme grille de lecture pour saisir celle du locuteur-aède avec son public (155).' I attribute a rather higher degree of significance to the *mise-en-abyme* in the *Hymn to Apollo*.

diegesis distinction after Pfister's comments on modes of presentation in drama.[41] She labels as 'diegetic' passages in which 'a story or description is being transmitted to a "reader"', reserving the label 'mimetic' for passages in which 'the speaker is either addressing himself as a fictional character or addressing other fictional characters'.[42] Interestingly, she includes under the 'mimetic' category passages which even minimally dramatise the situation of the primary speaker of the hymn, such as the 'response' of Zeus to Callimachus' question about his birthplace that appears suddenly in *h.Zeus* v. 8: 'Κρῆτες ἀεὶ ψεῦσται'.[43] She calls this a 'mimetic interruption in the text', noting that the sudden interjection of an unannounced speaker creates the illusion that the speaker and his discourse are 'fixed in space and time', like a dramatic character.[44]

The problem with Harder's schema of mimetic and diegetic modes is that it only takes into account the narrative presentation of fictional objects and events, although it is not at all clear that this representational function should be considered the primary function of the discourse of the *Hymns* or of their 'narrators'. The opening exposition of the *Hymn to Apollo* can, it is true, be said to 'present' objects and events in sequence; οὐχ ὁράᾳς; in v. 4 and εὐφημεῖτ' ἀίοντες ἐπ' Ἀπόλλωνος ἀοιδῇ (17) direct an audience to an audiovisual spectacle, which is then (at least notionally) set forth in the following lines, and in this sense the utterer of these words may indeed be thought of as acting as a kind of 'narrator'. Likewise, as per the usual understanding of the 'master of ceremonies' convention, the commands to begin the song and dance are really a kind of narration of the same, a presentation of the described events before an audience who cannot see them otherwise. To this extent it is understandable that some might consider the speaker as, in some sense, narrating the action of the *Hymn*. This conception of the speaker's role becomes problematic, however, when we consider some other utterances, such as the following:

(1) ἰὴ ἰὴ φθέγγεσθε· κακὸν μακάρεσσιν ἐρίζειν.
ὃς μάχεται μακάρεσσιν, ἐμῷ βασιλῆι μάχοιτο·
ὅστις ἐμῷ βασιλῆι, καὶ Ἀπόλλωνι μάχοιτο (25–7)

Cry '*hie! hie!*': it is wrong to strive with the immortals. Whoever fights with the immortals, may he fight with my king; whoever fights with my king, may he fight with Apollo too.[45]

---

41 Pfister 1988: 22–23.
42 Harder 1992: 386.
43 Harder 1992: 388.
44 Harder 1992: 388.
45 On the interpretation of the optatives here, see Williams 1978 *ad loc.*

(2) ὤπολλον, πολλοί σε Βοηδρόμιον καλέουσι,
πολλοὶ δὲ Κλάριον, πάντη δέ τοι οὔνομα πουλύ·
αὐτὰρ ἐγὼ Καρνεῖον· ἐμοὶ πατρώιον οὕτω (69–71)

O Apollo, many call you Cattle-herder, others the Clarian, and everywhere your name is manifold, but I call you Carneius; it is my birthright to do so.

(3) ἰὴ ἰὴ Καρνεῖε πολύλλιτε (80)

hie! hie! Much-beseeched Carneius!

(4) χαῖρε ἄναξ· ὁ δὲ Μῶμος, ἵν' ὁ Φθόνος, ἔνθα νέοιτο (113)

Hail, lord — and let Blame go the same way as Envy.

These utterances do not in any obvious way 'transmit' a 'story or description'; they primarily make assertions about the speaker's stance towards the act of praise he is performing, or else perform other speech acts closely aligned with hymnic discourse, such as invocation and praise. However we define their purpose or function, it seems clear that they are not 'diegetic' in the sense of performing a narration. By the same token, there is no good reason to attribute these utterances to a fictional character — thus labelling them 'mimetic' rather than 'diegetic' in Harder's terminology — unless we simply assume that all utterances in the *Hymn* must be categorised as either 'mimetic' or 'diegetic'. Such an attribution would not shed any light on these utterances, and would require special pleading. In fact, there is nothing at all to deter a reader so inclined from attributing them to Callimachus himself, either speaking in an individual capacity or else as the spokesperson of the chorus.

Despite this difficulty, I would suggest that something of Harder's discussion of 'mimetic' elements in the *Hymns* can nevertheless be carried over into our explication of the relation between the discourse and the events in the *Hymn to Apollo*, provided we drop the criterion of fictionality. Harder's discussion of 'mimetic interruptions in the text' shows that even when there has not been an overt *Szenerieveränderung*, the discourse can exhibit a minimal impression of *sequentiality*, i.e. the passing of narrative time alongside the unfolding of the hymnic discourse itself. We have of course already noticed this phenomenon in connexion with ἡγασάμην τοὺς παῖδας κτλ. (16), i.e. the implication that the song is a distinct event with its own temporality, not determined by the discourse of the speaker and its own sequentiality. To this extent the poem does indeed 'diegetically' present a hymn-performance and the ritual surrounding it. At the same time, however, that hymn-performance cannot be attributed exclusively to its own quotational frame within the diegetic universe of the poem, because, of course, the hymn to be sung is, by way of *mise-en-abyme*, identical with the present poem, the *Hymn to Apollo* of Callimachus.⁴⁶ This raises the question: in what sense do the 'mimetic' sections of the poem present a fictional narrative?

Now, it is widely acknowledged that Callimachus makes use in this poem of a well-established convention of choral poetry wherein the speaker announces the act of singing that is in fact already underway. According to this convention, originally outlined by Bundy, both the command to sing (ἐντύνεσθε, 8) and the future indicatives that respond to it (ὀψόμεθ', ἐσσόμεθ', 11) can be understood as 'self-fulfilling', conforming to a type of utterance that has been labelled 'performative'.⁴⁷ The 'performative future' is also a central feature of the *Homeric Hymns*, the primary models for Callimachus' own *Hymns*.⁴⁸ Often in the *Homeric Hymns*, the speaker announces the discourse as it unfolds with such a 'performative' utterance, typically either first-person futures or commands to the Muse.⁴⁹ This is in accordance with the function of the hymn as an ἄγαλμα offered to a god, aiming at the reciprocation of χάρις.⁵⁰ The opening is matched by a 'hymnic envoi', marked by a formula typically using a form of the word χαῖρε or ἵλαθι, which announces that the offering has been received successfully by the god, after which the poet typically goes on to promise another song. The χαῖρε-formula thus signals the fulfilment of the programme laid out at the beginning, representing the hymn as a whole as a completed and efficacious speech-act: by saying 'I will sing', the poet sings; by saying 'Rejoice in my hymn!' the poet demonstrates that the god rejoices in his hymn. Such utterances thus have the effect of objectifying the hymn as performed utterance, so that, as Calame says, 'the poem itself is transformed not only into an exchange commodity, but also into a musical performed object'.⁵¹

We can apply this understanding of 'performative utterances' to the *Hymn to Apollo* with one qualification. Pfeijffer, in an analysis of the 'performative future'

---

46 Cf. Calame 2005: 82; Bing 1993: 186.
47 Bundy 1986 [1962]: 21–22; see also Slater 1969: 86–94; Carey 1989: 550–2; Calame 1995: 144–6; Pfeijffer 1999: 34; D'Alessio 2004: 272–7. I see utterances of this type in Callimachus' hymn at vv. 7 (ἐντύνεσθε), 11 (ὀψόμεθ', ἐσσόμεθ'), 12–3 (μήτε...ἔχειν), 17 (εὐφημεῖτ'), 25 (ἰὴ ἰὴ φθέγγεσθε), 29 (τιμήσει), 30 (ἀείσει), and 113 (χαῖρε ἄναξ).
48 For performative futures in the *Homeric Hymns*, see Bakker 2005: 144–5. For Callimachus' imitations of the *Homeric Hymns*, see Faulkner 2011.
49 See e.g. the opening to *HH* 3, which resembles Callimachus *h.Ap.* 2.11 in structure: 'μνήσομαι οὐδὲ λάθωμαι Ἀπόλλωνος ἑκάτοιο'.
50 Calame 2011: 354; Nagy 2011: 328; García 2002: 29–34; Furley-Bremer 2001: 61–3; Pulleyn 1997: 4; Depew 2000: 60.
51 Calame 2011b: 132.

in Pindar, refutes the view that such uses of the future tense serve only to announce a present intention to sing and thus effectively lose their future-tensedness, arguing that all such 'performative futures' can be interpreted as referring to some future event, whether this event takes place during the performance of the ode or afterward.⁵² However he does concede that there is a certain use of the future in Pindar and other poets which he calls '"fictional" futures, announcing the ode as a whole.'⁵³ I concur in arguing that the 'performative utterances' in the *Hymn* can be read as having two simultaneous functions corresponding to two spaces of reference opened up in the text: a first-person future verb announcing singing does indeed refer 'constatively' to an event which happens in the future, as μνήσομαι in *HH*.3 refers to an act of singing which is about to begin; however, such a verb also discharges what can be called a *display* function, the function of foregrounding and drawing attention to the speech act of commemorative praise for which it stands.⁵⁴ The hymn is therefore both a 'musical performed object' which is involved in an honorific transaction between singer and god, *and* an event within the narrative of the poem, an event which has a beginning and an end, a temporal structure which is tied to the temporal structure of the discourse. It follows, then, that the speaker of such a poem can refer to the hymn either as an event which he is relaying in his capacity as 'narrator' — 'now the song is beginning, now it is ending' — or as the offering that is his discourse — 'Rejoice, lord!'

I argue, then, that the objectification of the song-performance in progress implied in v. 16 has the same 'objectifying' effect as the typical Homeric 'performative future', ὑμνήσω, μνήσομαι, ἀείσω. This effect, seen from the reader's point of view, can be conceptualised as a *lamination* of two experiential frames, borrowing the terminology of Goffman 1974 and Fludernik 1996.⁵⁵ We can label these two frames 'experience-report' and 'performed speech', to capture the sense that the

---

52 See his conclusion, Pfeijffer 1999: 67.
53 Pfeijffer 1999: 33–43. Cf. Fleischmann 1990: 39–40.
54 For the notion of the performance of praise poetry as an act of display, see Nikolaev 2012; see also Vamvouri Ruffy 2004: 85–90 on the theme of 'l'enchantement musical du dieu' in the *Homeric Hymns*, whereby '[on] offre une représentation narrative du plaisir que le dieu est invité à éprouver (88).' Incidentally, the tendency of inscribed cult hymns to include instructions on their own performance, which often shades into a narrative presentation of that performance (Vamvouri Ruffy 2004: 41), can be seen as a natural extension of this display function which, I argue, is already implicit in the 'performative futures' of the *Homeric Hymns*.
55 My use of the concept of experiential frames borrows something from Jahn's concept of 'story windows' (Jahn 1999). According to this model, it is not 'narrative instances' that are in question but rather the perspective offered on events and objects in the storyworld.

hymn oscillates between discharging a hymnic performance and relaying an audiovisual experience to a narratee.[56] The frame of performed speech is the angle from which the hymn can be considered a performance delivered in the here and now, whereas the frame of experience-report produces what could be called a *narrativisation* of this performance, which is accomplished by way of the figuration of the 'song to Apollo' as a *mise-en-abyme* of the enunciation of the *Hymn to Apollo*.[57] These frames are 'laminated' in that, while each represents a distinct 'point of view' on the hymnic discourse, they are superimposed together in such a way that both frames are equally available at all times. But here we come up against the narratological distinction between story and discourse, and between the world of the narrator and the world of the fiction. Let us try to bridge this gap.

Stanzel in his *Theory of Narrative* draws a useful distinction between a 'narrating "I"' and 'experiencing "I"' in first-person narratives.[58] In autobiography, this denotes the distance between the self as autobiographer and the self as subject, a distance canonically marked by a gulf in biographical time. However, in reflecting on the experiences of one's past self, one turns one's narrating self into the subject of the experience of reflection, and thus the boundaries between writer and subject are promptly blurred. It will, I believe, be agreed that, while Callimachus' *Hymn to Apollo* does indeed use the language of personal experience, the 'goal' of the poem is not to *reflect* on the experience implied in it in an autobiographical mode; rather, the node at which narrating self and experiencing subject coincide is in the performance of praise which constitutes the hymn. The performance of the hymn, whether conceived as the discourse of Callimachus' *Hymn to Apollo* or as the 'song of Apollo' referred to in the poem (vv. 8, 16, 17, 30, 97), can thus be seen as a single object which is viewed, as we have said, through two superimposed or laminated frames — the frame of experience-report and the frame of performed speech — and the perspectival 'switching' between these frames does not necessarily entail a change of speaker or a shift between diegetic levels, but is better conceived as a shift in modality that occurs not at the

---

56 These two frames correspond roughly to the Benvenistan dichotomy of *histoire* and *discours* which Calame employs to explain the primary modalities of the *Homeric Hymns* (Calame 2011a). However, where Calame applies these terms broadly to distinguish hymnic narrative from other typically hymnic utterance-types such as the *invocatio* and *preces*, I employ my frame model more specifically to explicate more minute shifts in the modality of the hymnic discourse as manifested in the experience of a reader.
57 The concept of the narrativisation of performance is derived in part from Nünning's concept of the *Mimesis des Erzählens* (Nünning 2001); cf. Ricœur's discussion of Günther Müller's distinction between *Erzählzeit* and *erzählte Zeit* (Ricœur 1988: 77–81).
58 Stanzel 1986: 90–104 and 209–14.

level of the 'characters' (whether 'narrators' or 'focalisers') but at the global level, the level of the mediacy of the *Hymn* itself.[59]

Approaching the poem in terms of experiential frames helps us to reconceptualise the fundamental disjunction pointed out by Albert between the discourse and the events which we have pinpointed at v. 16, where the speaker apparently reacts to the beginning of the chorus' song. The usual approach to this, as we have seen, has been to deduce that there has been a change of speaker, and either to apportion sections of text to various speakers or to conclude that the ambiguity of voice in the poem renders the decision impossible. I have argued, however, that it is more satisfactory to consider the discourse (Callimachus' *Hymn to Apollo*) and the events or story (the complex of auditory and visual phenomena that makes up the 'song of Apollo') as the same object viewed through the lenses of two distinct yet overlapping frames. According to this logic, the distinction between character-text and narrator-text basic to classical narratology is inapplicable to his poem, because the agents which critics have identified as the 'characters' of this poem (the chorus, the *choregos*, and the spectators) are doing the same thing (or a version of the same thing) that the 'narrator' is doing, that is, simultaneously performing and experiencing a hymn to Apollo. The 'enunciative ambiguities' of the poem cannot be solved by apportioning lines to characters because these ambiguities are a function of the composite multimodality of the song of Apollo, of its synaesthetic crossing of the experiential roles of singer and spectator, of subject and object positions in auditory and visual perception.

Our understanding of this poem has been debilitated by the Procrustean bed of classical narratology, which insists on defining the opposition of story and discourse in epistemological terms and regards the identification and classification of narrator-figures as the definitive solution to problems of voice and point of view. Thinking rather in terms of spaces and experiential frames permits us to move away from seeing the many and varied uses of person deixis in the poem as roll calls for a predetermined set of *dramatis personae* and towards considering them as orientating its participants in space, so that we cease to ask of the text 'who is this "I"/"we"/"you"?' and rather ask 'where am I/are we/are you in relation to the space of inclusion?' Once we accept that this space of inclusion is drawn around the experiential field of the 'song to Apollo', which acts in turn as an icon for the poem itself, we can appreciate how misguided it is to attempt to objectively reconstruct the *mise-en-scene* projected by the poem, since the hymn does not *depict* a scene but rather mobilises the very deictic field of its enunciation and the participants thereof to fill the indexical roles it produces.

---

59 See Fludernik 1996: 50.

Previous attempts to set the *Hymn to Apollo* in a performative setting have on the whole failed to take into account this *constitutive* role of deixis, instead operating under the misconception that close and attentive reading can uncover a determinate scene that lies behind the text and can be reconstructed deductively from it. This criticism applies equally to those like Calame who assume the poem is a 'literary fiction', those like Vestrheim who argue that it could be performed but that its enunciative ambiguities are unsolvable, and even those like Petrovic who in recent years have endeavoured to set the poem in a real-world performance context.[60] This deductive method overlooks the fundamental step of *concretisation*, the *creation* of communicative context and participant roles which occurs anew in every reception situation. This act of creation is not the sole reserve of the poet or the text, but must be seen as an intersubjective process, occurring between author, text, reader, and, in a performance setting, all those involved in the production and consumption of that performance. We need an interpretive method which takes into account this activity of contextualisation, of context-creation. I close with some comments on the question of fictionality raised at the beginning of this section.

1.6 Fictionality and epiphany

The most problematic entailment of applying the paradigm of classical narratology to this poem is the theory of fiction it presupposes. It suggests that wherever there is a verbal representation of a fictional object, there must be a creator (an extradiegetic narrator or an 'implied author') who is ontologically prior and exterior to the world of her creation.[61] Transgression of this boundary between the worlds of teller and told is called 'metalepsis',[62] a phenomenon which, according to Genette, 'produces an effect of strangeness that is either comical [...] or fantastic.'[63] This is precisely how Bing responds to the question in the opening lines of the poem addressed, unexpectedly, to a singular addressee: οὐχ ὁράᾳς; ('don't you see?', 4).

---

60 Calame 2005; Vestrheim 2012; Petrovic 2011.
61 For a critique of this model, see Walsh 1997 and 2007.
62 Genette defines metalepsis as 'any intrusion by the extradiegetic narrator or narratee into the diegetic universe (or by diegetic characters into a metadiegetic universe, etc.), or the inverse' 1980: 234–5. For some useful revisions of the concept see Fludernik 2003; for some applications to ancient Greek poetry, see de Jong 2009.
63 Genette 1980: 235. Cf. 236: 'All these [metaleptic] games, by the intensity of their effects, demonstrate the importance of the boundary they tax their ingenuity to overstep, in defiance of verisimilitude — a boundary *that is precisely the narrating (or the performance) itself*: a shifting

> The urgent question is obviously addressed to an unspecified bystander, a fellow celebrant in the ritual [...]. But a reader might well do a double-take at this question, glancing uneasily over his shoulder as though to ask 'Who, me?', for the style of the hymn clearly coaxes the reader into the role of one of the worshippers.[64]

For Bing, then, the question contributes to an overall effect by which 'the audience is unwittingly drawn out of its detached sense of self and into the scene'.[65] He considers the second-person address as stretching across two levels of communication, the fictional (narrator > narratee) and the extrafictional (author > reader).[66] Likewise, Hunter seems to regard the question as a deliberate absurdity: '"do you (sing.) not see?" asks the poetic voice, and we are compelled to answer, "well, no".'[67] But I have argued that the poem's lamination of the frames of experience-report and performed speech does not necessitate a change in speaker, let alone a shift between ontological levels. As it turns out, Reitzenstein offers a better formulation: according to him, the question 'den Leser selbst zum Zuschauer macht'.[68] Rather than parsing this statement into some monstrosity like 'Callimachus invites the reader to identify metaleptically with one of the spectators within the fiction', I suggest we keep it as it stands: the poet appeals to the reader's vision. Let us see how this works.

Consider again the verbal context in which the question appears:

> οἷον ὁ τὠπόλλωνος ἐσείσατο δάφνινος ὄρπηξ,
> οἷα δ' ὅλον τὸ μέλαθρον· ἑκάς, ἑκὰς ὅστις ἀλιτρός.
> καὶ δή που τὰ θύρετρα καλῷ ποδὶ Φοῖβος ἀράσσει·
> οὐχ ὁράᾳς; ἐπένευσεν ὁ Δήλιος ἡδύ τι φοῖνιξ
> ἐξαπίνης, ὁ δὲ κύκνος ἐν ἠέρι καλὸν ἀείδει. (1–5)

> How the laurel shoot of Apollo trembled, and the whole shrine as well! Begone, begone, whosoever is unworthy! Surely that is Phoebus knocking on the doors with his beautiful foot – don't you see? The Delian palm nodded sweetly of its own accord, and the swan is singing a beautiful song in the air.

---

but sacred frontier between two worlds, the world in which one tells, the world of which one tells.'
64 Bing 1993: 184.
65 Bing 1993: 184.
66 For a representative example of this structuralist schema of levels of communication, see Pfister 1988: 3–4.
67 Hunter 1992: 13.
68 Reitzenstein 1906: 160.

From the context it is clear that the question is asked not only to make sure the addressee is paying attention. Rather, the question is an appeal to the addressee to acknowledge the harbingers of Apollo's epiphany and so to back up the speaker's inference (signalled by the cluster of discourse particles καὶ δή που)[69] that the god is close at hand; that is, it both points to something visible and invites the addressee to share his interpretation of that thing. This is not the only instance in the poem of an appeal to an addressee in the second person singular:

> χρύσεα τὠπόλλωνι τό τ' ἔνδυτὸν ἥ τ' ἐπιπορπὶς
> ἥ τε λύρη τό τ' ἄεμμα τὸ Λύκτιον ἥ τε φαρέτρη,
> χρύσεα καὶ τὰ πέδιλα· πολύχρυσος γὰρ Ἀπόλλων,
> καὶ δὲ πολυκτέανος· **Πυθωνί κε τεκμήραιο.** (32–5)

> Golden is the dress of Apollo, his cloak, his lyre, his Lyctian bow and his quiver, and golden are his sandals, for Apollo is rich in gold, and rich in possessions too: **you may judge by Pytho**.

Surely Hunter or Bing would aver that this use of the 'empty' second person singular is of a different order than the 'metaleptic' οὐχ ὁράᾳς; However, the context in which it appears is strikingly similar. Whereas v. 4 appeals to the speaker's vision to substantiate the claim that Apollo is knocking on the temple doors, here the speaker appeals to the addressee's knowledge of Delphi to corroborate his assertions about the golden attire of the god. While 'you may judge by Pytho' does not appeal to the eyes directly in the way that 'don't you see?' does, it is nevertheless primarily an aspect of Apollo's physical appearance that is in question. The speaker acknowledges that the god is not (yet!) physically present to the addressee, and as such cannot affirm the assertion that he is rich in gold, so he asks her to recall the splendour of Delphi, which is an appeal to visual memory as much as anything else.

Reitzenstein is correct, therefore, to note that the reader is invited to become a spectator; but what she is invited to see is not only a series of fictional events which the poem 'mimetically' depicts, but also the presentation or *epiphany* of Apollo effected through the very argumentation of the hymnic discourse, if we stretch 'argumentation' to include its etymological sense of 'making manifest'. In both passages, then, the address to the second person singular functions as a *captatio beneuolentiae*, inviting the hearer to collude with the speaker in a certain way of seeing Apollo. I would therefore correct Bing's stratification of the communicative framework of the *Hymn* by positing that the very distinction between

---

[69] See Cuypers 2005: 41–45.

(extrafictional) reader and (intrafictional) spectator, which he supposes to be metaleptically transgressed by the question 'don't you see?', is itself of questionable validity, being justified only by certain rather precarious assumptions, most fully articulated by Calame in the passage quoted above (p. 14),[70] about the fictionality of the poem on the one hand and about the pragmatics of fictional texts on the other.

The way of seeing — the *epiphany* — that this poem brings into being is not readily classifiable according to a simple division of fact from fiction, of *deixis ad oculos* from *deixis ad phantasma*, because the object and field of this seeing, what I have called the 'space of inclusion', is not a determinate fictive space (and still less a determinate real space) but the product of a series of metaphorical mappings, which can now be delineated as follows.[71]

First,[72] the visual phenomenon of epiphany is equated by analogy with the aural phenomenon of song.[73] Second, the field of perceptibility of both epiphany and song is mapped onto the physical space of the temple and its spatial demarcation of sacred and profane.[74] Thirdly, this space is mapped onto the ideal reciprocity between worshipper and god that characterises prayer, which is of course already informed by the metaphorical conception that being 'in' the god's favour is equivalent to being in his presence and being able to see and hear him. Finally, the notion of reciprocity, mapped onto the field of perception, leads to a conception of the interchangeability of subject and object roles in the experience of sight and sound. This final mapping, in its interaction with the previous three, is in fact what produces the lamination of the frames of experience-report and performed speech which I have identified in the poem. Ultimately, then, despite the technical language which I have used to describe it, there is nothing more esoteric underlying this 'lamination' than the intuitive understanding that song is something which can be both produced and heard by humans.[75]

Peponi 2004 has some useful insights on the mediation of the choral performance through the poetry in the Louvre *Partheneion* of Alcman. On her view, the

---

70 Calame 2005: 80–82.
71 With 'metaphorical mappings' I am adopting the terminology of Johnson and Lakoff 1980, with a nod to the concept of 'conceptual blending' outlined by Fauconnier and Turner 2002.
72 My ordering is, of course, purely heuristic.
73 The aural and the visual are intermingled straight away with the portents described at vv. 1–5.
74 See Johnson and Lakoff 1980: 30 on the conceptual metaphor of the 'field of vision' as a container. For more on sacred space in the poem, see Petrovic 2011.
75 Here we may find some common ground with Albert in noting that the frames of experience-report and performed speech permit the 'song of Apollo' to be experienced at one and the same time as an objective 'process' (*Vorgang*) and a subjective 'event' (*Geschehnis*).

question ἦ οὐκ ὁρῇς; at v. 50 invites the spectator to apply the transformative power of the words to the spectacle before her so that her own eyes confirm the truth of the illusion conferred onto the performance by the poem. In the same way, I suggest, Callimachus' οὐχ ὁράᾳς; (4) acts as a *sense-suggestion* which transforms his own hymn into a spectacle which unfolds ἐξαπίνης (5), 'spontaneously', before his reader's or hearer's eyes, as if independent of his own act of poetic creation. The lamination of the frames of experience-report and performed speech ensure that, whatever the milieu of staging, the occasion is *made present* by the poem, in a way that makes it possible to comprehend an affirmative answer to the question 'do you not see?'.

1.7 *Mimesis* and the oral

At this point, I would like to expand on the conclusions drawn in my analysis of Callimachus' *Hymn to Apollo* in order to arrive at some general principles for the remaining sections of the book, as well as to further refine the definition of the fiction of occasion as presented in my introduction. It seems appropriate at this juncture to consider more directly the problem of *mimesis* and the oral raised in the analysis.

The theory of mimetic poetry is founded on a more general theory of *mimesis*, derived ultimately from Plato, which defines *mimesis* or representation as the production of a copy of some original object which it replicates, not in essence but only in appearance. The theory of mimetic poetry which describes the element of 'performance' present in the *Hymn to Apollo* as the product of *mimesis* reappropriates this representational theory of *mimesis* in a rather startling way which deserves a closer look. Falivene puts it most clearly when she argues that the purpose of this poem is to imitate an oral performance in writing. That is to say, it is not so much a particular kind of performance but rather *oral performance itself* that is the object of the poem's *mimesis*, and what makes this a technical tour de force, for Falivene, is that the medium in which this *mimesis* is performed is that of writing. The idea that writing can mimic the oral may at first glance seem unremarkable, even prosaic, but I would argue that it is in fact a rather surprising and indeed questionable claim. In essence, the claim that writing can imitate the oral in the same way that a portrait represents its object depends on a reification of the concepts of 'the oral' and 'the written' which is simply untenable, for reasons which I will attempt to demonstrate.

Oral theory in its modern form owes a considerable debt to the theory of media originating with Marshall McLuhan, encapsulated in the aphorism 'the medium is the message'. The central move here is the reconceptualisation of media, traditionally conceived as transparent vehicles of meaning-bearing content, as taking an active role in the meaning-making process, to the extent that the promulgation of new forms of media, from print to television to the internet, have the capacity to change the way we see the world.[76] Though classicists typically look to Havelock's *Preface to Plato*, oral theory proper attains its fullest and most robust expression in Ong's *Orality and literacy*, which feeds McLuhan's media theory into a cultural history of humankind wherein the advent of literacy is a seismic event, drastically altering not only communicative practices but also more fundamental aspects of culture and even cognition.[77] Once again, the crucial move here is the assertion that the medium of writing has powers all its own. That is, Ong argues not only that societies undergo a change when a certain portion of them adopts literacy, but also that the medium of writing has certain intrinsic properties which *effect* these changes when it grows to a certain degree of prominence.

It follows necessarily from this argument that societies unaffected by this change must have a certain set of characteristics which in turn are brought about by the intrinsic properties of something called 'orality'. The conceptual pair of 'orality' and 'literacy' thus forms a dichotomy, as the one is defined in contrast with the other, but because they are defined in terms of sets of *intrinsic* properties, this contrastive relationship can be expressed both diachronically (as a historical transition) and synchronically (as a clash of asymmetrical systems) — and this is one source of the theory's staying power. Oral theory directly negates the materialist principles from which media theory began by promoting its two great subdivisions of media, the oral and the written, to the status of transhistorical prime movers in human affairs. In order to get at the essential properties of these opposed forces, oral theory has to conceptualise them in the abstract, in isolation from the cultural practices in which they arise.[78]

The result is that, rather than elucidating the material grounds of communicative practices by analysing how the forms of media mould and shape their contents, oral theory only succeeds in reifying these forms and translating them back into content. A materialist critique of the orality/literacy dichotomy would ask of it, How can we possibly consider concepts such as 'the oral' or 'the written' in the abstract, if they are only knowable to us in the form of historically contingent practices? Consequently, how can we be sure that, when we are delineating the

---

76 McLuhan 1964.
77 Ong 1982.
78 For powerful critiques of oral theory along these lines, see Tannen 1982 and Sterne 2011.

various properties of orality/literacy or the 'oral/literate imagination', these properties are essential and not incidental, having some other cause entirely?

To return to the point with which we began, the commonplace idea that 'mimetic' poems like the *Hymn to Apollo* engage in a form of intermedial adaptation — written poetry mimicking oral poetry — is predicated on this reified notion of the oral and the written as separate and isolable domains.[79] Without this notion as a foundation, the argument that the *Hymn* presents a *mimesis* of oral performance in the medium of writing simply would not make sense. This is because the argument attributes certain properties of the poem to the element of 'performance', associates this element of performance with the domain of 'orality', and assumes that the written medium can only approach this domain through a kind of *mimesis*. But I would suggest that, if we do not approach this poem with the dichotomy 'oral (performance)/written (text)' already in mind, there would be little to convince us that there is anything particularly 'oral' or even 'pseudo-oral' about the performance we experience in this text, and no reason at all to suppose that this is a text which disavows or obfuscates its own writtenness in any way; this latter proposition, again, is only conceivable in the light of a theory which defines the oral in contrast to the written, and vice versa.[80]

Consider my own reading of the poem. I have suggested that the *Hymn* draws around the space of its own enunciation an experiential field which is also a 'space of inclusion', in order to foster the illusion that participation in the aural experience that is the hymn is also a participation in the visual experience of an epiphany, which in turn is also participation in a group which marks the experiencer out as a member of a privileged circle. One of the most salient components of this illusion is its positing of a *shared sensory field* between speaker and addressee, such that mutually perceptible objects can be indexed felicitously. It would be easy to conclude that this positing of a shared sensory field replicates what linguists refer to as the 'canonical speech situation', i.e., conversation between two mutually audible, mutually visible speech participants,[81] and subsequently to infer that the poem approaches the condition of the oral. But this ignores the possibility that writing models itself upon, or keys itself into, schemata

---

[79] Now, to say that Callimachus' *Hymn to Apollo* is a *certain kind* of written poetry imitating a *certain kind* of oral poetry is quite a different claim, and not subject to the critique I am posing here. But this is not the claim made by Falivene and others, since for them orality is an essential and not an incidental aspect of the *mimesis*.

[80] Harris 2000: 17–38 employs Aristotle's postulates on language and communication to critique the conception of written language as 'representing' spoken language, a conception which he argues is fundamental to Saussure's structuralist linguistics.

[81] E.g. Lyons 1977: 636–46.

derived morphogenetically from oral communication without therefore disengaging itself from the particular modalities of written communication.

In writing this chapter, it would be unforgivably odd for me to suddenly index an object in the room in which I am writing, as if it were manifest to my reader in the same way that it is for me; but this is a matter of the conventions of the genre in which I am writing and the institutional context within which I am working, and has little to do with the properties of writing itself. This set of conventions, it is true, is conditioned in part by the material properties of the text — not least the fact that it is digitally reproducible — but it is not wholly determined (let alone necessitated) by them.

It is completely within the bounds of the conventions of academic writing, for instance, to represent the ongoing discourse as a conversation taking place between the author and a projected reader or group of readers, as when I refer to assertions made in the text as something I 'said' or, indeed, that *we* 'said'; additionally, it is also perfectly ordinary to entertain the fiction that the temporal flow of the text represents a series of cognitive processes occuring in an imaginary space in between myself and my readers, as for example when I use phrases like 'let us consider'.

Despite the conventional and unmarked nature of such fictions, I submit that they are nonetheless *of the same order* as the fiction of occasion. Neither of these two kinds of fiction breaks the rules of written communication in a way that suggests a *mimesis* of the oral or any other communicative mode, because written communication does not have a set of predefined rules which determine what manipulations of the communicative situation fall within its domain to begin with. When I employ the vocabulary of oral communication in a written text, then, I may be creating the fiction of a conversation, but this fiction nevertheless forms part of the communicative situation in which the written text itself is bound up, and cannot be said to depart from it in any meaningful way. Similarly, the effect that produces the illusion of a shared sensory field in the *Hymn to Apollo* is a function of its rhetoric *as a text*, and not a property of a fictional 'oral performance' represented *by* the text.

So to expand this into a general conclusion: *the fiction of occasion is not a mimesis of oral performance*. This principle holds even in those cases (which, it turns out, are practically all of them) where a certain kind of oral performance, such as the choral song of the *Hymn*, forms an integral part of the fiction of occasion; for even in such cases I maintain that it would be an error to claim that (the) oral performance *itself* is the object of a *mimesis* performed by the text.[82] This conclusion certainly does not expel all the conceptual problems surrounding written and oral media, nor was this the purpose of the discussion. What I do hope to have shown, however, is that describing the fiction of occasion in terms of the oral/written binary misses the point. In the next part of this chapter, then, I will show how the approach to the *Hymn to Apollo* I have so far developed can point the way to an alternative conception which does not reduce the fiction of occasion to a matter of orality and literacy.

1.8 The 'epiphanic effect' and the fiction of occasion

Theoretical objections aside, then, what is the point of arguing, as I have, that the fiction of occasion is not a *mimesis* of oral performance? My proposed answer is that Ongian oral theory, on top of all its other faults, has the detriment of being a closed system. Because the domains of the oral and the written are posited as transhistorical constants, all that can really be done with them is to reaffirm their universal applicability by transposing their template in cookie-cutter fashion onto a given object of study. I see my project as an attempt to prise one such object of study from the grips of oral theory and to undo the straitjacketing effect that this theory has had in the scholarship on poems such as Callimachus' *Hymn to Apollo*.

Once we cease to interpret the fiction of occasion as a mere reflex or symptom of 'literacy', it emerges as a singular phenomenon with its own fascinating peculiarities, and we can approach a more nuanced and ultimately more positive engagement with it. The most attractive aspect of this conceptual shift, for me, is that it allows us to move away from the 'why' and towards the 'how', so that we cease trying to *explain* the fiction of occasion and explore rather how it works as a textual effect. My contention, then, is that what I have defined as the fiction of occasion belongs not to the history of 'orality and literacy', but to the history of *fictional effects*.

So if the fiction of occasion does not produce a *mimesis* of oral performance, what does it do? More to the point, if the fiction of occasion is a kind of effect

---

82 Related to this is the tendency to see the ritual event as the ultimate object of the poem. Stephens exemplifies this when she stresses the poem's capacity to 'capture the experience of actually being present' at such an event (Stephens 2015b: 68). I prefer to focus attention on the experience with which the text presents us, not the experience of a distant event which the text recalls.

aimed at producing an aesthetic illusion, how do we conceptualise the experience of this illusion if not as the pretense of oral performance? I hinted above at one possible way in when I suggested, in my discussion of the appeals to the reader's vision in vv. 4 (οὐχ ὁράᾳς;) and 35 (Πυθῶνί κε τεκμήραιο) of the *Hymn to Apollo*, that these phrases foster the experience of the poem as a 'way of seeing' comparable with epiphany. In order to explore this notion of epiphany as a 'way of seeing', let us consider the scene-painting in Sappho fr. 2.

δεῦρύ μ' ἐκ Κρήτας ἐπ[ὶ τόνδ]ε ναῦον
ἄγνον, ὄππ[ᾳ τοι] χάριεν μὲν ἄλσος
μαλί[αν], βῶμοι δὲ τεθυμιάμε-
   νοι [λι]βανώτῳ·
ἐν δ' ὕδωρ ψῦχρον κελάδει δι' ὕσδων   5
μαλίνων, βρόδοισι δὲ παῖς ὁ χῶρος
ἐσκίαστ', αἰθυσσομένων δὲ φύλλων
   κῶμα κατέρρει·
ἐν δὲ λείμων ἰππόβοτος τέθαλεν
ἠρίνοισιν ἄνθεσιν, αἰ δ' ἄηται   10
μέλλιχα πνέοισιν [
   [ ]
ἔνθα δὴ σὺ . . . . ἔλοισα Κύπρι
χρυσίαισιν ἐν κυλίκεσσιν ἄβρως
ὀμμεμείχμενον θαλίαισι νέκταρ   15
   οἰνοχόαισον.

Hither to me from Crete to this sacred precinct, where a lovely grove of apple trees awaits you, and altars asmoke with incense. Within, cold water murmurs through apple branches, and the whole place is in rose-shade, and sleep cascades from shimmering leaves. Within, a glade of horse-pasture blooms with spring flowers, and the breeze blows sweet [...] Once there, Cypris, take [...] and pour daintily into golden cups libations of nectar commingled with our festivities.

This is a model cletic hymn in which Sappho entreats Aphrodite to visit the sacred grove in which the song takes place. The poem alternates between two basic speech acts, entreaty (*epiclesis*) and description (*ecphrasis*). The two stanzas that describe the pleasures of the grove, each headed with with the topic phrase ἐν δ' ('Within...'), sit nestled in between the two stanzas of *epiclesis*, in which the goddess is entreated first to come 'hither to me' (δεῦρύ μ', 1) and then, having arrived (ἔνθα δὴ, 12), to 'pour libations of nectar commingled with our festivities' (ὀμμεμείχμενον θαλίαισι νέκταρ | οἰνοχόαισον, 14–5), so that the description serves as a lure for the goddess. Now, it is not only Aphrodite who must be convinced that this sacred grove is worthy of her presence, but the audience/participants as well; as such, the *ecphrasis* offers up the spectacle of the grove to them too. In this way, the scene-painting of the *ecphrasis* itself has a cletic, even epiphanic function, a function which is borne out by the temporal movement of the song: the action of the song-performance is set prior to the moment of fulfilment, before Aphrodite has answered the prayer with her presence so as to permit the festivities (θαλίαισι, 14) to begin, and yet the song itself iconically prefigures this wished-for celebration with a verbal rendition, so as to bring about the effect of the epiphany before it happens.

The epiphanic effect of the song works, like the *Hymn to Apollo*, by way of the overlapping frames of performed speech and experience-report. The description of the grove is the rhetorical means by which the epiphany of Aphrodite will be effected, both by virtue of its efficacy as a prayer directed at the goddess *and* by virtue of its efficacy as a description directed out towards the audience. The experience of the description is thus bound up directly with the experience of the epiphany, considered from the audience's point of view. If we look at epiphany from this angle, we can see the epiphanic effect as working backwards, so to speak: the prayerful act of summoning the goddess to a place hinges on the truly epiphanic act of calling into being a space in which the goddess' presence is possible.

If epiphany is in part the calling into being of an epiphanic space, this does not mean that this space is therefore necessarily fictional or otherwise perceptually absent to the participants. As Peponi argues in connexion with the Louvre *Partheneion*, an epiphanic song-performance engages the visual imagination of the audience, inviting them to imaginatively reconfigure the space they currently occupy in accordance with the spectacle offered up by the song. The grove of this poem has, then, a similar function to the 'space of inclusion' in the *Hymn to Apollo*, in that it serves as the manifestation in space of an epiphanic experience. Moreover, insofar as the θαλίαι which iconise Sappho's song-performance are offered up to the audience as part of this experience, we can say that this song exhibits an embryonic form of the more high-level switching between experiential frames that we observed in the *Hymn to Apollo*.

The sense-suggestions in the *Hymn to Apollo*, then, merely bring into sharper focus the perceptual dynamics of the epiphanic effect as manifested in cletic hymns such as Sappho *fr*. 2, in that they draw attention to this creative function of the discourse. οὐχ ὁράᾳς; paradoxically asks the audience to 'bear witness' to the spectacle which Callimachus is describing, namely the portents of the quaking temple and the singing swan, etc.; but to bear witness to a portent is necessarily an interpretative act, a feat of the imagination which in this case is guided by the epiphanic effect of the poem itself. As for the sense-suggestion in v. 35 (Πυθῶνί κε τεκμήραιο), Callimachus here evokes the splendour of Delphi as the τεκμήριον or 'visual proof'[83] of his assertion that 'Apollo is rich in gold, and rich in possessions too (πολύχρυσος γὰρ Ἀπόλλων, | καὶ δὲ πολυκτέανος, 34–5)'; but the τεκμήριον here is not a present proof but a memory of an absent place. The phrase prompts the reader to perform an act of visual recall which is structurally equivalent to the epiphanic effect of the poem, as the mind's eye surveys the mental image of Delphi for confirmation of the properties that the hymn attributes to the god himself, supplementing the verbal medium with the visual in an effort to unite them.

Roman poems which imitate the sense-suggestions of this poem have a similar effect. Take Catullus *c.* 61 for example:

> claustra pandite ianuae:
> uirgo adest. uiden ut faces
> splendidas quatiunt comas?
> [...]
> prodeas noua nupta, si
> iam uidetur, et audias
> nostra uerba. uiden? faces
> aureas quatiunt comas:
>   prodeas noua nupta.

> Throw open the door-bolt: the maiden is here. See how the torches shake their radiant hair? [...] Come forth as a new bride, if it please you now, and hear our words. See? The torches shake their golden hair: come forth as a new bride.

The dramatic action of Catullus' wedding-ceremony is articulated as a series of commands and spontaneous events which follow each other in rapid succession. The causal relation of the spectacle of the flickering torches to the 'production' of the bride shifts from one stanza to the next: first the torches herald her emergence through the door, and next they seem to coax her to come more fully into the light, ushering in her transformation from *uirgo* to *nupta*. The effect is to make each ritual action — the procession of the bride, the movement of the torches, and the verbal performance itself (*nostra uerba*) — seem to be the spontaneous reaction to some other equally spontaneous event, such that the whole poem gives the impression of being composed of a series of epiphanic visions, which we experience alternately through the eyes of the bride and through the eyes of the audience.

Tibullus' *lustratio* poem plays with a similar effect:

---

[83] See Ar. *Rh.* 1357b 8–9.

> casta placent superis: pura cum ueste uenite
>   et manibus puris sumite fontis aquam.
> cernite, fulgentes ut eat sacer agnus ad aras
>   uinctaque post olea candida turba comas.
> [...]
> euentura precor: uiden ut felicibus extis
>   significet placidos nuntia fibra deos? (Tib. 2.1.13–6, 25–6)

The gods favour what is undefiled: come with pure vestment and take up water from the font with purified hands. Observe how the sacrificial lamb approaches the glistening altars, and after it the white-robed train, hair bound with olive sprigs. [...] My prayer is coming to fulfilment: do you see how the messenger entrails signify with propitious organs that the gods are appeased?

Of the two sense-suggestions here, *cernite* [...] *ut* (15) and *uiden ut* (25), the former makes the ritual action of the sacrifice into a spectacle, whereas the latter invites the audience to participate in the divinatory activity of the *haruspex* at the climax of the rite. Even more explicitly than the previous examples, this passage superimposes the experiential structure of the portent onto the series of events that makes up the dramatic action of the poem, to foster the illusion that they unfold of their own accord as if emerging in response to the performance of prayer (*euentura precor*, 25). Once again, the epiphanic effect of these two poems has nothing to do with their incorporating a *mimesis* of oral performance, but is rather a function of the experiential structure built up by the text.

1.9 Conclusion

What I have called the epiphanic effect is intended only as an explanatory model for the fiction of occasion more generally. Indeed, as I will show in further chapters, the fiction of occasion as an effect extends well beyond the bounds of poems which deal directly with epiphany. However, the idea of the epiphanic effect carries with it some key postulates which can serve as instructive principles for the case studies that make up the remaining sections of the book. Two elements in particular that have been borne out in the preceding discussion have been a focus on *space* and a focus on *experience*. In conclusion, I would like to expand a little more on what these terms do for us conceptually.

My emphasis on these two terms is intended as a corrective to the theoretical framework that underlies the concept of 'mimetic poetry.' We have already discussed the problems with interpreting poems such as Callimachus' *Hymn to Apollo* as involving a *mimesis* of oral performance, which is Falivene's interpretation of the term 'mimetic'; but the preceding discussion also implies a critique of another meaning of 'mimetic' that has been put to work in previous treatments. This is the sense that what marks out a poem as 'mimetic' is its representation of fictional 'processes and events' (Albert's terms), or of a fictional world more generally. Representative of this approach are Harder and Bing, for whom the term 'mimetic' denotes the creation of a fictional communicative situation; they are largely followed in this by Morrison, Vestrheim, and Payne.

The latter provides a succint summary of this view when he says that the 'mimetic *Hymns*' have an 'unsettling quality' which he ascribes to the fact that the poems use the 'device of the fictional addressee' to 'project their world outward, into the world of the reader.'[84] Following Bing in particular, Payne assumes that poem and reader by default occupy separate worlds: the fictional world of the poem is populated by the fictional speaker and the other participants in the fictional scenario of the poem, and the reader can only gain access to these fictional objects — at least in *normal* cases — by way of the mimetic medium of the text. The 'device of the fictional addressee', however, assures that this is not a normal case, since the direct appeal to the reader's vision transgresses the onto-epistemological boundary that separates the worlds of poem and reader, with a disorienting effect.

My conception of the fiction of occasion, both in the *Hymn to Apollo* and in general, quite simply does away with this boundary altogether, on the strength of the intuition (if nothing else) that this effect is a primary and not a residual component of the fictive rhetoric of texts like these.[85] As such, I argue, it deserves to be treated not as a curious anomaly, but as a unique development in the history of fictional effects, one which follows its own rules, so to speak, rather than peevishly deviating from the standard mechanics of fiction.

What the fiction of occasion does, then, is not to *represent* a fictional object but rather to expand the experiential domain of the material event of the poem's enunciation. My spatial metaphor of expansion corrects Payne's metaphor of projection, in accordance with the conviction that the space opened up by the fiction of occasion does not (at least by default) present itself as being 'elsewhere', as the worlds of narrative fiction typically do, but rather as linked to the production of the poetic utterance by way of the logic of *occasion*. The production of space that

---

[84] Payne 2007: 55.
[85] Not to mention the conviction that we should not impose structural abstractions such as boundaries, frames, and levels on texts *a priori*, but should rather use them as a means to an end.

the fiction of occasion performs is therefore not the creation of a 'pocket universe', as possible-worlds theory would have it, but in fact a *spatialisation* or extension in space of the poem itself.

My adoption of 'experience' as an operative term is what makes this concept of space and spatialisation meaningful. To invoke 'experience' is to turn away from the objective structures observable in poems and turn instead to the *affordances* of those structures and the intersubjective encounters which they make possible. This means that my project has more in common, in terms of its final aims, with approaches drawing on phenomenology and cognitive science than those grounded in traditional hermeneutics, whether formalist, (post-) structuralist, or (new) historicist. The remaining chapters will be dedicated to defending this approach and expanding its horizons into new trajectories.

2 Figuring Occasion in Propertius 4.6 and Bion's *Adonis*

2.1 Introduction

The previous chapter concluded with the argument that the fiction of occasion is not a mimesis of oral performance. This rejection of the mimetic model entails a radical resituating of occasion in relation to texts on the one hand and performances on the other. According to the mimetic model, poems with fictional occasions mimic or reproduce within themselves the condition of poems with 'real' occasions, i.e. poems which are embedded in specific real-world performance settings. Encouraged by the mimetic conception of writing as a medium for the representation of speech, proponents of the mimetic model of occasion understand fictional occasions as attempts to supply the written medium with those aspects of the oral that it lacks, such as the sense of situatedness and involvement associated with oral performance. My alternative approach, as demonstrated in the discussion of Callimachus' *Hymn to Apollo*, stresses that the poem fosters a sense of space and spatiality through features like deixis, 'sense-suggestions', and the figure of epiphany, and that these features are best seen not as properties of a fictional world represented by the poem, but rather as fictional effects which address themselves directly to the reader and attach themselves to her experience of the poem *qua* poem.

In this chapter I will turn to Propertius 4.6 and Bion's *Lament for Adonis*, two poems which are linked to the *Hymn to Apollo* both by similarities of form and by their association with the 'mimetic' qualities attributed to Callimachus' poem. My aim will be to show how, in both of these poems, the occasion is not an external event which the poem represents for the reader but is rather constituted by poetic effects such as metaphor and versification. The first part will discuss how Propertius 4.6 uses the figure of the 'path of song' as a means of guiding the reader both through the poem and through its occasion, the commemoration of the dedication of the temple of Apollo Palatinus. The second part will consider the novel use of address and refrain in Bion's *Lament for Adonis*, which, I argue, allow the reader to bond empathically with the mourning love-goddess Aphrodite. Together, these two readings are intended to show how the fiction of occasion arises from poetic figures which traditionally would be considered peripheral features of 'style'.

2.2 The path of song in Propertius 4.6

Propertius 4.6, an aetiological elegy on the foundation of the temple of Palatine Apollo with an inset narrative of the battle of Actium, has earned a reputation among its academic readership as something of an anomaly, if not a paradox. Following Gordon Williams' famous condemnation ('a thoroughly bad poem';[1] 'one of the most ridiculous poems in the Latin language'),[2] a generation of more cautious scholars has come to regard the centrepiece of Propertius' book of Roman aetiologies as a locus of contradiction and incongruity, both internally and against the background of Propertius' elegiac corpus.[3]

This assessment is largely a product of the interpretive context within which Propertius' poetry in general has traditionally been set. Propertian elegy is most often considered in the light of a politically charged metapoetic programme which the poetry is thought to articulate: the elegist vaunts his own light, erotic poetry inspired by Callimachus and the carefree lifestyle associated with it over warlike epic poetry and the values of career and conquest derived from hegemonic ideals of Roman masculinity.[4] In the light of this metapoetic programme, Propertius 4.6 is nothing short of a scandal: the otherwise peace-loving poet now presents a grand accolade for Augustus' victory at Actium, and all couched in the same metapoetic symbolism that informed his previous elegiac output.

My approach to this poem will push this programmatic approach to the background in order to bring the fiction of occasion to the fore. This is not so as to dismiss either metapoetics or politics *per se* as privileged terms in regard to this poem; my rationale for this move, rather, is to advocate a shift of focus to those aspects of Propertian poetics that do not fall under the rubric of 'programmatics' proper, insofar as we understand by this term the working out in poetry of an imaginary economy of metapoetic/political values which can be formulated as a set of clearly-defined propositional statements. Instead, I will begin from problems of form and style, focussing on the often-remarked ecphrastic or descriptive mode of the Actian battle narrative as well as on the transitions between this central tableau and the proem and epilogue sections. My argument is that a complex of spatial figures runs through these apparently disparate scenes: the proem sets up the metaphor of the 'path of song' to serve as an orientational figure which

---

1 Williams 1968: 51.
2 Williams 1962: 43.
3 Hutchinson 2006: 152–5; Welch 2005: 96–103; Debrohun 2003: 210–35; Janan 2001: 102–8.
4 Among recent scholarship Hutchinson 2006: 7–16 and Keith 2008: 45–85 are broadly representative.

guides the reader through the poem, while the narrative section uses fictional effects to fashion the bay of Actium into monumental space.

Sacra facit uates: 'The poet performs the rites'. The opening utterance of the poem brings together poetic performance and ritual action perhaps more explicitly than any passage of Latin literature. The sentence takes up the two divergent senses of the word *uates* — soothsayer and poet — and invites us to conceptualise the one in terms of the other, and to imagine them as partaking of a shared field of action:

> sacra facit uates: sint ora fauentia sacris,
>   et cadat ante meos icta iuuenca focos.
> serta Philiteis certet Romana corymbis,
>   et Cyrenaeas urna ministret aquas.
> costum molle date et blandi mihi turis honores,
>   terque focum circa laneus orbis eat.
> spargite me lymphis, carmenque recentibus aris
>   tibia Mygdoniis libet eburna cadis.
> ite procul fraudes, alio sint aere noxae:
>   pura nouum uati laurea mollit iter.
> Musa, Palatini referemus Apollinis aedem:
>   res est, Calliope, digna fauore tuo.
> Caesaris in nomen ducuntur carmina: Caesar
>   dum canitur, quaeso, Iuppiter ipse uaces!

The poet performs the rites: let your mouths be favorable to the rites, and let a slain heifer fall before my altar fires. Let Roman garlands vie with Philetas' grapes, and let the urn dispense Cyrenean water. Give me fragrant spikenard and offerings of pleasing incense, and let the ball of wool circle the fire thrice. Sprinkle me with spring water, and on the fresh altars let the ivory flute pour a libation of song from Phrygian jars. Begone deceit; let the air be cleared of malice: untainted laurel smooths a new path for the priest. Muse, we shall recall the temple of Palatine Apollo: the subject is worthy of your favour, Calliope. My songs are on a path to the name of Caesar: while Caesar is sung, I pray, let even Jupiter himself stand clear!

The standard critical response to this passage is to take it as one of a series of type-scenes in Augustan poetry which allusively reenact the scene of initiation in Callimachus' *Aitia* prologue, where the poet is instructed by Apollo to offer a 'fat sacrifice', but to keep his Muse slender. The next step in this line of interpretation is to note the variations on the model and the ways in which these subvert expectations and create new meanings. So we might note that Propertius innovates by closely echoing Callimachus' *Hymn to Apollo*, drawing links between his predecessor's praise of the god and his own;[5] that he incorporates into the sacral imagery metapoetic language proper to his own brand of love elegy;[6] or, finally, that he verges on paradox by invoking Callimachus — who elsewhere in Propertius appears as the model of the unwarlike poet — in a panegyric of Augustus' military victories.[7]

This metapoetic approach is valid and useful as far as it goes, but it carries with it a certain reductiveness. As noted above, metapoetic theory views passages like this against the backdrop of a poetic 'programme', which is essentially a list of propositions about the poet's project. This focus on the propositional transforms metapoetics into a series of coded messages to be cracked by the critic. This is an ideal method for mobilising poetic imagery to map out complex intertextual relations between the poet and the traditions into which he inserts himself, but it has little to say about how these images contribute to the poem *as a poem*. A poem is not its programme, and metapoetic metaphors in a poem are also, crucially, poetic metaphors. This poem, however, has suffered from a tendency to treat metapoetic metaphors as working on a higher, more abstract level of signification from the 'body' of the poem. This is illustrated by Hutchinson's remark that '[this] is a metaphorical rite, not, like that of Callimachus, *Hymn* 2, fictitious but literal.'[8] The comparison should give us pause: its implication is that while the *Hymn to Apollo* is aimed at drawing readers into an imagined performance *of* the poem, the ritual performance of Propertius 4.6 is an allegorical one,[9] aimed at divulging a coded meaning *about* the poem. It is to be interpreted, not imaginatively recreated; deciphered, not experienced.

The presence of metapoetic metaphor in this passage is undeniable, but whether we are in the realm of allegory (at least in the more restrictive modern sense)[10] is far from certain. Firstly, there is nothing here that can justly be called an allegorical narrative, only an opaque sequence of ritual actions and an assembly of symbolically charged objects. But allegory can be pictorial as well as narratival, so perhaps we might allow that the passage presents the reader with a tableau of objects which gather to form an allegorical message. Here another problem raises itself, however. Allegory prototypically forms a layered semiotic

---

5 Cairns 1984; Pillinger 1969; Heyworth 1994.
6 Debrohun 2003: 210–35.
7 Keith 2008: 84–85.
8 Hutchinson 2006: 155.
9 He describes this passage as allegorical at Hutchinson 2006: 20 and 155.
10 See Quint. *Inst.* 8.6.44–9 on *allegoria*; for the concept of a non-narrative allegory, see Aviram 1994: 229–30.

structure in which the surface meaning conceals a hidden 'true' meaning, the ὑπόνοια. For this to work, there can be no significant overlap between the layers; each allegorical signifier on the surface layer must point to something analogous but distinct on the hidden layer, or else the concealing-revealing structure of *allegoresis* is destabilised.[11]

A truly allegorical interpretation of this passage, then, would locate 'poetry' (or 'this poem', or 'Callimachean poetry', or 'elegy') on the hidden layer and the 'ritual performance' on the surface layer.[12] But such an interpretation must fail, since the element 'poetry' is already present on the surface layer. *Vates* to the Augustans means 'poet', not allegorically but literally; insofar as there is a metaphorical link drawn between the sense 'poet' and the sense 'soothsayer', it obtains not in the figure of the *uates* itself but in the action ascribed to it: *sacra facit*. Consequently, the *uates* who performs rites in the poem is not a proxy for Propertius,[13] but Propertius himself, in his capacity as poet.

One of the commands that the *uates* issues to his attendants is to 'let the ivory flute pour on the fresh altar a libation of song from Phrygian jars (7–8)'. The allegorical interpretation would take 'Phrygian pipe music' as a symbol for 'elegiac poetry', and therefore relegate this expression to the surface layer of the allegory; but how then do we reconcile this 'allegorical' use of the word *carmen* with the use of the word at vv. 13–4 ('My songs are on a path to the name of Caesar: while Caesar is sung, I pray, let even Jupiter himself stand by')? It would be perverse not to recognise a fundamental continuity between the libation of pipe-song at vv. 7–8 and the declaration of intent at vv. 13–14.

One could answer that *carmen* appears in these two couplets in two different modes, one symbolic and one literal,[14] but that would ignore the fact pointed out by Heyworth that the phrase *Caesaris in nomen ducuntur carmina* employs a metaphor for the performance of poetry no less figurative than the image of 'libations of song': his suggested translation is 'songs are led to the name of Caesar'.[15] In

---

11 Even in the case of what Quintilian calls 'mixed allegory' (*Inst.* 8.6.48), the literal meaning is thought to be introduced as a clarification of what is otherwise concealed.
12 Hutchinson employs the 'vehicle/tenor' dichotomy, calling 'poetry' the tenor and 'the rite' the vehicle (Hutchinson 2006: 157).
13 *contra* Williams: 'In this poem, as in Horace, a *vates* speaks, not the private individual Sextus Propertius (Williams 1968: 53).'
14 So e.g. Eisenhut 1956: 126 perceives a clear-cut alternation between literal and symbolic imagery across each of the first five stanzas, and Williams 1968: 52 (followed by Günther 2006: 374–5) sees the passage as drifting between poetological imagery, dramatic depiction of the sacrifice, and an ambiguous mix of the two.
15 Heyworth 2007: *ad loc.*

both these couplets, the element 'song' inhabits both the figured world of the poem and the material world in which the poem comes to being through the act of reading. There is, then, no ontological barrier between the world in which Propertius is the poet of this poem and the world in which a ritual involving song is being performed. Instead, the ritual proem seizes upon the enunciative situation created by the actual event of reading the poem, and modifies it.

This 'modification' of the enunciative situation can be elucidated using the framework employed in the previous chapter to theorise the epiphanic effect. There, I argued that Callimachus' *Hymn to Apollo* and related poems make use of aesthetic illusion achieved through 'sense-suggestions', modulations of voice, and other techniques to 'expand' the experiential domain of the text. The *Hymn*, according to this theory, does not merely represent an epiphany ritual; it creates an epiphanic experience. The spatiality of the poem — the underlying spatial logic which orients and gives meaning to its various deictic expressions — obeys the logic of this epiphanic quality of experience, and not the other way round. It is therefore proper to call the space of the poem an 'epiphanic space', in that it is space as imaginatively (re)configured by epiphanic experience.

If we apply this theory of space (viz. space as the *product* of qualitative, intersubjective processes)[16] to the ritual performance space of Propertius 4.6.1–14, we will find there is no need to follow Hutchinson in drawing up a barrier between the 'literal' and 'symbolic' elements of the scene, or to join with Williams in puzzling over the 'curious' cross-contamination of the 'sphere of the sacrifice' and the 'sphere of poetry'.[17] The force of these dichotomies stems from a perceived need to make our performance space conform to the laws of mimetic coherence ('mimetic' in the sense of adhering to an objectivist realism). Thus, Hutchinson declares the ritual performance as a whole a 'metaphorical rite' because it contains individual metaphorical elements which, to him, destabilise the conception of the scene as a mimetic whole. He concludes therefore that 'The poem does not present itself as written for an occasion'; on the contrary, '4.6 is experienced by the reader as a poem in a book.'[18] But there is no need to draw a line between the interior space of a poetry book (where metaphor has free rein) and the exterior

---

16 See esp. Merleau-Ponty 2012: 253: 'Space is not the milieu (real or logical) in which things are laid out, but rather the means by which the position of things becomes possible.' Cf. Lefebvre 1991: 26 ('(Social) space is a (social) product').
17 Williams 1968: 53.
18 Hutchinson 2006: 153.

space of a fixed performance occasion (where language is locked in to referentiality) if we consider the possibility that space, and therefore occasion, can themselves be constructed and configured through metaphor.

2.3 Leading songs to Caesar

The proem presents us with the tracing of two spatial figures which intersect. The demand for auspicious silence in the first line, ringed with the epanalepsis of the word *sacra*, constructs a sacred space coextensive with the space of the poem, in imitation of the 'space of inclusion' in Callimachus' *Hymn to Apollo*. The *uates* then proceeds with a series of jussives ordering participation in the auspicious completion of the rite; their purpose is to usher into this charmed circle items marked out for their aesthetic value. *Mollis* and *blandus* here are not merely metapoetic tagwords outlining an elegiac programme; rather, we should take the jussives as functioning like 'sense-suggestions', fostering the illusion that the poetic performance is an event happening before our own eyes.

Once we reach the fifth couplet (vv. 9–10), the previously stationary sacred space is modified by the introduction of locomotion:

> **ite** procul fraudes, alio sint aere noxae:
>   pura nouum uati laurea mollit **iter**.

> Begone deceit; let the air be cleared of malice: untainted laurel smooths a new path for the poet.

Two divergent trajectories are traced: the departure of 'deceit' and 'malice' toward an outer, profane space (lit., 'another air'), and the onward movement of the *uates* along a 'purified' path. We thus move from centripetal motion (the assembly of ritual objects and actants around the space of the song) to linear (the advancement toward a desired goal), while still retaining the dichotomy of sacred vs. profane space.[19] The next pair of couplets pinpoints the destination of this sacred procession:

> Musa, Palatini referemus Apollinis aedem:
>   res est, Calliope, digna fauore tuo.

---

[19] Notice the mirrored structure of the two expressions *costum molle date* (5) and *laurea molle iter* (10): first the *uates* draws 'soft' spikenard to himself, then 'soft' laurel guides his onward path.

> Caesaris in nomen ducuntur carmina: Caesar
>   dum canitur, quaeso, Iuppiter ipse uaces!

> Muse, we shall recall the temple of Palatine Apollo: the subject is worthy of your favour, Calliope. My songs are on a path to the name of Caesar: while Caesar is sung, I pray, let even Jupiter himself stand clear!

It has been noted that the name 'Caesar' rings v. 13 in the same way that *sacra* rings v. 1, suggesting a quality of sanctity in the very name.[20] What has been less appreciated is how the verb *ducuntur* resumes the 'path' image introduced in v. 10. The expression transfers the notion of movement from the *uates* himself to his poem, figuring the temporal progression of the verse as physical movement along a path according to the traditional figure of the 'path of song'.[21] This conception of the song as moving along a path is however promptly modified by the pentameter, which introduces the idea of the 'singing of Caesar' as a privileged time-span within which Caesar takes centre stage and Jupiter is requested to 'stand by', to 'make space for' the poem (*uaces*, 14). The couplet 13–14 thus conceptually defines the song to be performed both in terms of temporal duration and in terms of extent in space, and Caesar presides over both of these dimensions: he is both the goal towards which the song proceeds and the presence which conditions its temporality. The performance space or occasion of the poem is to be sought out nowhere else than in the conceptual space opened up by these metaphors.

The path of song metaphor, and the superimposition of the spatial and temporal dimensions that it makes possible, is not active only in the opening section of the poem; rather, I propose, it functions as an extended metaphor sustained with subtle modulations throughout the course of the poem. Most suggestive for this hypothesis are the mirrored couplets that close each of the ritual frame-scenes:

> Caesaris in nomen **ducuntur carmina**: Caesar
>   dum canitur, quaeso, Iuppiter ipse uaces! (13–14)

> My songs are on a path to the name of Caesar: while Caesar is sung, I pray, let Jupiter himself stand by!

> sic noctem patera, sic **ducam carmine**, donec
>   iniciat radios in mea uina dies. (85–86)

> Thus will I spend the night in drink and in song until dawn casts its rays into my wine.

---

[20] E.g. Williams 1968: 252.
[21] For examples of the 'path of song' metaphor, see Hes. *WD* 659; *Hom. Hymn* 4.451, 464–5; Pindar *O*. 1.11, 9.47; Call. *h.Zeus* 78. For an overview, see Giannisi 2006.

These two couplets are bound together by echoes of both sound and sense and by their complementary structural roles in the poem (respectively, introducing the song of Caesar and capping off the sympotic coda). Each couplet places a form of *ducere* and a form of *carmen* immediately before a sense-break, followed each time by a single spondaic word in enjambment (the only two examples of such enjambment in the poem),[22] creating a pronounced echo. The effect is enhanced by the complementary use of verbal repetition in *Caesaris* [...] *Caesar* (13) and *sic* [...] *sic* (85), each of which contributes to the staccato feel produced by the enjambment.

In content, both couplets are statements on the current path and trajectory of Propertius' song, and both are followed by a temporal clause of duration, governed in the first case by *dum* and in the second case by its near-synonym *donec*. Given these parallelisms, the differences are intriguing, particularly in view of the polysemy of the verb *ducere*. *Ducuntur* (v. 13), by virtue of the triumphal imagery and the association with the victorious general Caesar, naturally calls up military connotations of 'marching' or 'leading into battle',[23] whereas *ducam* (v. 85) primarily denotes the passive activity of 'spending' the night, while also bringing to mind the activity of the symposiarch who 'leads' the group in song (*carmine*) but also 'quaffs' wine from the jar (*patera*).

The difference between the temporal clauses themselves is also suggestive: *dum* + indicative is durative, while *donec* + subjunctive is limitive, and thus the two expressions propound two contrasting figures of the temporal span of the song. In the first couplet, the interval of the song is the durative limit within which Jupiter is asked to 'stand by'; in the second, the temporal span of song is itself limited by the length of the night. The act of 'leading', then, has a different force in the two couplets: Propertius' turn as symposiarch is subject to the limits of time, whereas the procession of Caesar sets its own time limit, its own span. The contrast between the 'expansive' song of Caesar and and the 'terminal' song of the symposiarch is encoded in spatial terms as well, for while the song of Caesar moves outwards toward its goal (*Caesaris **in** nomen*), the sympotic song passively awaits the *incoming* rays of the morning sun (*iniciat radios **in** mea uina dies*). In both couplets, the notion of duration or extent in time finds expression

---

22 The only other examples I can find in Propertius of the final word of the hexameter beginning a new clause (as opposed to the much commoner two-word enjambment) are at 1.15.13, 2.1.53, *ibid*. 65, 2.13.39, 3.8.35, and 4.3.13.
23 Cf. the closing line of Apollo's speech, ***ducam** laurigera Iulia rostra manu* (54).

at the syntactic level too, as anaphora (*Caesaris...Caesar*;[24] *sic...sic*) evokes a sense of rhythmic pacing and regularity which is then 'interrupted' by the enjambment.

These remarks should serve to demonstrate how the path of song metaphor not only provides a convenient conceptual framework for the poet to articulate his poetic aims in accordance with a 'programme'; it also helps the reader to conceptualise the experience of reading. Ford remarks that the path of song metaphor introduces a conception of poetry as 'spatially extended',[25] and according to contemporary theories of cognitive embodiment, activating this conception means literally enacting it in the experience of reading.[26] Caracciolo argues that readers make sense of space in fictional narratives by projecting a 'virtual body' into the fictional world of the text.[27] He suggests that certain fictional devices, such as focalisor-characters in narrative texts, function as 'anchors' which aid the orientation of the virtual body in the fictional world. Insofar as the path of song metaphor figures the reader's virtual journey through the text, I submit that it also has this same anchoring or orienting function, allowing the reader to conceptualise her experience of reading the poem as a journey with a starting point and a goal.[28]

Once the schema of the path of song is activated, I suggest, it can become modified or reconfigured by the introduction of figures of space and time which play on the concepts of duration, extent, expansion and contraction, as we saw above with the metaphor of 'leading' (*ducere*). By virtue of its orienting function, then, the path of song metaphor comes to serve as a 'megametaphor' which guides the reader through the spatial experience of the poem.[29] This can be demonstrated in our analysis of the central tableau of the poem, the narrative of the battle of Actium.

---

[24] Interestingly, the pairing *Caesaris...Caesar* (v. 13) forms an anaphora if considered at the syntactic level (mirroring *sic...sic*, v. 85), but an epanalepsis if considered at the metrical level (mirroring *sacra...sacris*, v. 1).
[25] Ford 1994: 43.
[26] See e.g. Zwaan 2004.
[27] Caracciolo 2011.
[28] See Johnson and Lakoff 1999: 32–4 on the 'source-path-goal' schema.
[29] See Werth 1994 on 'megametaphors'.

2.4 Actium as monumental space

Hutchinson and Williams agree that we are encouraged to conceive of the untrodden path of the *uates* as a processional route which will end at the temple of Palatine Apollo.[30] Propertius does not set this out in so many words, however; what he does say is 'Muse, we shall recall (*referemus*) the temple of Palatine Apollo'. *Referre* literally means 'bring back', and thus implies movement in *reverse*; as a metaphor for acts of memory such as 'recalling' and 'relating' past events, it connotes travelling back in time to 'retrieve' information which is not presently at hand.[31] How do we reconcile the retrograde movement of *referre* with the forward trajectory of the path of song? I will argue here that the spatial metaphor implicit in the verb *referemus* is informed by a certain spatial logic — the logic of monumental space — which in turn informs Propertius' ecphrastic treatment of the Actian battle-narrative. Let us look first at the pair of couplets which manage the transition from the proem to Actium:

> est Phoebi fugiens Athamana ad litora portus,
>   qua sinus Ioniae murmura condit aquae,
> Actia Iuleae †pelagus†[32] monumenta carinae,
>   nautarum uotis non operosa uia. (15–8)
>
> There is a harbour receding into Phoebus' Athamanian shores, where a bay curbs the roar of the Ionian sea; †that water is† the Actian monument of Caesar's vessel, a passage untroubled by sailors' prayers.

The transition from the declaration of intent to 'recall' Apollo's temple on the Palatine in Rome to an ecphrasis of the bay of Actium on the opposite side of the Ionian sea is one of the paradoxes of this poem.[33] Propertius' other aetiological narratives start with a monument in modern Rome (the shrine of Vertumnus in 4.2, the Tarpeian grove in 4.4, the Ara Maxima in 4.9, the temple of Jupiter Feretrius in 4.10) and follow with an origin-story from the city's mythical past.[34] At vv. 15–18, on the contrary, the origin-story of the Palatine Apollo transports us not through time but through space, to visit another monument which will, paradoxically, tell the story of our local Roman monument. That is, in order to 'call to

---

[30] Hutchinson 2006: *ad* 10, Williams 1968: 252.
[31] See Short 2016: 388-94 on the usage in Latin of the spatial metaphor of past time as 'behind'; Short 2008 on spatial metaphors of mental activity in Latin.
[32] For the crux, see below, n. 40.
[33] Welch 2005: 96–103.
[34] For more on monuments in Propertius 4, see Welch 2005 and Hutchinson 2006.

mind' (*referemus*) the temple of Palatine Apollo, Propertius has to *refer* us to another monument.³⁵

The aspect of monumentality in the poem comes to the fore when we consider the mode of presentation of Propertius' narrative. Vv. 15–18 present the bay of Actium not only as the scene of the battle-narrative but as the actual *monumentum* or 'memorial' of the events to be narrated there.³⁶ It is therefore precisely the word *monumenta* which effects the transition from the present-tense description of the site of Actium to the narrative of the battle. Place and memory thus coincide inextricably in this poem, as they do with monuments. Monuments like verbal narratives are media of memory, but unlike narratives, monuments cannot be 'related' (another meaning of *referre*);³⁷ they have to be visited, whether physically or in the mind's eye. The logic of monumentality thus pulls the meaning of the word *referre* from the verbal act of 'relating' (or the graphemic act of 'retracing') to an act of mental transport; we must 'visit' the monument in memory in order to remember what it commemorates.

'Visiting' is a felicitous word for conceptualising the experience of monuments because it unites the act of viewing with the act of travelling, *theoria* or pilgrimage;³⁸ but the word *referre* in the sense 'recall' is equally apt in that it evokes the centripetal force exerted by monuments themselves, their capacity to salvage the past from the flow of time and tether it to fixed points of surveyable, 'eusynoptic' space.³⁹ With monuments, the act of recall is tied to the act of surveying or scanning, and if the ecphrastic mode overtakes the diegetic in this poem, it is as a function of Propertius' transformation of Actium itself into monumental space. When we are introduced to the site of Actium, it is perfectly empty of content and activity: it is a void or 'gap' (*sinus*) opened by the 'receding' (*fu-*

---

35 Lewis and Short, *referō* def. II.B.4, 'Referre aliquid ad aliquid, *to trace back, ascribe, refer* a thing to any thing'.
36 This is not entirely surprising given that Suetonius (*Vit. Aug.* 18.2) records no less than three works intended to 'extend the glory of his victory at Actium': the building of a victory monument comprising ten captured enemy ships (to which Propertius alludes at vv. 67–8), the expansion of the ancient temple of Apollo, and the foundation of the colony of Nicopolis. The synecdochic notion that the entire geographical region was transformed into a monument of the battle does not seem too far off from historical reality.
37 Propertius uses *referre* of relating hymnic narrative (the aretalogy of Bacchus) at 3.17.39.
38 Cf. the Latin root word *uisere*, used e.g. by Catullus of travelling to see the monuments of Caesar's far-flung conquests at *c.* 11.10.
39 On the Aristotelian term 'eusynoptic' for easily surveyable space, see Purves 2010: 24–64.

giens) of the coastline, a negative space in which the sea's habitual roar is punctuated with silence.[40] The participle *fugiens* offers a striking example of what Talmy refers to as 'fictive motion', the cognitive-linguistic phenomenon whereby static formulations in space such as a dip in the coastline are conceptualised in terms of movement.[41] This fictive 'fleeing' of the coast inland to form the bay of Actium depicts the site as an empty receptacle waiting to be filled with activity,[42] and this demand is answered by the introduction of the battle narrative:

> huc mundi coiere manus: stetit aequore moles
>   pinea, nec remis aequa fauebat auis.
> altera classis erat Teucro damnata Quirino,
>   pilaque feminea turpiter acta manu:
> hinc Augusta ratis plenis Iouis omine uelis,
>   signaque iam Patriae uincere docta suae. (19–24)

> Here joined the armies of East and West: a great mass of pine stood on the water, and fortune did not favour their oars equally. On this side was the fleet doomed by Trojan Quirinus and the javelins shamefully wielded by a woman's hand; on the other was the Augustan ship, her sails full with good omens from Jupiter, and the standards that had now been taught to lead the fatherland to victory.

The transition from the present to the past is made not with an adverb of time but with the directional deictic *huc* ('hither', 19) in emphatic verse-initial position, which suggests a relation of linear causation between the emptiness of Actium and the entrance of the combatants, as if the stillness of the water were the quiet before the storm – even though logically the quiet of Actium is in the present, while the battle is in the past. Propertius' ecphrasis of Actium thus follows a sequence not of narrating but of monumental viewing: the spectator surveys the empty space of Actium and, with the act of 'recall' (*referemus*), *fills* it with monumental content.[43] Just as the ritual space of the proem had to be emptied of ill-

---

[40] If we accept the problematic manuscript reading, the bay is empty of sailors too; Heyworth's not unattractive reading *celebrant* would have this otherwise vacant space filled only by the monuments. See Heyworth 2007: *ad loc.* for a full discussion. Hutchinson obelises the whole couplet 17–18; this seems to me unnecessary.
[41] Talmy 2000: 99–175.
[42] The first hemistich of v. 15 (*est Phoebi fugiens*) finds a strong verbal echo in the first hemistich of v. 27 (*cum Phoebus linquens*), suggesting a parallelism between the 'fleeing' of the coastline and Phoebus' 'leaving' Delos for Actium, as if both god and coast were attracted by the centripetal force of the bay.
[43] This sequence of viewing is exemplified in the first couplet of the first poem of the book: *hoc, quodcumque uides, hospes, qua maxima Roma est, | ante Phrygem Aenean collis et herba fuit.*

omened noise before it could be filled with libations of Propertius' song,[44] Actium must be populated by the act of recall before it can be refashioned into monumental space.

This act of recall renders Actium visible to the (eu)synoptic gaze, and we are treated to a bird's-eye view which allows us to appreciate the huge scope of the events we are witnessing: the opposed fleets are a 'great mass of pine' and their meeting is the joining of the 'hands of the world' (to preserve the metaphor in *manus*, 'armies'). Our view on the events is also that of the bird of omen (*auis*, 20), for we are allowed to see which side is favoured by fortune. Antony's fleet is introduced by *altera*, which in augural terminology refers to the unfavorable side of the augural field or *templum*;[45] in this way we are encouraged to become augurs and to declare Antony's fleet doomed (*damnata*, 21) by virtue of its very position on the field of battle.

The verb which expresses fortune's favour is *fauebat* (20); this harks back to the ritual space of the proem, where the success of the rite is dependent on the *fauor* of both the attendants and the Muse Calliope (1, 12). Similarly, Jupiter is asked to 'stand by' for the singing of Caesar in the proem (14), and fills Augustus' sails with good omens in the narrative section (23). The *fauor* (ritually regulated goodwill or complicity) which made possible the creation of the sacred space of the proem is thus also the *fauor* which guided Augustus to victory, and which is now made *visible* to the attendants of the ritual (the readers of the poem) through the medium of monumental space. We can now see how the poem's optical sojourn in Actium picks up the thread of the path of song established in the proem, which, as noted above, leads 'to the name of Caesar' (*Caesaris in nomen*, 13). The path to the name of Caesar is a path to the monumental space filled *by* Caesar himself, just as the temporal span of the song is said to be filled by the singing *of* Caesar (13–14).

---

44 There is an attractive parallel here between *murmura condit aquae* and the silenced sea of Callimachus' *Hymn to Apollo*.
45 Lewis and Short, *alter* def. II.D. The metaphor of the 'hands (= armies) of the world' in v. 19 also naturally suggests a lucky right hand (Augustus, the West) and an unlucky left hand (Antony, the East); cf. the 'womanish hand' (*feminea...manu*) of Antony and Cleopatra's soldiers in 22. We might perhaps follow Welch 2005: 101–02 in detecting in *remis* (20) a pun on Remus, the losing side in Rome's foundational augury.

2.5 *Inauguratio* and Augustus

Propertius' use of augural tropes in this poem becomes more intelligible once we look back to the mission statement set out in the first poem of the book, where Propertius frames his aetiological project as a 'rebuilding' of the walls of Rome:

> moenia namque pio coner disponere uersu:
>   ei mihi, quod nostro est paruus in ore sonus!
> sed tamen exiguo quodcumque e pectore riui
>   fluxerit, hoc patriae seruiet omne meae.
> Ennius hirsuta cingat sua dicta corona:
>   mi folia ex hedera porrige, Bacche, tua,
> ut nostris tumefacta superbiat Vmbria libris,
>   Vmbria Romani patria Callimachi!
> scandentis quisquis cernit de uallibus arces,
>   ingenio muros aestimet ille meo!
> Roma, faue: tibi surgit opus: date candida, ciues,
>   omina, et inceptis dextera cantet auis!
> sacra deosque canam et cognomina prisca locorum:
>   has meus ad metas sudet oportet equus. (4.1[A].57–70)

Indeed, I will try to array [Rome's] walls in dutiful verse: alas, that this whimper lives in my mouth! Yet whatever stream flows from my meagre breast, all of it will go to serve my country. Let Ennius wreathe his words with a shaggy crown: extend to me the leaves of your ivy, Bacchus, so that my books may swell Umbria with pride, Umbria, homeland of the Roman Callimachus! Whoever sees the tall buildings climbing out from her valleys, let him rate those walls by the measure of my talent! Favour me, Rome: my work rises for you: give me happy omens, citizens, and may my undertaking be attended by auspicious birdsong! I will sing of rites and gods and ancient place-names: my horse must sweat towards this goal.

As Macleod demonstrates, Propertius here draws a sustained analogy between the writing of his book of Roman aetiologies and the founding of Rome itself.[46] Macleod further notes[47] that the explicit augural imagery of vv. 67–68 coupled with the motif of 'growing' and 'increasing' aligns Propertius' activity with the ritual of *inauguratio*.[48] Linderski explains *inauguratio* (alternately *auguratio*) as the ceremony through which units of sacred space or *templa* are demarcated and

---

[46] Macleod 1976: 143–44.
[47] Macleod 1976: 143.
[48] Viz. in *surgit opus* (67), *tumefacta…Vmbria* (63), *scandentis…arces* (65); cf. *creuerunt moenia* (56) and *resurgentis Troiae* (47). For Propertius as augur, see 2.21.2; 3.1.36; 3.4.9; and cf. 2.10.19–20.

set apart from profane space,⁴⁹ an activity which is conceptualised metaphorically in terms of 'augmenting' or 'increasing' that space, in accordance with the etymology *augurium < augeo*.⁵⁰ As Linderski and Short emphasise, this act is largely a visual one of traversing the space with the eye.⁵¹ Fittingly, then, the paratactic phrase *Roma, faue: tibi surgit opus* (67) assumes a direct link between the *fauor* of Rome (i.e. her cooperation in the augural rite) and the 'rising' of the work in her honour; but Propertius' poem will also perform the re-inauguration of Rome herself, through the singing of her 'rites and gods and ancient place-names' (69).⁵² Compare this with Propertius' mission statement in 4.6:

> Musa, Palatini referemus Apollinis aedem:
>   res est, Calliope, digna fauore tuo.
> Caesaris in nomen ducuntur carmina: Caesar
>   dum canitur, quaeso, Iuppiter ipse uaces! (11–14)

> Muse, we shall recall the temple of Palatine Apollo: the subject is worthy of your favour, Calliope. My songs are on a path to the name of Caesar: while Caesar is sung, I pray, let even Jupiter himself stand clear!

Propertius' subject (*res*) is the temple of Palatine Apollo and its origin, but the key to this aetiological puzzle is the *name* of Octavian — or more specifically, his two *cognomina*, Caesar and Augustus. This is fitting when one considers that Octavian's adoption of the name Augustus is often conceptually linked with his victory in the civil war, as e.g. in the *Res Gestae*.⁵³ The fact that Caesar's two *cognomina* appear no less than eight times in the poem⁵⁴ certainly reinforces this link, but the focus on the name Augustus in particular also calls to mind the etymology of the name. Suet. *Vit. Aug.* 7.2 records that Augustus chose his new *cognomen* over 'Romulus' because of its association with augury and the foundation of Rome⁵⁵ by way of the term '*loca augusta/inaugurata*' — places made sacred

---

49 Linderski 1986: 2262–71.
50 Linderski 1986: 2290–91.
51 Linderski 1986: 2265–6; Short 2008: 122–26.
52 It is well known that Propertius only follows through on this plan in a handful of poems: 4 on the Tarpeian grove, 9 on the Ara Maxima, and 10 on the temple of Jupiter Feretrius. The other poems only gesture at the aetiological programme (e.g. in the Lanuvium vignette in poem 8). Poem 6 is arguably Propertius' most concerted effort to live up to the title of Roman Callimachus.
53 *RG* 34.16–21.
54 *Augustus*: 23, 29, 38, 81; *Caesar*: 13 (twice), 56, 59.
55 Suetonius cites Ennius' line augusto augurio postquam incluta condita Roma est.

through *inauguratio*.⁵⁶ Octavian becomes Augustus, then, through his (re-)*inauguratio* of Rome, an act symbolised in the *Res Gestae* and the *Aeneid* by the founding of the temple of Palatine Apollo.⁵⁷

Propertius' poem makes this act of *inauguratio*, the 'Augustification' of Octavian, visible. After Apollo makes his fiery appearance atop Octavian's prow, he gives an oracular speech which draws a link between Augustus' impending victory and Romulus' augury on the Palatine, the pivotal moment in the history of Rome's foundation:

> solue metu patriam, quae nunc te uindice freta
>   imposuit prorae publica uota tuae.
> quam nisi defendes, murorum Romulus augur
>   ire Palatinas non bene uidit auis. (41–4)

> Free the fatherland from fear; she now rests the hopes of her people on your prow, depending on you as her protector. If you do not defend her, it was an evil sign when Romulus, the augur of her walls, observed the flight of the Palatine birds.

Propertius alludes to the story that Romulus and Remus called an augury competition to decide in whose name the new city would be founded. According to the prevailing account, Romulus stood on the Palatine hill, and Remus stood on the Aventine,⁵⁸ and it was decided — though not without dispute — that Romulus' vantage point was the true one, proving him to be the rightful king. The magnitude of the oracular pronouncement here cannot be overstated: its implication is that Augustus' victory proves once and for all that Romulus was correct, and that the foundation of Rome in his name rather than Remus' was in fact achieved in accordance with divine will — a truth which was evidently concealed until this very moment. The defeat of Antony is thus figured as a divine epiphany, the revelation of the destiny of Rome, embodied in the person of Augustus.⁵⁹ The epiphanic aspect of Augustus and his victory is made explicit in the concise pair of couplets which concludes the battle:⁶⁰

> uincit Roma fide Phoebi: dat femina poenas:
>   sceptra per Ionias fracta uehuntur aquas.

---

56 See Ov. *F.* 1.609–10.
57 See *RG* 34.16–21.
58 e.g. Liv. 1.6; Ennius famously has the stations reversed, and other versions have Remus in some other place, but Romulus on the Palatine is fairly consistent.
59 An analogous idea might be found in Hector's statement at Hom. *Il.* 12.243 that 'the single best (bird of) omen is to fight for one's country' (εἷς οἰωνὸς ἄριστος ἀμύνεσθαι περὶ πάτρης).
60 See Cairns 1984 on the relation of this passage to the language of epiphany.

> at pater Idalio miratur Caesar ab astro:
> 'sum deus; est nostri sanguinis ista fides.'

> Rome is victorious, Phoebus' faith (*fides*) is kept: the woman is put to justice: her broken power is carried away across the Ionian main. Looking down from the star of Venus, the elder Caesar exclaims: 'I am a god: this is the confirmation (*fides*) of my bloodline.'

Apollo's support of Augustus is a manifestation of his *fides*, faith or loyalty, the same principle which permits Julius Caesar to bear witness to his adoptive son's divinity. *Fides* emblematises the harmonious relationship of past to present, the fulfilment of prophecy and the ratification of vows, and the principle of *continuity* which is visible only through the (eu)synoptic gaze made possible by monumental space.

The image of Romulus' eye following the flight path of the birds across the space of the unsettled Palatine Hill — which, as Newman notes, falls squarely at the middle point of the poem[61] — is a figure of monumental space as the medium for the visual manifestation or staging of *fides*, much like the appearance of Caesar's comet and the fiery epiphany of Apollo. As the only use of the adjective *Palatinus* in the poem other than at the beginning, this passage is the one place where Propertius intimates the aetiological link between the Palatine Apollo and the Actian, thereby retroactively justifying the plotting of his song as a path leading from the Palatine to Actium and finally to the 'name of Caesar'. Apollo's pronouncement reveals how Romulus' augural foundation of Rome and Augustus' epiphanic refoundation are bound together in the space of the Palatine, which is both the *templum* formed by Romulus' augury and the *templum* founded by Augustus in honour of Apollo. Just as Romulus' *templum* was formed by an act of visual scanning (*ire Palatinas non bene uidit auis*), so too does the path of Propertius' song make possible the monumental viewing of Apollo's Palatine temple, the traversing with the eye or 'contemplation' which pulls together past and present into a eusynoptic whole.[62]

---

[61] Newman 1997: 369.
[62] The Palatine temple is also made into a privileged site of monumental viewing at Hor. *CS* 61–68, where the *augur* Apollo (61) is said to ensure the future prosperity of Rome 'as long as he looks with equity on the Palatine altars (*si Palatinas uidet aequus aras*, 65).'

2.6 The path of Apollo

As noted above, Apollo's speech presents Augustus' victory as an epiphany of *fides*. According to this logic, the end of the civil war marks both a radical break from the past and a reaffirmation of it — a paradox not unknown to Augustan ideology. In this final section, I will show how Propertius' path of song breaks its own line of continuity and thereby effects the dispersal of the eusynoptic gaze. To reiterate, the epiphany of Apollo is a manifestation of his *fides* to Augustus and thereby of the *fides* that confirms Augustus' divine parentage and his destiny to restore Rome to greatness. The epiphany of Apollo is thus, in a way, the *medium* of the epiphany of Augustus.[63] It is fitting, then, that Propertius emphasises the physical appearance of Apollo, stressing that he came dressed for the occasion:

> non ille attulerat crinis in colla solutos
>   aut testudineae carmen inerme lyrae,
> sed quali aspexit Pelopeum Agamemnona uultum,
>   egessitque auidis Dorica castra rogis,
> aut qualis flexos soluit Pythona per orbis
>   serpentem, imbelles quem timuere deae. (31–6)

> He had not come with hair hanging loose onto his neck or with a peaceful song from his tortoise-shell lyre, but with the countenance with which he looked on Pelops' descendant Agamemnon and emptied the Doric camp into hungry pyres, or as he was when he slew the serpent Python whom the unwarlike goddesses feared, unravelling his writhing coils.

Propertius adopts the common topos of the dual aspects of Apollo — the avenger armed with a bow and the peacemaker bearing a lyre[64] — expressing them in terms of outward appearance and dress, as one would normally describe a statue.[65] The comical implication of this is that, for Apollo, the transition from peace to war and back again is as simple as a costume change, and that is precisely what happens once Propertius reaches the end of the battle narrative:

---

[63] Compare vv. 47–50, where Apollo exhorts Augustus not to be deterred by the spectacle of the enemy fleet painted with monstrous figures, setting up an implicit contrast between the 'true' appearance of Apollo and the deceptive appearance of the enemy's 'painted terrors (*pictos...metus*, 50).'
[64] Miller 2009: 87.
[65] In fact, as Welch discusses, this description forms an interesting counterpoint with Propertius' memorable description of the statue of *Apollo citharoedus* (i.e. Apollo in his *un*warlike aspect) at 2.31 (Welch 2005: 96–103).

> bella satis cecini: citharam iam poscit Apollo
>   uictor et ad placidos exuit arma choros,
> candida nunc molli subeant conuiuia luco,
>   blanditiaeque fluant per mea colla rosae,
> uinaque fundantur prelis elisa Falernis,
>   terque lauet nostras spica Cilissa comas.
> ingenium potis irritet Musa poetis:
>   Bacche, soles Phoebo fertilis esse tuo. (69–76)

> I have sung enough of war: now victorious Apollo calls for his lyre and sheds his battle-gear in preparation for gentle choruses. Now let banqueters proceed in white robes to the pleasant grove, and let the caress of roses stream about my neck; let wine from Falernian presses be poured, and let the Cilician spikenard anoint our hair. Let the Muse rouse inspiration in drunken poets: Bacchus, you are known to be fruitful for your brother Phoebus.

It is well known that *bella satis cecini* is an example of the break-off formula or *Abbruchsformel*, a technique associated with Pindar by which a poet cuts short a narrative or a topic of song. In Pindar, the break-off formula is often articulated within the path of song metaphor, allowing the poet to dramatise his movement from topic to topic in the course of his performance. Here, however, it is not only the poet who makes an end, but Apollo as well: the god is envisioned as a triumphant general returning home to his victory feast (*uictor*, 70), and steps out of his military garb to re-emerge as Apollo *citharoedus*, miming Propertius' thematic transition from war to peace. This Apolline conceit depends on a complex manipulation of narrative time. If the god's costume-change only takes place once Propertius' battle-narrative is over, then we must imagine that he has been in his war costume up until the moment indexed by the word *iam* (69). This naturally refers us to the battle narrative immediately preceding, in which Apollo was specifically described as geared up for war (vv. 31–6), and suggests a linear progression in time between the two episodes — despite the fact that the first of these occurred within the frame of the historical battle-narrative, while the second is contemporaneous with the time of utterance. The effect is that the time of narration is grafted onto the narrated time, and we are made to imagine that Apollo's costume-change and the 'gentle choruses' for which he is outfitting himself are to occur *directly after the battle of Actium*.[66]

The god's costume-change cues another set of ritual directions as in the proem, this time aimed at the creation of a convivial space. This convivial space

---

[66] Hutchinson 2006: *ad* 71. Cf. the temporal distortion between the ecphrasis of Actium and the start of the battle narrative at v. 19.

is introduced both as a scene-change (*subeant*, referring to the banqueters entering the grove) and as a costume-change (*candida*, referring to their white dress),⁶⁷ and thus the movement of the banqueters mimics both Apollo's transformation and Propertius' thematic *volte-face*, integrating them into a synchronised manoeuvre within the path of song. The path of song metaphor thus forges its own fictive temporality, within which the gap between the narrated time of the battle and the time of utterance is bridged.

Applying the frames of experience-report and performed speech to this will elucidate some of the complexities involved.⁶⁸ Within the frame of experience-report, the path of song takes on the aspect of a journey through which the poet guides the reader; within this frame, Apollo's two outfittings form part of the 'story' or *fabula* of the song-performance, and Apollo is made present to the reader through the medium of this *fabula*. Within the frame of performed speech, however, Apollo enjoys another modality of presence, for he functions not as a (fictional) character but as himself the medium of song. As both medium and matter of Propertius' poem, Apollo maintains an irreducibly metaleptic presence: he is both revealed through the path of song and guides its movement.⁶⁹

The path of song thus in a significant way *follows* Apollo, just as the god's costume-change ushers in Propertius' transition to the convivial scene in the epilogue. We noticed above how the directional deictic *huc* (19) harnesses the forward momentum of the path of song in order to depict the start of the battle-narrative as a 'filling up' of the empty space of Actium. This deictic introduction is mirrored in the couplet that effects the transition between the battle-narrative and the convivial epilogue with the obverse deictic, *hinc* ('hence'):

Actius **hinc** traxit Phoebus monumenta, quod eius
    una decem uicit missa sagitta ratis. (67–8)

From this Actian Phoebus derived his monument, because he sunk ten ships with one loosed arrow.

---

67 This line is ambiguous: *conuiuia* can refer to 'banquets' or metonymically to 'banqueters', and thus *subire* can refer to the movement of the banqueters 'entering' into the grove (taking *molli luco* as dative) or else to the 'arising' or 'occurring' of the banquet itself (taking *molli luco* as ablative). Either way, the verb *subire* resumes the path of song metaphor, as well as the theme of costume-change; if we take *candida* as denoting the white dress of banqueters, then the scene-change of the *molli...luco* is put on like a dress in an epiphanic act of *mise-en-scene*.
68 For the terms, see ch. 1.
69 Klooster 2013a: 156 makes a similar observation about the embedded apostrophe to Apollo in a narrative context at Hom. *Il.* 15.365. Refer to the remainder of her article for an application of the term 'metalepsis' that dovetails with my application of it here.

To be sure, *huc* (19) is literal in its spatial deixis, serving to set the scene for the battle-narrative ('*hither* they came together'), while *hinc* (67) is figurative, denoting the causality of Apollo's monument ('*from this* he derived his monument'); but placed as they are respectively at the opening and close of the battle-narrative, they suggest a mirrored relation between the centripetal force of the battle-scene and the winning of Apollo's monument from that battle. v. 67–8 also form a strong ring-composition structure with vv. 17–8, in which the word *monumenta* and the adjective *Actius* each stand in the same metrical *sedes*:

> **Actia** Iuleae †pelagus† **monumenta** carinae,
>   nautarum uotis non operosa uia.

> ††that water is† the Actian monument of Caesar's vessel, a passage untroubled by sailors' prayers.

Here, in the ecphrasis of Actium, the adjective *Actia* is applied to *monumenta*, whereas after the battle is won, it is *Phoebus Actius* who 'derives' his monument *from* the site of Actium. In the intervening time, we witnessed Apollo departing his birthplace of Delos for the battle of Actium (27–8), so we are not unjustified in conceiving of the god's act of 'deriving' (or perhaps 'dragging') his monument *from* Actium (*hinc*) as an act of travel. How can Apollo conceivably travel away from Actium and still remain *Actius*? An answer is offered in vv. 27–8: the god departs from the floating island of Delos but leaves it 'unmoved thanks to his guardianship' (*stantem se uindice*, 27). With the word *uindex*, we move into the sphere of Roman imperialism, and we begin to conceive of Apollo as an expansionist with a number of provinces under his management.[70]

Within this context, we may view *Actius* as a *cognomen* won through military conquest on the model of e.g. *Africanus*, and the *monumenta* of v. 67 as military trophies to be deposited in a temple at Rome. This representation resonates with much that scholars know and guess about the real monument at Actium (the 'monument' at Actium was in fact a naval trophy deposited at the site of Augustus' camp, and apparently the restored temple of Apollo Actius was fitted with memorials of the battle as well) in addition to the supposed thematic presence of the victory at Actium in the real Palatine temple at Rome.[71] For our purposes, however, it will suffice to note that the image of Apollo dragging his Actian monument back to Rome enacts an imperialist fantasy which is embodied in the monumental space of Actium itself: the fantasy of condensing the breadth of foreign conquest

---

[70] Apollo names Augustus the *uindex* of the Roman people at v. 41.
[71] Miller 2009: 227.

into a single eusynoptic view. As Propertius' path of song follows Apollo on his journey from Delos to Actium and back to the Palatine, seeing him veer between the incompatible guises of local guardian and expansionist conqueror, the god performs a complex dialectic of presence which finally problematises the epiphany of *fides* at the heart of the narrative, as well as the promise of monumental space to 'recall' the past into the present. Amid this dialectic of presence the figure of Augustus is thrown into relief, and the question is raised: conqueror, founder, protector, god — what are we really looking at?

2.7 Recall and refrain in Bion's *Lament for Adonis*

The preceding discussion helped to bring to light two significant aspects of the fiction of occasion which reinforce and expand upon the conclusions drawn in the previous chapter. Firstly, we saw an example of how figures such as the path of song metaphor can be essential to the construction of a spatial experience and to the production of occasion. This approach transcends the restrictive conception of performance space as a static container by recognising the capacity of mere words — even 'non-literal' language — to shape and construct space. Essential to this is a rejection of the notion that figurative language is secondary to or parasitic on literal language,[72] and hence a rejection of the common distinction (noted above) between 'literal' (real, realistic, or mimetic) performance spaces and 'metaphorical' spaces. Secondly, this section took up the Apolline thread of the previous chapter in exploring how Propertius' poem enacts modalities of divine presence which serve as an experiential anchor for the fiction of occasion. This approach offers an alternative to the mimetic schema challenged in the previous chapter by suggesting that Apollo is not so much a character *in* the poem as a medium which the poem coopts to create its own presence effects.

Propertius' poem is virtually a hymn to Apollo, but it is curiously lacking one key hymnic touch: Propertius never addresses the god directly.[73] I think it fitting, then, to turn to a poem where address plays a central role, namely Bion's *Lament for Adonis*. In this section of the chapter, I will offer another example of how a pervasive trope can function as an experiential anchor for the fiction of occasion. Specifically, I will show how the poem takes up the idea that invoking the name of Adonis can bring him back from the dead and makes it a reality. It does so, I

---

72 Johnson 1987.
73 Although oddly he does apostrophise Bacchus at v. 76.

argue, through the fractured quasi-refrain of the poem and the rhythmic soundscape created thereby. This will feed into a discussion of how the fiction of occasion of the poem relates to the real-life rituals documented as part of the Adonia festival.[74] I will argue that interpreting the poem as a 'mimetic' account of a particular ritual performance[75] is not only unnecessary and unproductive, but in fact hinders our ability to appreciate the fictional effects which the poem produces within the apparatus of its native medium.

2.8 Measureless measures: the Adonis-cry and refrain

Unlike Propertius 4.6 and Callimachus' second *Hymn*, the *Adonis* begins not with the creation of a sacred space but with the announcement of a vocal performance:

> αἰάζω τὸν Ἄδωνιν· 'ἀπώλετο καλὸς Ἄδωνις'·
> 'ὤλετο καλὸς Ἄδωνις' ἐπαιάζουσιν Ἔρωτες. (1–2)

> Adonis is my cry: 'Fair Adonis is dead!' 'Fair Adonis is dead!', cry the Loves in reply.

The verb αἰάζω both announces and intones the mourning cry αἰαῖ, folding the act of mourning and the sound of the mourning voice into one. Insofar as the verb announces an act of mourning, its direct object, τὸν Ἄδωνιν, denotes Adonis, the subject of the dirge; but insofar as the verb indexes the production of a voice, 'Adonis' is simply its sonic content.[76] Adonis' name in fact takes up a large share of the sonic content of the poem, appearing no less than 33 times in the poem's 98 verses, and in three of those instances (32, 90, 94), the name is mentioned as part of an exclamation introduced by the cry αἰαῖ (32, 90) or αἴ (94), and is thus nothing more than mere sound.[77] Likewise, the cry ἀπώλετο καλὸς Ἄδωνις, 'fair Adonis is dead' is reduced by its repetition from an informative statement to a ritualistic chant; the event of Adonis' death is subordinated to the act of mourning him, an act which is implied in the very act of uttering his name.

---

74 On the Adonia, see Luc. *Syr. D.* 6, Plut. *Alc.* 18.3, *id. Nic.* 13.7, Theoc. 15.110–35, Ar. *Lys.* 387–98.
75 Reed 1997: 16, 21–23; Fantuzzi 1985: 155–56; Wilamowitz 1900: 10. Alexiou 2002: 56 suggests that the poem was intended for performance on the second day of the *Adonia* but does not comment on how she envisions the interaction between poem and rite.
76 Verg. *G.* 4.523–7, in a related context (the story of Orpheus' death), produces a similar effect through the ambiguous use of the name *Eurydicen*; see Butler 2015: 214 n. 27.
77 The accusative of the name preceded by the article (τὸν Ἄδωνιν) appears no less than eleven times (1, 6, 15, 32, 34, 50, 57, 67, 85, 90, 94).

The gratuitous repetition of the name throughout the poem reproduces at the level of enunciation the antiphonal structure adumbrated by the first two verses in the form of an exchange of laments between a chorus leader and a chorus of Loves. The second verse produces a kind of jumbled echo of the first by reversing the two metrico-syntactic units formed by each hemistich,[78] while introducing a pointed variation: ἀπώλετο, transferred to the first hemistich, loses its prefix ἀπ(ο)-, while αἰάζω, now in the third person plural, gains the prefix ἐπ(ι)- to fill the slot left vacant by ἀπ(ο)-. Sitting right in the spot where the second hemistich takes over from the first, these mirrored prefixes thematise the very call-and-response scheme of which they form a part: the passing *away* (ἀπ-) of Adonis is answered with an image of motion *towards* (ἐπ-), as if the chorus' supplementation of the dirge with their own cries (the literal sense of the prefix) had the power to reverse the youth's passage into death.

The song-form evoked by these first two lines — monody interpuncted by a regular choral refrain — draws on traditional analogues both from Greek lament in general[79] and from Bion's direct literary model, the *Lament for Daphnis* of Theocritus 1.64–142.[80] Bion's use of refrain naturally bears comparison to that of Theocritus' shepherd Thyrsis:

> ἄρχετε βουκολικᾶς, Μοῖσαι φίλαι, ἄρχετ' ἀοιδᾶς   (Theoc. 1.64 etc.)
> ...
> λήγετε βουκολικᾶς, Μοῖσαι, ἴτε, λήγετ' ἀοιδᾶς   (Theoc. 1.127 etc.)
>
> Begin the bucolic song, dear Muses, begin.
> ...
> Leave the bucolic song, come, Muses, leave.

Thyrsis' refrain has no bearing on the narrative content of his song — the pining of Daphnis — but only on its musical shape and rhythm. Its function is to interpolate a stanzaic cadence into the stichic procession of the hexameter and thus to form a kind of rhythmic frame or 'hook' to mark out Thyrsis' bucolic song from

---

[78] Reed 1997: *ad loc.*
[79] Alexiou goes so far as to claim that 'There seems to be no example in Greek antiquity of a lament which has lost all traces of refrain (Alexiou 2002: 134).'
[80] For Bion's debt to the *Lament for Daphnis*, see Reed 1997. It is noteworthy from an intertextual standpoint that Ps.-Moschus' *Epitaph for Bion*, among all its close imitations of Bion's poetry and in particular the *Adonis*, incorporates a refrain closely modelled on Theocritus': ἄρχετε Σικελικαὶ τῶ πένθεος, ἄρχετε Μοῖσαι.

the surrounding verses.⁸¹ This is helped along by the self-enclosed regularity of the refrain itself, a feature which obtains at both the syntactic and the stylistic level: the address to the Muses sets off the utterance as parenthetical, while the singsong anaphora of ἄρχετε ('begin') and λήγετε ('leave') figures the timekeeping function of the refrain within the refrain itself.⁸²

Bion's poem exhibits nothing like this kind of rhythmic regularity. What we find instead is fragmentary echoes of the first two lines scattered unevenly throughout the text and intermingled with other motifs picked up along the way. First, the second hemistich of the first line ('ἀπώλετο καλὸς Ἄδωνις') is repeated at v. 5, but this time in a different quotational context, namely the voice of Aphrodite. Next, at vv. 6 and 15, we hear a truncated version of the first two lines which sounds like the start of a one-line refrain, but this pattern is quickly broken off by the introduction of a new element in the first hemistich at v. 28: 'αἰαῖ τὰν Κυθέρειαν' ἐπαιάζουσιν Ἔρωτες ('Alas for Cytherea!' cry the Loves in answer). This half-line is heard twice more in combination with the familiar ἀπώλετο καλὸς Ἄδωνις (37, 63) and once with ἐπαιάζουσιν Ἔρωτες (86). Finally, a direct echo of v. 1 comes at v. 67, but this time without the reply of the Loves (2) to accompany it. Estevez helpfully catalogues all these verse-segments and assembles them in such a way that they seem to add up to a refrain with hemistichal variations,⁸³ but Reed does more justice to the acoustic effects of the poem when he avers that it 'does not simulate a song [...] but a festival atmosphere punctuated by irregular cries.'⁸⁴

This effect is achieved not only by the lack of internal consistency in the 'refrain', but also and crucially by its use of quoted speech. The first two lines each comprise a *verbum dicendi* (αἰάζω, ἐπαιάζουσιν) accompanied by a phrase in quoted speech ('ἀπώλετο καλὸς Ἄδωνις', 'ὤλετο καλὸς Ἄδωνις'). As noted above,

---

81 Rosenmeyer observes that refrain in bucolic 'has the function of reemphasizing the point of origin; the beginning, the source, reaches out to form a frame, much like the ivy whose tendrils surround the panels on the cup. [...] wherever the refrains are prominent, the idea of going back to the beginning, of periodically re-anchoring the imagination in a fundamental motif, is present (Rosenmeyer 1969: 94).' See also Goldhill 1991: 241–43 on refrain in Theocritus, which he links to the 'mimesis of song'.
82 For this aspect of refrain in general cf. Wills 1996: 96. *id.* 96–99 is a good overview of refrain in Roman and some Greek poetry.
83 Estevez 1981: 35–6. He lists the half-lines as follows: A: αἰάζω τὸν Ἄδωνιν; B: ἀπώλετο καλὸς Ἄδωνις; C: ὤλετο καλὸς Ἄδωνις; D: ἐπαιάζουσιν Ἔρωτες; E: αἰαῖ τὰν Κυθέρειαν. These half-lines, as he explains, occur in the following lines in the following combinations: 1: A, B; 2: C, D; 6: A, D; 15: A, D; 28: E, D; 37: E, B; 63: E, B; 67: A, B; 86: E, D.
84 Reed 1997: 1–2n. We will return below to the mimetic theory implied in Reed's use of the word 'simulate'. Cf. Rutherford 2001: 70–71 and 315–16 on 'quasi-refrains' in Pindar's paeans.

the first variation on this 'pattern' is the transference of one of these blocks of quoted speech to Aphrodite (λέγε πᾶσιν 'ἀπώλετο καλὸς Ἄδωνις', 5). The formula is repeated verbatim, but outside of the scheme formed by the strophic responsion of chorus and chorus leader in vv. 1–2. Once we are introduced to the wilderness scene of Adonis' death, this same formula is distributed all across the natural environment in typical bucolic fashion:

> 'τὰν Κύπριν αἰαῖ'
> ὤρεα πάντα λέγοντι, καὶ αἱ δρύες 'αἲ τὸν Ἄδωνιν.'
> καὶ ποταμοὶ κλαίουσι τὰ πένθεα τᾶς Ἀφροδίτας,
> καὶ παγαὶ τὸν Ἄδωνιν ἐν ὤρεσι δακρύοντι,
> ἄνθεα δ᾽ ἐξ ὀδύνας ἐρυθαίνεται· ἁ δὲ Κυθήρα
> πάντας ἀνὰ κναμώς, ἀνὰ πᾶν νάπος οἰκτρὸν ἀείδει
> 'αἰαῖ τὰν Κυθέρειαν, ἀπώλετο καλὸς Ἄδωνις.'
> Ἀχὼ δ᾽ ἀντεβόασεν 'ἀπώλετο καλὸς Ἄδωνις.'
> Κύπριδος αἰνὸν ἔρωτα τίς οὐκ ἔκλαυσεν ἂν αἰαῖ; (32–40)

'Cypris, alas' say all the mountains, and the oaks say 'Alack for Adonis.' Even the rivers cry sorrow for Aphrodite, even the mountain springs weep for Adonis, and grief turns the flowers red; all along her dells, all amongst her thickets the island of Cythera piteously sings, 'Alas for Cytherea; fair Adonis is dead', and Echo cried back 'Fair Adonis is dead'. For the doomed love of Cypris who would not cry 'Alas'?

At this point in the text, the 'refrain' expands beyond a simple call-and-response scheme into a diffuse reverberation to be sounded by any voice within its range; as Bion says, who *wouldn't* join in? This diffusive effect is made possible by the very quotability of quoted speech, permitting the nesting of one echoic fragment within another and their recombination in various permutations throughout the text. Whereas refrain is measured repetition within fixed bounds, the cry for Adonis rebounds like an echo from place to place, an echo which is sounded in each iteration of the cry in the text itself. But this echoic quality is not limited to the Adonis-cry; a welter of verbal repetitions suffuses the entire poem with a pulsing, incantatory quality.[85] Reed observes that Bion's expository style occasionally exhibits a 'spiral' structure of successive repetitions whereby 'each return to a word [...] is a launching place to the next idea, until the culminating point is reached.'[86]

---

[85] ὀδόντι, | λευκῷ λευκὸν ὀδόντι (7–8); τὸ φίλημα [...] τὸ φίλημα (12–3); ἄγριον ἄγριον (16); ὤλεσε [...] συνώλεσεν (29); ὡς ἴδεν, ὡς ἐνόησεν [...] | ὡς ἴδε (40–1); μεῖνον Ἄδωνι [...] μεῖνον Ἄδωνι (42–3); χείλεα χείλεσι (44); με φίλησον | [...] με φίλησον (45–6); φεύγεις, | φεύγεις (50–1); χέει | [...] χέει (64–5); καὶ νέκυς ὢν καλός ἐστι, καλὸς νέκυς (71); ῥαῖνε [...] ῥαῖνε (77); μύροισιν | [...] μύρα [...] μύρον (77–8); Ὑμήν, | Ὑμήν (88-9); πάλιν [...]πάλιν (98). See Reed 1997: 45–8.
[86] Reed 1997: 52; he points in particular to vv. 42–53.

If refrain's regularity allows it to be set off as a 'figure' against the 'ground' of the surrounding text, then, Bion's Adonis-cry gets lost among the dense texture of clustered repetitions that makes up his poem. The result, though, is not that the refrain disappears altogether from view, but that we begin to see hints of refrain — to hear snatches of it — at every turn.

We may turn here to Hollander's searching remarks on refrain:

> Refrains can time a poem, tolling its strophic hours in the tongue of bells that may be wholly foreign to the noises of the stanzas' daily life. And poetic refrains can enact tropes, as well as schemes, of time and memory. [...] Thus we again observe that refrains *are*, and *have*, memories – of their own prior strophes or stretches of text, of their own pre-occurences, and of their own genealogies in earlier texts as well.[87]

We might take this a step further and suggest that the echoic reverberations of Bion's poem carry the memory of Theocritus' bucolic refrain with its orderly rhythm. This can be seen for example in the conclusion of the poem:

> λῆγε γόων Κυθέρεια τὸ σάμερον, ἴσχεο κομμῶν·
> δεῖ σε πάλιν κλαῦσαι, πάλιν εἰς ἔτος ἄλλο δακρῦσαι. (97–8)

> Leave your lament for today, Cytherea, cease your wailing; you must weep again, cry again another year.

This ending does not only directly echo the Theocritean refrain with λῆγε and ἴσχεο in the same metrical *sedes* as Theocritus' λήγετε...λῆγετ'; it also resumes a trend of timing the end of a bucolic song with the end of the day, tying the song-performance to what we now call circadian rhythm.[88] The refrain-like repetitions of λῆγε...ἴσχεο and πάλιν...πάλιν work to lull the goddess back to sleep after her rude awakening immediately following the opening refrain:

> μηκέτι πορφυρέοις ἐνὶ φάρεσι, Κύπρι, κάθευδε·
> ἔγρεο δειλαία κυανόστολε καὶ πλατάγησον
> στήθεα καὶ λέγε πᾶσιν 'ἀπώλετο καλὸς Ἄδωνις.' (3–5)

> Sleep no longer, Cypris, in crimson-dyed sheets; arise, poor thing, dressed all in black, and beat your breasts, and say to all 'Fair Adonis is dead!'

---

[87] Hollander 1985: 77.
[88] Theoc. 1.144–45, 2.163–66, 15.147–49, 18.54–57. Vergil makes good use of this trope at *Ecl.* 1.82–3, 6.85–6, and 10.77; cf. 9.51–5. Finally, Milton's *Lycidas* ends with these verses: 'And now the sun had stretch'd out all the hills, | And now was dropp'd into the western bay; | At last he rose, and twitch'd his mantle blue: | To-morrow to fresh woods, and pastures new.'

This framing device figures the occasion of the lament as a brief episode of sleeplessness in the life of the goddess. If refrain is a figure of the recurring cycle of day and night, waking and sleeping, the scattered reverberations of the Adonis-song signify an interruption in this cycle for a festive period of vigil. But there is more at stake here than the goddess' beauty sleep. The command with which she is roused, ἔγρεο (4), reappears in the same emphatic line-initial position in the middle of Aphrodite's speech to the fatally wounded Adonis:

>   μεῖνον Ἄδωνι,
> δύσποτμε μεῖνον Ἄδωνι, πανύστατον ὥς σε κιχείω,
> ὥς σε περιπτύξω καὶ χείλεα χείλεσι μίξω.
> **ἔγρεο** τυτθὸν Ἄδωνι, τὸ δ᾽ αὖ πύματόν με φίλησον,
> τοσσοῦτόν με φίλησον, ὅσον ζώῃ τὸ φίλημα,
> ἄχρις ἀποψύχῃς ἐς ἐμὸν στόμα κεἰς ἐμὸν ἧπαρ
> πνεῦμα τεὸν ῥεύσῃ, τὸ δέ σευ γλυκὺ φίλτρον ἀμέλξω,
> ἐκ δὲ πίω τὸν ἔρωτα, φίλημα δὲ τοῦτο φυλάξω
> ὡς αὐτὸν τὸν Ἄδωνιν, ἐπεὶ σύ με δύσμορε φεύγεις... (42–50)

Stay, Adonis, stay, ill-fated Adonis, that I may lay hold of you one last time, that I may enfold you and intertwine my lips with your lips. **Rise** for a little, Adonis, and kiss me again at the last, kiss me for as long as your kiss yet lives, until you breathe out your life into my mouth and pour your breath into my liver, and I will drain the sweet potion from you and drink up your love, and I will keep this kiss as if it were Adonis himself, for you are slipping away from me, hapless one...

The poem's two central events of rousing — the chorus leader's waking of Aphrodite and Aphrodite's plea for a last kiss from the dying Adonis — are united by the command ἔγρεο ('rise', 4, 44). Whereas the rousing of Aphrodite interrupts her sleep, the rousing of Adonis is a delay of his inevitable death. In both cases, the command to rise expresses a desire to still the passage of time in order to capture a fleeting moment, a desire which is embodied in the kiss of Adonis. The time-arresting fantasy of the kiss is encapsulated in the near-oxymoron τὸ δ᾽ αὖ πύματόν ('again at the last' 45), where αὖ ('again') entertains for a moment the notion that this kiss is only one more kiss among many to be had, a notion belied by the knowledge that this must be the last one (τὸ πύματον). Aphrodite's stolen kiss is thus itself a repetition in the full sense of the word, an attempt to reassert the continuance of desire in the face of the tragic cycle of mortality.

2.9 Sensing Adonis, (ad)dressing Aphrodite

In vv. 46–50 we see how Aphrodite's kiss preserves the object of her desire by transforming it into something capable of being consumed into her immortal body. The macabre imagery of this passage is motivated by a play on the metaphor of dying as 'breathing out the soul' (ἀποψύχειν). Since the inhaling of vapour or smoke in Greek and many other languages is conventionally expressed using verbs of drinking, Bion here can depict Aphrodite's last kiss as a kind of love-draught, a conceit which permits him to dwell on the morbid pleasure the goddess derives from the act. The striking depiction of Adonis' kiss / spirit as a 'sweet potion' which Aphrodite will 'drain' (lit. 'milk') from him (49) intimates that the drinking is both a pleasurable act in itself and an attempt to bottle that pleasure as in a vial for further use.

The pleasure that Aphrodite takes in the kiss is predominantly oral (if I may borrow a term from psychoanalysis),[89] but Aphrodite is using her mouth in this passage for more than just kissing / drinking: she is also, of course, using it to produce a lengthy speech, and one which comprises the most intensive sequence of obsessive repetitions in the entire poem. Among them is the repeated ending -ksō (περιπτύ**ξω**, μί**ξω**, ἀμέλ**ξω**, φυλά**ξω**), which might be heard as mimicking the repeated sucking sound of nursing (an association evoked by ἀμέλξω, 48).[90] But it is above all Adonis' name that is on the goddess' lips,[91] and her repeated invocation of the youth by name forms a linguistic counterpart to the fantasy of conservation embodied in the kiss.[92] After the erotic energy of her speech with its exuberant repetitions, the subsequent recurrence of the 'refrain' in the terse reply of the chorus of Loves comes like a death knell:

ὣδ' ὀλοφύρατο Κύπρις· ἐπαιάζουσιν Ἔρωτες
'αἰαῖ τὰν Κυθέρειαν, ἀπώλετο καλὸς Ἄδωνις.' (62–3)

---

89 Suggestive here is the metaphorical use of φίλτρον to refer to the 'Cupid's bow' dimple, which would make the φίλτρον simultaneously the object of Aphrodite's sucking and the liquid drawn thereby. Fantuzzi 1985: *ad loc.* is however certainly wrong to argue that this sense crowds out the primary sense of 'potion' here; see Reed 1997: *ad loc.*
90 With this cf. Abraham's psychoanalytic study of poetic rhythm, where he writes, 'There is no better illustration of the primordial structure of the creation of time than a cadence divided into strong and weak beats, a figure for sucking the breast, the child's first relational act (Abrahams and Rand 1986: 9).'
91 She repeats his name at vv. 42, 43, 45, 50, 51, and 57, and elsewhere at v. 5.
92 In a sense, the simple act of addressing a deceased person by name is already necromantic in itself, in that it entertains the fiction that the person is able to hear and respond.

> So mourned Cypris: the Loves mourn in reply,
> 'Alas for Cytherea! Fair Adonis is dead!'

From this we can see how the play of Aphrodite's desire is encoded in the rhythmic repetitions of the verse: where these repetitions verge on echo, they signify the deferral of death through the continual reawakening of desire; where they approach the closural cadence of refrain, they bring to mind ending, sleep, and death.[93]

Aphrodite's oral eroticism thus forms a vital link between the pleasure of the kiss and the pleasure of the verse as it plays on the reader's lips. When the chorus leader commands the goddess to 'rise' and begin the lament with the same word that Aphrodite uses to rouse Adonis for a last kiss, the reader is invited into a kind of love triangle with the divine couple, reproducing Aphrodite's desire for Adonis in a readerly desire to reach both goddess and youth through invocation. Like most love triangles, this one is marked by unidirectional desire rather than reciprocity. From the moment of Aphrodite's awakening to the end of the poem, we see the world through her eyes and feel what she feels; Adonis, by contrast, is emphatically deprived of all his senses.[94] The result is that the poem transforms Aphrodite into an assemblage of sense organs mobilised for the consumption of Adonis' beautiful body, a body which is offered up to the reader through a very specific set of sensory motifs.

Our first glimpse of Adonis is heralded by a flash of colour (vv. 7–11). His fatal wound is introduced as the product of the boar's 'white tusk' piercing his 'white thigh' (μηρὸν ὀδόντι, | λευκῷ λευκὸν ὀδόντι τυπείς, 7–8), and this monochrome field throws into relief the black blood dripping along the 'snowy flesh' (τὸ δέ οἱ μέλαν εἴβεται αἷμα | χιονέας κατὰ σαρκός, 9–10), followed by the 'rose' — Bion's striking figure for the red hue quickly draining from the lips (τὸ ῥόδον φεύγει τῶ χείλεος, 11). Colour here is stark and vivid, drowning out other visual impressions, but the mention of 'wounding' and the 'dripping' of blood also incorporates the tactile dimension, which comes into play more fully in vv. 19–28. Here, Aphrodite is depicted running through the woods barefoot to find her lover, pricked by brambles which draw her 'sacred blood' (21–2), and her 'sharp' cry (ὀξύ, 23) matches her pain.[95] With the emendations convincingly defended by Reed, vv. 25–8 have Aphrodite tearing in grief at her breasts (again 'snowy':

---

93 Cf. Hollander 1985: 74 on the 'broken refrain' of Poe's *The Raven*: 'the return of "Nevermore" denies the return of dead beauty to memory.'
94 Reed 1997: 25–26 rightly stresses the poem's focalisation through Aphrodite.
95 ὀξύ is used of the sound of mourning also at v. 93.

χιόνεοι, 27) and drawing more blood there, emphasising the intense physical pain involved in mourning.

The tactile sensation of dripping or trickling liquid runs through the poem, not only in the love-draught passage discussed earlier, but also in vv. 64–6, where Aphrodite's empathy for Adonis' pain is bodied forth in the synchronised dripping of their blood and tears:

> δάκρυον ἁ Παφία τόσον ἐκχέει ὅσσον Ἄδωνις
> αἷμα χέει, τὰ δὲ πάντα ποτὶ χθονὶ γίνεται ἄνθη·
> αἷμα ῥόδον τίκτει, τὰ δὲ δάκρυα τὰν ἀνεμώναν.

> The Paphian sheds a tear for every drop of blood shed by Adonis, and every drop turns into a flower on the ground: blood begets the rose, and tears beget the anemone.

Tears and blood thus together tap out a rhythm to accompany the rhythm of the lament itself, and soon after, Aphrodite is urged to cease her mourning with a verb which literally means 'drip' (μύρεο, 68). Another dripping sensation derives from the prominence of unguents which imbue the lament with an Asiatic flavour, as e.g. in the command to 'sprinkle' the corpse with Syrian oils and perfumes (77); and here the ethnonym echoes the 'Assyrian cry' which Aphrodite is said to make (Ἀσσύριον βοόωσα, 24), hinting at a transference of the tactile and olfactory properties of unguents to the sound of the lament itself.[96] The following verse resumes this sensory catachresis by transforming Adonis' dying body itself into an unguent:[97]

> ὀλλύσθω μύρα πάντα· τὸ σὸν μύρον ὤλετ' Ἄδωνις. (78)

> Let all perfumes die: your perfume Adonis is dead.

Smell of course comes to the fore with the mention of perfume, but we can also detect its presence in the repeated mention of dyes throughout the poem, both to describe clothing and flowers and as a metaphor for the colour of blood;[98] Bradley points out that Phoenician purple dye carried a characteristic odour which would have been inseparable in memory from the colour itself.[99] Finally, the sense of

---

[96] Compare the highly aestheticised imagery of 'dripping' song at Theoc. *Id*. 1.7–8, noted by Gutzwiller 1991: 85.
[97] On the comparison of Adonis with perfume, see Detienne 1994: 63.
[98] vv. 3, 4, 26, 27, 35, 72, 79; φοίνιον (41) is not a cognate of φοῖνιξ (deriving instead from φόνος), but there is no such thing as a false friend in poetic language.
[99] Bradley 2013: 135–38.

taste is indulged heavily in the kiss scene discussed above, but it also figures in this passage later in Aphrodite's speech:

> λάμβανε Περσεφόνα τὸν ἐμὸν πόσιν· ἐσσὶ γὰρ αὐτὰ
> πολλὸν ἐμεῦ κρέσσων, τὸ δὲ πᾶν καλὸν ἐς σὲ καταρρεῖ (54–5)

> Take my husband, Persephone, for you are far greater than I, and all that is beautiful trickles down to you.

If we take the metaphor in καταρρεῖ seriously, we can conceptualise the souls of the beautiful dead as drops of liquid seeping down into the underworld, as if to be drunk up by Persephone in the same way Aphrodite drinks up Adonis' kiss. Perhaps we could even detect in the word πόσις, 'husband' (54, used previously of Adonis at v. 24), a sly pun on the homonym in the feminine gender meaning 'drink'. From all this we can see how the poem presents the experience of mourning Adonis as a synaesthetic feast for the senses which is at the same time focused by the repetition of a fixed set of motifs.

The poem does not begin, however, as an account of Aphrodite's experience of Adonis' death; it starts with a song-performance, involving a first-person speaker and a chorus of Loves. This brings us back to the topic with which we began, namely, the relation of the poem to the rite of the Adonia. The problem can be phrased as follows: what is the link between the song-performance and the mythical event of Adonis' death? There is a general agreement that the song, announced as it is with a *verbum dicendi* in the first person singular, takes place in the 'present', while the mourning of Aphrodite is a mythical event taking place in the 'past'. No temporal transition attends our introduction to the world of the myth, however: Adonis simply 'lies in the mountains', in the present tense (7). D'Alessio explains this use of tense with reference to a ritual re-enactment of a mythical event, pointing to the specification of the time of the lament as 'today' (τὸ σάμερον, 97) and the promise of a repeat performance in 'another year' (εἰς ἔτος ἄλλο, 98).[100] However, if the ritual itself is a re-enactment, what relation does the poem have to the ritual? Reed offers one possible answer to this question:

> [The *Lament for Adonis*] is a mimetic mythological narrative akin to Callimachus' mimetic hymns, and like them descended on one side from the festival odes of Archaic lyric. The referent of Bion's representation, however, is removed two degrees from the reality of an Adonis festival: it is not the actual performance, nor the literary, constructed festival world

---

100 D'Alessio 2004: 294.

of Callimachus' hymns, but the very mythological event the ritual commemorates (which thus becomes the tacit aetiology of the rite).[101]

In Reed's view, Bion's poem is a 'mimetic' representation of a ritual which is itself 'mimetic', and in the latter instance the term approaches the sense of 're-enactment' as developed by Gregory Nagy.[102] The resultant definition of the poem as a mimesis in the second degree is complicated by Reed's own observation that, unlike the 'mimetic' hymns of Callimachus, the *Lament* does not exhibit a concern with representing the rite as such.[103] No ritual participants are mentioned; besides the unidentified first person speaker, the only persons in the poem are Aphrodite, Adonis, and the series of divine or mythological beings and personifications who join in with the mourning.[104] At no point does the poem step outside this enchanted realm in such a way that we can perceive a boundary between the world of the myth and the world of the ritual.

Reed insists, however, on locating the point of mediation between the two worlds in the first-person voice, whom he identifies as a woman leading the ritual lamentation.[105] Once this identification is made, Reed can assert that the repeated addresses to Aphrodite to sing the lament form part of a game of make-believe, wherein the 'real' addressees of her commands are participants in the rite who play parts in the re-enactment of the mythical narrative.[106] This approach rests on circular reasoning: in order to define Bion's poem as 'mimetic' on the model of Callimachus' 'mimetic' hymns, Reed assumes the background of a 'mimetic' Adonis rite and proceeds to transfer the 'mimetic' qualities of this putative ceremony to Bion's poem.[107] Within this framework, the burden of fictionality, so to speak, is conveniently but erroneously off-loaded from the text to its represented object. The fault line of this approach lies in the first-person speaker: Reed wants this figure to mediate our entry into the world of the myth while at the same time existing as a fictional *persona* within the fiction of the rite (and hence a 'she'). The

---

[101] Reed 2006: 220; cf. Reed 1997: 16–17.
[102] For a succinct statement of Nagy's 'mimesis as re-enactment' theory in relation to occasion, see Nagy 1994–5.
[103] Reed 1997: 16, 21-22.
[104] The Loves, *passim*; hounds and oreads, 18-9; mountains, oaks, rivers, springs, and flowers, 31–5; the island of Cythera, 35–7; Echo, 38; Hymenaeus, 87–90; the Graces, 91–3; the Fates, 94–5.
[105] Reed 1997: 16, 24–26.
[106] Reed 1997: 16.
[107] Reed's term for the relation between Bion's poem and the Adonis-rite in his view is 'metalepsis' (Reed 1997: 23). In ancient sources for the rites of the Adonia (Luc. *Syr. D.* 6, Plut. *Alc.* 18.3, *id. Nic.* 13.7, Theoc. 15.110–35, Ar. *Lys.* 387–98), the only element of *mimesis* apparent is in the effigies of Adonis (and in Theoc. of Aphrodite and Adonis).

result is that the fiction which produces this first-person voice and the space of its enunciation — the fiction of occasion — becomes unthinkable.[108]

The hypothesis that Aphrodite is addressed as part of a game of make-believe is encouraged by the analogy of Sappho fr. 140a L-P:

κατθνα‹ί›σκει, Κυθέρη', ἄβρος Ἄδωνις· τί κε θεῖμεν;
καττύπτεσθε, κόραι, καὶ κατερείκεσθε κίθωνας.

Pretty Adonis is dying, Cytherea; what can we do?
Beat your breasts, maidens, and tear your tunics.

Here we have a dramatic dialogue between the goddess herself and a group of girls who are ordered to perform the lament. D'Alessio argues that the present tense of κατθνα‹ί›σκει entails a deictic shift whereby the 'now' of the performance is transferred back in time to the mythical moment of Adonis' death, adding that this fictive mythical frame of reference is not indicated in the text but postulated by the 'ritual situation' in which the poem is embedded.[109] The assumption is that it is only possible for Sappho to speak a poem addressing Aphrodite at the moment of Adonis' death within the context of a ritual occasion which sets the scene in such a way as to make such an enunciative situation possible. Once again, this approach leaves no room for the actual working of the *fiction* which brings this 'ritual situation' into being; it is simply given in advance in accordance with a putative tradition of play-acting Aphrodite.[110]

If we are to approach poems like Sappho's and Bion's as poems rather than documents of rituals, we must appreciate that addressing Aphrodite is itself a fictive act, no less so than speaking in her voice, and is thus a fiction of *poetry*, not one mediated by ritual. Let us return to Bion's framing of the address to the goddess:

μηκέτι πορφυρέοις ἐνὶ φάρεσι, Κύπρι, κάθευδε·
ἔγρεο δειλαία κυανόστολε καὶ πλατάγησον
στήθεα καὶ λέγε πᾶσιν 'ἀπώλετο καλὸς Ἄδωνις.' (3–5)

---

108 Cf. the discussion of the 'author'/'narrator' distinction in fiction in Walsh 2007: 69–85.
109 D'Alessio 2004: 294; cf. 292. Alexiou 2002: 55 surmises that this fragment was 'probably part of a lament performed antiphonally as a dialogue between Aphrodite and the Nymphs'.
110 Burnett 1983: 3–7 and 229 offers a welcome critique of this approach to Sappho and other archaic poetry, which she interestingly labels 'occasionalism'. D'Alessio 2018 takes a broader and more nuanced perspective on the relation between Sappho's pragmatics and ritual performance contexts.

> Sleep no longer, Cypris, in crimson-dyed sheets; arise, poor thing, dressed all in black, and beat your breasts, and say to all 'Fair Adonis is dead!'

The command to emerge from sleep is fundamentally a variation on the *epiclesis* (e.g. Sappho's 'come to me from Crete'),[111] but instead of being summoned from one place to another, Aphrodite here is transported psychically from tranquility to grief. This state of grief, which occasions the Adonis-cry itself, is corporealised in the goddess' black garb and the act of breast-beating (4), making the lament a performance not only of the voice but of the body.

This mobilisation of Aphrodite's body, her transformation into a mourning subject, finds grammatical expression in the curious 'predicative vocative' κυανόστολε, so identified by Fantuzzi.[112] According to his interpretation, κυανόστολε does not carry the force of invocation associated with the vocative case, but is rather a predicative nominative which takes on the vocative case by way of attraction to the imperative verb. This is based on the premiss that the attribute 'black-robed' marks a change from Aphrodite's previous state (viz. 'sleeping in crimson-dyed sheets'), a development which is signalled by the pair of commands 'arise' and 'beat (your breasts)' (ἔγρεο [...] πλατάγησον, 4).

Fantuzzi is too rigid, however, in implying that κυανόστολε is completely empty of vocatival force; in the examples adduced by himself and Reed as parallels, the predicative vocative is never vocative in form only, but always carries a sense of address. For example, at Soph. *Phil.* 828, the chorus prays to Sleep as follows: εὐαὲς ἡμῖν ἔλθοις ('may you come well-disposed [voc.] toward us'). The vocative here is at odds with the syntax of the sentence but perfectly at home in the communicative context of prayer. We may reconcile these two conflicting frames of reference by explaining the vocative as proleptic, projecting a future time within which the prayer will have been answered and the god can rightly be addressed as 'one who is well-disposed to us'.

I suggest that Bion's κυανόστολε has a similar two-pronged illocutionary force: as a virtual predicative nominative, it dictates the manner in which the goddess is to 'arise'; as a vocative, it projects a future time within which Aphrodite will have obeyed this command and thus can rightly be addressed as 'she who is dressed in black'.[113] These two interpretations happen to correspond respectively to the frames of experience-report and performed speech; in the frame

---

111 See Fantuzzi 1985: *ad loc.*
112 Fantuzzi 1985: *ad loc.*, followed by Reed 1997: *ad loc.*
113 This solution would obsolete Reed's assertion (which he does not himself explain) that καὶ is postponed after κυανόστολε, since, on my reading, there is no difficulty involved in the two vocatives (δειλαία and κυανόστολε) occurring within the same clause (Reed 1997: *ad loc.*).

of experience-report, the command to 'arise dressed in black' relays to the reader the unfolding of a scene in which Aphrodite arises dressed in black in response to the command, while in the frame of performed speech, the command to 'arise' and the adjective κυανόστολε both form part of the same invocation. Only within the frame of experience-report, then, can κυανόστολε be seen as either descriptive or narratival; within the frame of performed speech, the adjective is not descriptive of the enunciative situation but constitutive of it. The predicative vocative permits us to read the adjective within both frames at once, and thus creates a fictive space within which the causal progression between commanding the goddess to dress in black and invoking the goddess as 'dressed in black' is elided.[114] Within this fictive space, the goddess' bodily performance of mourning can be conceived as an extension or sympathetic projection of the poem's act of mourning, a projection which is itself performed through the act of address.

2.10 Bion *bucolicus* and resonant space

We can now refine our earlier observation that Aphrodite serves as a sensory vehicle for the experience of mourning Adonis. Aphrodite in fact embodies the lament itself, acting as the experiential anchor for the fiction of occasion, much as the path of song functions in Propertius 4.6 as argued above. We saw earlier how the echoic rhythms of the poem are tied to the play of Aphrodite's desire by virtue of the pathetic fallacy. Echo, however, is not a property of sounds but of acoustics, and hence of space; and this same pathetic fallacy informs the creation of space in the poem. The poem moves between two rather generic locations: Aphrodite's bed, which seems from a reference in v. 59 to be in her palace,[115] and the site of Adonis' death, a generalised wilderness area. These locations are fleshed out in the goddess' movement through them, as we can see e.g. in vv. 19–24:

ἁ δ' Ἀφροδίτα
λυσαμένα πλοκαμῖδας ἀνὰ δρυμὼς ἀλάληται
πενθαλέα νήπλεκτος ἀσάνδαλος· αἱ δὲ βάτοι νιν
ἐρχομέναν κείροντι καὶ ἱερὸν αἷμα δρέπονται·
ὀξὺ δὲ κωκύουσα δι' ἄγκεα μακρὰ φορεῖται
Ἀσσύριον βοόωσα πόσιν καὶ παῖδα καλεῦσα· (19–24)

---

114 The parallel here with Propertius 4.6, where Apollo sheds his war costume at the turning point of the poet's path of song, is remarkable.
115 The palace of Aphrodite seems to be an invention of Apollonius Rhodius, who might be Bion's source for v. 59 (*Arg.* 3.36–40); the context implies that it is located on or near Olympus.

> Aphrodite wanders through the thickets with her hair undone, grieving, unbraided, unsandalled, and the brambles prick her as she goes and draw her sacred blood; she wanders crying sharply through meandering glens, calling on her husband and her boy with the Assyrian shout.

It was noted above that the pain of Aphrodite's mourning is transferred to her environment in the form of the pricking brambles, and that this tactile sensation is transferred to the lament by the metaphor in ὀξύ (24). We can now synthesise these remarks with the observation that lament is conceptualised metaphorically in this poem in terms of movement through a hostile environment. If the ideal is a straight paved road (like Propertius' untrodden path smoothed with laurel), Aphrodite's wilderness is just the opposite, hindering progress with both physical impediments (the brambles and thickets) and orientational obstacles (the meandering glens). In this wilderness, Aphrodite's cry becomes more than just an expression of emotion; it is also an attempt to utilise the voice to penetrate spaces which she has difficulty reaching through normal movement.

With the personification of the island of Cythera, Aphrodite's Laconian haunt, this metaphor takes a surprising turn:

> ἁ δὲ Κυθήρα
> πάντας ἀνὰ κναμώς, ἀνὰ πᾶν νάπος οἰκτρὸν ἀείδει
> 'αἰαῖ τὰν Κυθέρειαν, ἀπώλετο καλὸς Ἄδωνις.'
> Ἀχὼ δ' ἀντεβόασεν 'ἀπώλετο καλὸς Ἄδωνις.' (35–8)

> All along her hillsides and through every grove the island of Cythera piteously sings, 'Alas for Cytherea; fair Adonis is dead', and Echo cried back 'Fair Adonis is dead'.

Here the repeated preposition ἀνά + acc. ('up and down', 'along', 'through') conceptualises the island's song as coursing through the wild spaces of her own landscape in the same way that Aphrodite traipses toward Adonis' final resting place;[116] but whereas the wilderness stymies both the goddess and her song, the song of Cythera is free to resonate and expand, transforming the whole island into an echo chamber. The reply of Echo (which uses the same root as Aphrodite's 'Assyrian shout', 24)[117] clinches the irony: the lament has no power to traverse the space separating the dead from the living, only to fill that space with its own reverberation.

---

116 This is another example of 'fictive motion' (Talmy 2000).
117 βοόωσα, 24; ἀντε**β**όασεν, 38.

The wilderness echoes precisely because it is full up, overgrown with hiding places for supernatural presences;[118] but Aphrodite's palace on the contrary echoes because of its emptiness:

χήρα δ' ἁ Κυθέρεια, κενοὶ δ' ἀνὰ δώματ' Ἔρωτες. (59)

Cytherea is bereaved, and the Loves all through the palace are orphaned (lit. 'empty').

Here again a prepositional phrase with ἀνά + acc. denotes the filling of space, only now it is filled with emptiness; and in this glimpse of the empty space of the palace we are offered a spatial frame in which to locate the echoed laments of the Loves heard throughout (ἀνά) the poem itself.[119] Presenting resonant spaces for the lament to inhabit in this way does more than add emotional colouring; as implements of the fiction of occasion, such spaces can act as sounding boards for the poem, permitting its expansion from a string of text into a virtual environment.[120]

One model for how a reader may inhabit Bion's poem as a virtual environment is offered by a persistent trope that runs through the bucolic tradition, namely, the conceit that the bucolic poet is not only an imitator of herdsmens' songs but is in fact himself a herdsman.[121] Bion indulges this fiction memorably in his fr. 10, which may in fact be a complete poem.[122] This comprises a poetic initiation narrative in which Aphrodite visits the poet (whom she addresses as 'dear herdsman', φίλε βούτα, v. 4) in a dream and requests that he teach Eros to sing; Eros, however, ignores his 'bucolic' songs (βουκολίασδον, 5) and teaches him his own erotic material. There is no need to establish definitively that this narrative is to be taken as programmatic for Bion's poetry as a whole (although this is a possibility I would not rule out) in order to entertain some measure of continuity between the world in which Bion is a herdsman inspired by Aphrodite and the world in which the lament for Adonis takes place.

---

118 See Lucr. 4.570–93, with Hollander 1981: 12.
119 2, 6, 15, 62, 80 (a variant), 86.
120 See Fitzgerald 2016a on resonance and what he calls the 'sonic environment' of Vergil's *Eclogues*.
121 For an overview of this trope, see Gutzwiller 1991: 176–9.
122 See the discussion of Reed 1997: 7–14.

This possibility certainly attracted the author of the *Lament for Bion*, an anonymous poem attributed to 'Moschus'[123] which places the figure of Bion the herdsman in the setting of his own poetry, lamenting him in the same way that Bion lamented Adonis.[124] 'Moschus'' adulatory fiction is of course the product of an independent poetic enterprise, but it is also bound up with a certain reading of Bion's own fictions, a reading which departs radically from Reed's interpretation of the *Lament for Adonis* as a 'mimetic' account of a ritual. For a reader who attributes the poem's opening αἰάζω not to an anonymous festivalgoer but to Bion the herdsman-poet, the world of the poem would look entirely different.

One significant entailment of the poet-as-herdsman fiction is the merging of the aesthetic qualities of the bucolic landscape with the aesthetic qualities of bucolic verse. Bion's Doric accents,[125] which come across as a mere stylistic affectation on a 'mimetic' reading, blend in seamlessly with the virtual environment on a 'bucolic' reading, so that we can truly hear Echo's name as *Ā*-cho (Ἀχώ, 38).[126] Such a reading would also give point to Bion's use of Cythera as a resonant space (35–8, discussed above, p. 41), since this island, unlike some of Aphrodite's other haunts, is in the Doric-speaking Peloponnese. More important for our purposes, however, is that such a reading would not require the postulate of a 'mimetic' rite to mediate between the world of the lament and the mythic world of Adonis' death. The world of bucolic is already inhabited by poets and divinities alike, so that the striking up of bucolic song and the visitation of a dying demigod go hand in hand.

2.11 Conclusion

I have sought in this chapter to expand the fiction of occasion beyond the realm of the 'epiphanic effect' delineated in the previous chapter. To this end, I have attempted to show how figures or 'megametaphors' like the path of song in Propertius 4.6 and the concomitant schemes of refrain and address in Bion's *Adonis* can serve as experiential anchors for the fiction of occasion. A secondary aim of this chapter was to call into question the theoretical strategy of labelling the first-

---

123 Gutzwiller 1991: 177 suggests that 'Moschus' may in fact have originated as a pseudonym, suggesting a tradition of imitation analogous to the Anacreontics.
124 See Gutzwiller 1991: 176–78 and Reed 2006: 222–24.
125 On dialect forms in Bion see Reed 1997: 31–36.
126 Doric is of course the dialect of bucolic, and 'Moschus' puts great store by Bion's Doric provenance (despite the fact that Bion was from Smyrna, where Aeolic was historically spoken): [Mosch.] 3.1, 12, 18, 96, 122

person speaking voice a fictional *persona* who 'mediates' the fiction of the poem. I argued that conceiving of the speaker of Propertius 4.6 or its proem as a '*uates*-figure' or some other such character, and of the speaker of Bion's *Adonis* as an anonymous chorus leader or master-of-ceremonies figure at a putative Adonia, is an oversimplification, if not an error, and only serves to suspend some of the most intriguing questions surrounding the fiction of occasion. The next chapter, which turns away from the ceremonial mode to explore the more intimate spaces of Horace's *Odes*, will expand on both these conclusions, building on the critique of the fictional *persona* as well as delving deeper into the role of metaphor in the fiction of occasion.

3 Occasion and Presence in Horace, *Odes* I

3.1 Introduction

If the term 'occasion' has any claim to be considered a keyword of classical literary scholarship, it will be largely thanks to Horace and his collection of *Odes*. While Horace was certainly not the only Hellenistic or Roman poet to try his or her hand at transposing the forms of archaic Greek lyric for a latter-day public, his attempt has attained an exemplary status which no other author, canonical or otherwise, can claim. Horace's *Carmina* are widely recognised as a crucial turning point in the history of lyric poetry in the West, and since Richard Heinze's seminal 1923 essay, if not earlier, lyric's Horatian turn has been conceptualised as a radical shift in the poet's relation to his medium. This shift is rarely considered as occurring in a vacuum, of course; the importance of the influence of Hellenistic poets and the previous innovations of Catullus and other Roman poets is well documented in the scholarship. What I am trying to highlight here, rather, is the well-established practice of reading this shift into the *Odes* themselves, seeing in them a poet coming to terms with the genre's putative dissociation from the elements that once defined it: oral performance, communal settings, musical accompaniment.

When used in relation to the *Odes*, the term 'occasion' reifies this primeval state of (lyric) poetry in order to make Horace's departure from his models all the more visible. This formulation of the problem of occasion in Horace can be attributed to Heinze, who both authoritatively established the essential occasionality of the *Odes* and defined their particular mode of occasionality in opposition to that of their archaic models. He observed that the *Odes*, like archaic lyrics, are typically cast as personal addresses rather than soliloquies, and that these addresses tend to comprise dialogic acts of communication subtended by external circumstance ('occasions'), rather than constituting the unmediated expression of the author's thoughts in a monologic format. This distinguished the *Odes* decisively from 'modern lyric' broadly conceived; but what set Horace's lyric occasions apart from those of the early Greeks, for Heinze, was the fact that Horace's were the product of a grand fiction:

> it is fiction that the poet stands opposite his addressee, fiction — except where general admonitions are concerned — that he wishes to affect his interlocutor, fiction that the listener should, from the songs, recognize the occasion in which they were composed. We must therefore be clear that Horatian lyric made greater demands of his contemporaries than his archaic metrical form: he required of their imagination nothing less than to transport themselves back to the times of an Alcaeus or Anacreon, to a sympotic practice that must have

seemed unfamiliar to them, to understand the form containing the Horatian ode's thoroughly modern content. (30)

With this passage, Heinze helped instigate a pattern of thought which dominates Horatian scholarship up to the present day, namely the conception of Horace's lyric poetry as founded, on the most basic level, upon a problematic of presence. He argues that the occasional nature of the monodic song tradition from which Horace drew inspiration demands that the '[address] to a person imagined as present'[1] be always in view, but that this presence — that is, the co-presence of the poet, the interlocutor, and a situation of utterance in which both are directly implicated — is itself necessarily belied by the patently anachronistic fictions that Horace employs in setting the scenes for his lyric performances. The metaphor of 'transport' underlines the dissonant effect of reading Horatian lyric as Heinze conceives it: even those readers who were the least historically removed from Horace's time needed to radically displace themselves from their everyday world if they hoped to participate in the imaginary present of their contemporary's lyric addresses.

The work of Michèle Lowrie exemplifies a more recent trend of expanding Heinze's problematic of presence into a post-structuralist thesis concerning the ideological bases of the rhetoric of Horatian lyric discourse.[2] For Lowrie, the incongruities between the world of Horace's performance occasions and the realities of his contemporary Rome are not only a stumbling block for his readers but an embarrassment to his entire poetic enterprise, which, she argues, is predicated on the construction of a lyric voice which in turn embodies an ultimately illusory ideal of lyric presence. She employs the term 'poetics of presence' for the rhetorical strategies employed in the *Odes* to defend the privileged space of lyric utterance from influences that threaten to dispel the illusion, strategies which she unites under the banner of Derrida's concept of phonocentrism.[3] Horatian lyric maintains the pretence of oral performance, she proposes, precisely in order to occlude and suppress its own written status, so as to absolve itself of the inherent capacity of writing to detach itself from its author and from all originary contexts.[4] In Lowrie's view, then, to recognise the fictionality of the *Odes*' occasions is to read against the grain of the poetics of presence, calling into question the very grounds for the authority of Horatian lyric discourse.

---

1 Heinze 2009: 15.
2 Lowrie 1997, 2009a.
3 Lowrie 1997: 57–58 and 75–76; cf. Barchiesi 2007: 151. See Barber 2014 for a critique of the concept of Horace's poetics of presence.
4 Lowrie 1997: 49–76 and 2009: 72–117.

Barchiesi's contributions to thought on occasion in the *Odes* similarly begin from a problematic of presence. He sees in every gesture towards lyric performance in Horace the thematisation of the irretrievable absence of any enabling social context for such performance, an absence which poses an 'existential problem' for Horatian lyric as a whole.[5] For Barchiesi, the very fact that Horace takes up occasion as a theme, linking it to philosophical meditations on time and metapoetic discourses on lyric decorum, only serves to accentuate the fact of its functional obsolescence for his own poetry, heightening the 'sense of rift and loss' that pervades the collection.[6]

This problematisation of the idea of presence that crops up whenever we try to conceptualise Horace's *Odes* in terms of performance and occasion has obvious implications for the current project. If we follow Lowrie and Barchiesi, occasion is a phenomenon that only really comes into view in Horace once it is destabilised, once its pretensions of unmediated presence are exposed by the telltale signs of the fictionality inherent in poetic discourse. According to this view, to talk of the 'fiction of occasion' in Horatian lyric is necessarily to talk of the disruptions and subversions of presence. However, the conception of fictionality vis-à-vis presence adopted by Lowrie and Barchiesi is not the only one available. Heinze's account of the imaginative effort required of Horace's contemporary readers to transport themselves into a fictional world already hints at the other side of the coin: fiction is undoubtedly productive of (fictional) presences to at least the same extent that it disrupts or obstructs (factual) presence. It should in principle be possible, therefore, to say something useful about the 'positive' aspects of the poetics of presence, and this is what I hope to do in this chapter and the following.

3.2 *c.* 1.20: The merry echo

Lowrie points to *c.* 1.20 as an example of the effects of distancing and deferral that are produced wherever Horatian lyric attempts to establish itself as performative

---

[5] Barchiesi 2000: 176.
[6] Barchiesi 2000: 167, 176. Cf. Barchiesi 2007: 148: 'it is all about the music – the absent music. [...] The music is present (and richly so) at the level of *theme*, not of *performance*, just as [...] the treatment of time in the poems provides a thematic ersatz, a thematisation, of the missing performance culture.' See also Lowrie 2009: 50 and 103. P. Hardie 2002: 1–29 articulates a similar problematic of presence with regard to Ovid. Attridge 2019: 98–104 takes a rather oversimplified approach to this problem by pointing to Horace's 'dislike' for public performance as a mode of delivery.

utterance grounded in occasion. The poem invites Maecenas to enjoy some cheap Sabine wine which Horace had bottled personally to commemorate an occasion on which his powerful friend was given the honour of an acclamation in the theatre. Horace fills the short space of the ode's three stanzas with a colourful description of the applause reverberating throughout the Roman landscape followed by a comparison of the fine vintages available to Maecenas with his own meagre stores of wine. Heinze's theory of occasion presupposes that all this must be underpinned by a face-to-face situation of utterance in which Horace hopes to act upon his interlocutor in some concrete way; in this case, the poem offers praise to Maecenas. As Lowrie points out, however, Heinze's model of efficacious address to a person imagined as present does not sit comfortably with this ode.

> Vile potabis modicis Sabinum
> cantharis, Graeca quod ego ipse testa
> conditum leui, datus in theatro
>   cum tibi plausus,
> clare Maecenas eques, ut paterni   5
> fluminis ripae simul et iocosa
> redderet laudes tibi Vaticani
>   montis imago.
> Caecubum et prelo domitam Caleno
> Tu bibes uuam ; mea nec Falernae   10
> temperant uites neque Formiani
>   pocula colles.

> You will drink from modest vessels a common Sabine which I myself sealed and stored away in a Greek jar at the time when you were given applause in the theatre, illustrious knight Maecenas, such that the banks of your ancestral river and the merry echo of the Vatican hill returned your praises to you both at once. Enjoy your Caecuban and the grape crushed by the Calenian press; neither Falernian vines nor Formian hills infuse my cups.

Lowrie points to 'several levels of deferral' which intervene in the ideally unmediated co-presence of poet and addressee in this ode.[7] Firstly, the invitation format naturally presupposes that Horace and Maecenas are apart at the time of utterance, only to come together at a future time which lies beyond the scope of the poem. Even if, as the standard interpretation holds, the offer of wine stands in for the offering that is the present poem,[8] it is hard to gloss over the fact that the wine remains sealed for the time being (vv. 2–3); now is not the time for its enjoyment.

---

7 Lowrie 2009: 69.
8 See e.g. Commager 2009.

However, if what we are looking for is an occasion for the enactment of praise, not even this future rendezvous over cheap Sabine quite fits the bill; the wine may have been bottled in Maecenas' honour, but the event that it commemorates is itself a commemoration, the offering of applause for some unspecified accomplishment. In place of a unified and originary occasion of performance, Lowrie argues, the poem offers us glimpses of isolated events (the applause, the bottling, the invitation, the party) which individually gesture toward notions of enactment and lyric presence without actually embodying these concepts in any substantial way.[9] The ode *qua* utterance turns out to coincide precisely with none of these tangential 'occasions', and thus unmasks itself in its materiality as a mediate piece of writing rather than an immediate vocal performance.[10] In this way — and this is Lowrie's overarching thesis on the *Odes* — presence is exposed as a chimera, a metaphysical conceit employed to mystify the mundane realities of Horace's poetic production.

Lowrie's reading hinges upon the failure of Horatian lyric to foster a sense of presence that transcends its medium. What happens, we might ask, once the veil is lifted? Such a question, of course, breaks the rules of deconstructive criticism. I suggest, however, that Lowrie's critique of the poetics of presence leaves open another avenue which she does not explore. The thesis that poetry's mediality always asserts itself against lofty metaphysical pretensions, framed by Lowrie and Barchiesi in terms of absence and loss, can just as easily be framed in terms of presence if we simply adopt an approach which privileges the material over the ideal.

Take for example Lowrie's reading of the 'merry echo' which sounds Maecenas' praise abroad (*iocosa* [...] *Vaticani | montis imago* vv. 6–8), itself an echo of the same phrase in an earlier ode, at 1.12.3–4.[11] She suggests that Horace's dwelling on the echoed sound of the applause rather than on the theatrical event itself or the praiseworthy occasion it celebrated reflects the fundamental incapacity of his poetry to truly participate in such live enactments of praise; as writing rather than speech, she implies, Horatian lyric can only capture such events at a distance, i.e. through representation, just as echo can only replicate utterances, not produce them.[12]

---

9 Lowrie 2009: 69–70.
10 '[The poem] falls temporally between the theatre and the party, a piece of writing between two celebrations (Lowrie 2009: 70).'
11 Lowrie 2009: 67–71.
12 Breed 2006: 74–94 employs a similar conception of echo as an illusory projection of vocal presence in connexion with Vergil's sixth *Eclogue*.

However, an echo does not only betoken an absent origin; it also makes a sound of its own. Accordingly, rather than emphasising the echoed ovation for Maecenas as an occurrence irretrievably removed from the poem's situation of utterance, we might turn our attention instead to the echo itself and its capacity to 'return' or 'render (again)' (*redderet*, 7) acts of praise which have already been discharged. The middle stanza of this poem is devoted to expounding this special power of echo. Occasionally in Greek and Roman poetry, echoes are conceptualised as travelling from the source of a sound to a far-off hearer, as in Pin. *Ol.* 14.21–24, where the personified Echo is instructed to bring the message of Asopichus' victory to his father in the underworld.[13] Implicit here, of course, is the claim that epinician song can traverse unfathomable distances, and can even cross the threshold between the living and the dead.

However, we have already seen in our discussion of Bion's *Adonis* an example of a different kind of poetic echo, one which fills spaces with its reverberations rather than carrying a verbal message from one place to another. That Horace's echo is of the latter kind is evidenced by the use of the word *simul* in v.6: the echo joins together two great Roman landmarks, the Vatican hill and the river Tiber, by making them reverberate with the same sound at the same time. The emphasis falls not on the faithful transmission of semantic content relayed in a linear fashion from sender to receiver, but rather on the amplification of sound *qua* sound for the benefit of anyone in earshot; the mere volume of the echoed applause as it reaches Maecenas' ears is enough for it to register to him as offered praise.[14] Instrumental here is the account of sound distortion presented at Lucretius *DRN* 4.549–71 and 603–11, which relies on the Epicurean theory of the materiality and corporeality of the voice (4.524–48) to explain both how the sound of a voice can reach the ear without being intelligible (4.557–62, 603–11) and how a single voice can reach multiple ears (4.563–67).

---

13 Cf. Verg. *E.* 6.84, where echo carries Silenus' song up to the stars.
14 Related to this is the description in Verg. *E.* 6.82–86 of the reverberations of Silenus' song, which Breed discusses as an *imago uocis*: 'The echo ascribes presence to the voice of Silenus within the fictional world, and in representing Silenus' voice through its presence rather than by any verbal communication it might accomplish, the poem gives us not the words, but the voice as phenomenon (Breed 2000: 328).' Cf. also Fitzgerald's reappropriation of Northrop Frye's concept of lyric '*melos*' or 'babble' to describe the phenomenon of resonance in the *Eclogues*: 'Resonance in this sense is reduction, a degrading that is at the same time the sound that is made by sense when stripped of its communicative function, as though heard by an alien ear (Fitzgerald 2016a: 4–5).'

The echo, in other words, optimises amplitude at the expense of fidelity. Putnam and Macleod both judge this to be a negative within the value system of Horatian lyric, arguing that Horace contrasts the intemperate applause of the crowd at the theatre with his own humble offering of cheap Sabine.[15] However, it seems to me that the way in which Horace positions himself and his poetry in relation to the echo is not quite so one-sided. In particular, when Horace says that the Tiber river and the Vatican hill 'returned your praises to you both at once', he is ascribing to them a performance of praise which is comparable to the act of praise Horace is performing in this very poem. He prefaces his invitation to Maecenas with the disclaimer that the wine he offers is *uile*, common or cheap; it derives its value not from its quality but from the fact that he bottled it as a personal tribute to his friend on the date of his ovation. The wine thus compliments Maecenas by recalling a previous occasion of praise, and in this sense, the dinner-party will be a kind of re-enactment or 'echo' of the original event. Without echo's amplification, the applause would have been confined to the space of the theatre; likewise, without the commemorative wine-bottle and the accompanying poem, the occasion of the applause might have been forgotten.

The paradox here is that the echo prolongs the occasion precisely by negating its very occasionality. As Lowrie argues, the ovation is hypostasised in this poem as a model occasion for the enactment of praise; the communion between Maecenas and the audience makes the theatre into a 'space of inclusion', to borrow a term from chapter 1, that is, a privileged space of communicative presence. The echo, however, decouples this enactment of praise from its communicative context and distributes it across the landscape, a sonic effect which Horace renders in verbal form in the prosopopoeia of vv. 5–8, where the riverbanks and the hillside themselves are invested with agency in the speech act of giving praise.[16] These Roman landmarks do not only repeat the sound of roared applause in the theatre; they create with their reverberations a new occasion of praise-giving in the new sonic space formed by their geographical contours.

Horace's poem is analogously positioned in relation to the theatrical event. As a past occasion of communion between the man of the hour and his adoring public, the ovation by definition resists being subsumed within the present of address that informs the poem; but by figuring praise itself (viz. the *laudes* of v. 7) as an auditory percept rather than an item of communicative content, Horace hints at a means of escaping the narrow confines of the one-off occasion. Only

---

15 Putnam 1969; Macleod 1979.
16 Here we may compare the theory of echo articulated at Lucr. *DRN* 4.568–71, which links the phenomenon to the striking of hard surfaces by voice-atoms which have failed to reach ears.

when conceptualised as pure sound detached from any originary font of communicative intention can the *laudes* given to Maecenas in the theatre be given to him again after the fact in an ode of Horace. By accentuating Maecenas' role as the *hearer* of the *laudes*, Horace foregrounds his present role as the hearer of the poem, thereby creating a space within which the two aural experiences may intersect and merge into a single act of audition. The *laudes* of Maecenas appear in this poem both as a past experience to be recounted and as a present speech act to be performed (here the theoretical framework developed in ch. 1 concerning the frames of experience-report and performed speech is fully applicable), and it is, I argue, in this imaginative overlaying of past on present that the poem can be said to achieve the 'presence' that Heinze and Lowrie see as instrumental for Horatian lyric.

However, the diffuse and echo-mediated form of presence generated by this reading is a far cry from what the term denotes in Heinze and Lowrie. By opting to line up our conception of 'presence' with material, perceptual presence rather than metaphysical presence, we effectively turn the established problematic of presence on its head. Rather than dismissing the conceit of the co-presence of poet and addressee as a mere prop for the lofty pretensions of Horatian lyric, a transparent device to be exposed and demolished, we can shift our attention to the involved work of *producing* presence as a function of the experience of reading the *Odes*.

Paul de Man pointed in this direction when he argued in an often-quoted passage that '[the] principle of intelligibility, in lyric poetry, depends on the phenomenalization of the poetic voice', adding that 'this voice is in no circumstance available as an actual, sensory experience' but must be '[made] manifest' by a 'poetic labor' that 'can take several forms and adopt a variety of strategies.'[17] Whereas Lowrie reads this passage as an exposé of the self-contradictions involved in the concept of the lyric utterance,[18] I would suggest that de Man's essay also admits of a quite different and perhaps more productive reading, one which privileges the 'poetic labor' of making the poetic voice manifest as itself a central issue for the theory of the lyric.

De Man's critique is aimed above all at the notion of the voice of the poet as a wellspring of interpretive authority to which well-trained readers can achieve direct, unmediated access as though in face-to-face conversation with the author. The point, however, is not quite that this phenomenalised poetic voice is a pernicious illusion which must be shattered, but rather that a theory of lyric reading

---

17 de Man 1985: 55.
18 Lowrie 1997: 26.

should not take this poetic voice for granted by glossing over the process by which it is brought into being, a process which de Man traces in his essay as a sequence of 'figural substitutions [and] material inscriptions'.[19]

It is with de Man's challenge in mind that I propose a new direction for the theory of occasion and 'presence' in Horatian lyric, to be explored in this and the following chapter. The central points to be advanced are as follows. Firstly, the presence of the speaking voice and of the addressee, and hence of the whole staging ground of lyric presence which we can refer to as the occasion, is never supplied in advance but is typically posed as a problem which the ode sets out to solve for itself. The *Odes* can thus rightly be said to *perform* presence rather than simply to depend upon it as an assumption. Another corollary of this first point is that 'presence' in the *Odes* is always dialectical in nature. The product of this dialectical, performative process of presence-making is what we have been calling the fiction of occasion.[20]

Secondly, in order to bring out this dialectical aspect of Horace's lyric presences, we must recognise the element of materiality that abides in them, whether we are speaking of the material form of the text, the materiality of the social and economic relations that govern poetic production (which will receive less emphasis here), or, most critically, of the materiality of the reader as a sensing, bodied being. We saw in our discussion of *c.* 1.20 above how the recollection of a low-fidelity echo serves as a kind of perceptual ground on which a novel kind of lyric presence is built. In the next section, I will turn to *c.* 1.9, the 'Soracte ode', a poem in which the exploration of the possibilities of presence is concentrated on the modality of vision rather than that of hearing. This serves as an opportunity to take a closer look at the legacy of Heinze's theory of occasion as it has played out through successive scholarly readings of the Soracte Ode, and thereby to arrive at a more precise formulation of the concept of the fiction of occasion in Horatian lyric.

---

[19] de Man 1985: 56.
[20] McCarthy 2019: 86–113 advances an argument that shares many points of contact with my own here, though with a fundamental difference of orientation. She is persuasive in her claim that Horace's aim in the *Odes* is 'not to re-create a performance context or to airbrush the difference between that context and his own literate poems, but to create a new kind of discursive force that is native to writing (2019: 92).' However, her conception of this new kind of discursive force is founded on the vision, untenable in my view, of the *Odes* as an experiment in shifting the power away from ritual/performative 'contexts' and towards the autonomously performative 'text' (see esp. 2019: 99). The problem of the text/context distinction cannot be so absolutely resolved.

3.3 Seeing Soracte: *c.* 1.9

Heinze illustrates the fictionality of Horatian lyric occasion through two distinct frames of reference, one which is concerned with the author's perspective and another which deals with the reader's perspective. The fiction, for Heinze, consists not only in Horace's simulation of communicative contexts reappropriated from the poetry of a distant time and place, but also in the 'requirement' of imaginative collusion in those communicative contexts on the part of contemporary readers. It is this readerly perspective that authorises Heinze to define the occasions of the *Odes* as fictions rather than as mere falsehoods or pretenses; the point is not simply that 'the songs were not composed and sung in the occasion in which they claim to have been composed and sung',[21] but that they require their readers to make a positive effort to imagine them as though they were composed and sung on such occasions.

Heinze stresses that occasion in the *Odes* is an essential feature of Horace's lyric project, not a peripheral or ornamental one. It is, he argues, not only when Horace uses deictic pronouns to allude to 'the situation in which he and his interlocutor find themselves, or an action that his utterance sets in motion',[22] that the reader is required to perform the act of mental transport he describes; rather, he argues that the fiction of occasion is evoked simply through the '[address] to a person imagined as present',[23] which, he maintains, forms part of practically every poem in the collection.[24] On this theory, the Horatian ode is a medium predicated on the imagined co-presence of the poet, the interlocutor, and a situation of utterance in which both are directly implicated. 'Occasion' is Heinze's generic term for this imagined co-presence in all its forms. Moreover, Heinze's insistence on occasion as a formal precondition for the lyric ode implies that the imaginative act of 'recognising' the occasion is not only necessary for the reader's understanding of a given lyric utterance; it also entails recognising Horace's authority to perform that utterance. The reader who colludes in this all-important act of recognition effectively transports herself to a fictional world in which Horace is a

---

[21] Heinze 2009: 30.
[22] Heinze 2009: 14. His examples are 1.27, 2.11, 2.14.22, and 3.19.
[23] Heinze 2009: 15.
[24] Heinze 2009: 11–12: he counts 'six exceptions out of 103 poems, oddities that do not constitute their own type'.

lyre-brandishing bard always ready with a song, and it is in this world that all the occasions of the *Odes* take place.²⁵

The premiss that Horace's *Odes* presuppose a specified dialogic situation of utterance which the reader must mentally reconstruct has proved influential, but it has also been a major point of contention in Horatian scholarship. Eduard Fraenkel sparked a lively debate in his 1957 monograph when he discounted *c.* 1.9, known as the Soracte ode, as a failure due to its violation of dramatic unity, arguing that the winter scene with which the poem begins is utterly irreconcilable with the springtime setting with which it ends.²⁶ The ensuing flood of responses to Fraenkel's charge, incorporating numerous attempts to rehabilitate the poem by establishing its unity as well as critiques of the principle of dramatic unity itself, had the salutary result of bringing into sharp focus the question of how far Heinze's model of the imaginative basis of the Horatian ode is theoretically tenable. In more recent years, the debate on dramatic unity has given rise to a strong thesis, formulated separately by Davis 1991 and Schmidt 2002, that Horace's lyric occasions do not in fact have the character of fictional worlds, and that dramatic setting is not as significant a factor in the *Odes* as previously thought. I would like to re-open this question through a reading of *c.* 1.9 which will reevaluate both Heinze's proposals on occasion in the *Odes* and the counter-proposals set out by Davis and Schmidt in the light of the theory of the fiction of occasion so far developed.

uides ut alta stet niue candidum
Soracte, nec iam sustineant onus
   siluae laborantes geluque
      flumina constiterint acuto?
dissolue frigus, ligna super foco   5
large reponens, atque benignius
   deprome quadrimum Sabina,
      O Thaliarche, merum diota.
permitte diuis cetera, qui simul
strauere uentos aequore feruido   10
   deproeliantis, nec cupressi

---

25 Heinze draws a telling analogy to what he calls the 'Romantic world (28)' ... 'the phrase *harum quas colis arborum* ("those trees you grow", 2. 14. 22) transports us into Postumus' arboretum (14).' He suggests further that the lyre, along with the appurtenances of musical performance generally, is the emblem of this authority, since 'the prerequisite of [Horace's] lyric is that the lyre be always at hand, at the feast, in a stroll in the park, at a tryst with his beloved, and before the deity's altar (28).'
26 Fraenkel 1957: 176–77. Nauta shows that Fraenkel's concerns had already been raised in a number of 19th century readings (Nauta 1994: 225).

>   nec ueteres agitantur orni.
> quid sit futurum cras fuge quaerere et
> quem Fors dierum cumque dabit lucro
>   appone nec dulcis amores   15
>   sperne puer neque tu choreas
> donec uirenti canities abest
> morosa. nunc et Campus et areae
>   lenesque sub noctem susurri
>   composita repetantur hora,   20
> nunc et latentis proditor intimo
> gratus puellae risus ab angulo
>   pignusque dereptum lacertis
>   aut digito male pertinaci.

> Do you see how Soracte stands all white with high-piled snow, how the struggling forests no longer support their burden and the streams are frozen with jagged ice? Thaw the cold: fetch a generous supply of logs to place on the fire and with a freer hand, O Thaliarchus, break out the four-year-old wine in the Sabine jar. Leave the rest to the gods: once they have quelled the winds that fight with the seething waves, the cypresses are no longer shaken, and the old ash trees.
>   Leave off asking what will happen tomorrow and mark down as profit each day that Fortune brings, and do not scorn, young man that you are, sweet love and the dance while you are in bloom, untouched by peevish gray. Now is the time to [reclaim/revisit] the Campus and the playing fields, and soft whispers in the night at an appointed hour; now, too, the lovely laugh from a secluded nook that gives away the girl hiding there, and the love-token snatched from her arm or from a not-so-resistant finger.

The problems posed by the Soracte ode are problems central to the theory of occasion in general, namely, the problems of sense-perception, deixis, and literal and figurative reference. The poem begins with a word signalling an act of visual perception, *uides*, which serves to introduce one of the most well-known descriptions of a natural scene in Latin literature. In the second stanza, we discover who is viewing this scene — a youth named Thaliarchus — and the relevance of the description to the current situation of that viewer. The ode is thus, as Mayer points out, 'a characteristic example of "situation and response": the situation, winter weather, is sketched in the first stanza, and the rest of the poem offers advice on what to do in such circumstances.'[27] Critics are divided, however, as to how this situation is to be conceptualised, and what its elements are. Heinze's model would dictate that the figure of direct address itself assumes the co-presence of Horace and Thaliarchus in a place where both can view the snowy moun-

---

27 Mayer 2012: 112.

tain and both can be warmed by the fire; on this model, details such as the fireplace and the jar of Sabine form part of the backdrop of Horace's unfolding lyric utterance.[28] This view entails firstly that Horace's utterance is a (fictional) event which unfolds in time, and secondly that this utterance is perceptible to Thaliarchus in the same way as the snows on Mt. Soracte are visible to him. Thaliarchus' act of visual perception would then coincide with the time of the poem's utterance.

Up until the fifth stanza, there is nothing to deter us from imagining the discourse of the poem as taking place in some kind of indoor setting with a fireplace from which snow-capped Soracte is visible. At line 18, however, Horace declares that *now* (*nunc*) is the time to 'seek once again the Field of Mars and the grounds' and to pursue sexual escapades by night. Fraenkel reads this statement as implying an abrupt and incongruous change of scene from an initial winter setting evoked by the fireplace and the cold to a spring or summer setting when it is warm enough to roam the open spaces of the city after dark; the result, he argues, is that 'the picture of the season at the end of the ode is not compatible with the beginning.'[29] The most widely accepted response to this objection is the one adopted e.g. by West and Mayer, namely that *nunc* refers not to the time of year but to the youthful phase of Thaliarchus' life; West glosses *nunc* as 'while you are still young'.[30] Such an interpretation would decouple the closing description of nighttime rendezvous from the act of visual perception signalled by *uides* and thus sever the temporal reference of *nunc* in lines 18 and 21 from the immediate present of the poem's utterance.

According to contextual framing theories of text comprehension, the conceptual shift that would allow the reader to understand *nunc* in line 18 as specifying a different 'now' from the 'now' of the present-tense verb *uides* in line 1 would require the activation of a new temporal frame of reference within which this new

---

28 'When Horace describes nature, it serves the purpose of justifying some demand: [...] since it is bitterly cold, and snow lies on the mountains and trees, Thaliarchus should make a proper fire and let flow streams of warming wine, and so on (22–23).'
29 Fraenkel 1957: 177 n. 1.
30 West 1995: 43, restating his argument from West 1967: 7; cf. Nisbet and Hubbard 1970: *ad loc*. Another attempt to preserve the poem's dramatic unity, represented by MacKay 1977 and Clay 1989, would read *nec* in v. 2 as disjunctive (Clay reads *nec iam* as '[but] not yet'), drawing a distinction between the snowy peak and the still uncovered forests lower on the mountain's slopes; this line of argument has not seen much support, presumably due to the incongruity of emphasising the snow-free portions of the mountain in the middle of a description the main topic of which is the abundance of snow and ice.

'now' can be situated. West and Mayer argue that this frame of reference is activated by the use of time and age as a theme in lines 13–18, where Horace urges Thaliarchus to enjoy youth 'while green and free from peevish gray [i.e. old age] (17–18)'. As they point out, this metaphorical use of the colours green (*uirenti*) and gray/white (*canities*) harks back to the opening imagery of trees blanketed with white (*candidum*, 1) snow, introducing a symbolic layer of meaning on top of the natural scene of snowy Mt. Soracte: Thaliarchus' 'green' youth is threatened by the prospect of old age just as the forests on the mountain slopes are beset by the crushing weight of the snow.[31]

The shift from the 'now' of the viewing of Soracte to the 'now' of Thaliarchus' youth would thus coincide directly with a shift from literal to figurative reference. Mayer concludes that we can in fact recognise a distinction between two situations involving a threat to Thaliarchus — the literal cold and the metaphorical frostiness of old age — to which Horace recommends two separate responses: '[w]inter can be dealt with by warmth and wine; the prospective miseries of old age must urge us to make the most of [...] our springtime youth.'[32] Mayer's metaphorical phrase 'springtime youth', however, attests to the sliding between the literal and the figurative in this poem which ensures that his two situations cannot ultimately be kept entirely separate.[33] Williams observes that, while the sense-suggestion of *uides ut* evokes an 'immediate visual effect', 'the details which follow are conceptual: [...] the words *laborantes* and *constiterint* explore a non-visual level whose interest lies in the application to nature of terms that apply to human behaviour.'[34] This initial pathetic fallacy permits us to understand the relation between the snow and ice on Soracte and the 'cold' that Thaliarchus is to 'thaw' (*dissolue frigus*, 5) in more ways than one. We can understand Thaliarchus as being chilled by the same inclement weather that besets Soracte, while at the same time understanding Horace as drawing an analogy between the snows on the mountain and another kind of 'frost' in his interlocutor.[35]

This is not to say, of course, that Mayer's reading fails to recognise the metaphoricity of the opening description or of the phrase *dissolue frigus*. Rather, I am

---

[31] Nisbet and Hubbard 1970 note *ad loc.* that *uirenti* is 'less specifically a colour-word than English "green", yet here obviously contrasted with *canities*.' Cf. Commager 2009: 39–40, Cunningham 1957: 101, and Lee 1969: 25–28 on the green/white contrast.
[32] Mayer 2012: 113.
[33] Cf. Clay 1989: 103.
[34] Williams 1968: 635–36.
[35] Cf. Moskovit 1977: 121–22, who recognises that '[the] chill cannot be understood in only a literal sense' and that 'the imperative in stanza two is both particular and general.'

arguing that this metaphoricity destabilises the structure of 'situation and response' which Mayer uses to determine which of the poem's referents are to be considered as objects within the situation of utterance.[36] The difficulty stems from the fact that we are not provided with any cues to distinguish between the source domain (or 'vehicle') and the target domain (or 'tenor') of its metaphor. If the opening description were phrased as a simile (e.g. 'Just as Soracte…'), we might be able to neatly relegate everything that follows to the target domain, but as it is, Horace offers no such explicit framing device to manage the transition from the Soracte scene to Thaliarchus' state of being.[37] Because the determination of the source-target relation has been left in suspense, we are deprived of the tools needed to make hard distinctions between poetic imagery and scene-setting.

This problem is evident in the much-worried third stanza (vv. 9–12): 'Leave the rest to the gods: once they have quelled the winds that fight with the seething waves, the cypresses are no longer shaken, and the old ash trees.' West scoffs at commentators who understand the passage as transporting us jarringly from the Soracte scene to a tree-lined coast,[38] arguing that the sequence of tenses points to 'a general law, not a particular description' and that the maxim about the impermanence of suffering which Horace expresses using weather and trees 'could be said of a plague of locusts or a broken ankle or a professor with tenure'.[39] He

---

[36] The same criticism applies to Cameron's attempt to restore the unity of the dramatic setting by interpreting *nunc* […] *repetantur* (18–20) as 'now (while I am speaking) let these things be recalled (Cameron 1989: 153).' He advises us to select from all the possible senses of the verb only the one which can describe a *literal* action which fits into his conception of the literal situation of Horace and Thaliarchus' interaction, but he offers no justification for excluding from our reading all the other equally suggestive interpretations of the word which do not happen to conform to this model. Edmunds similarly argues that Horace's advice slides into recollection of his own erotic adventures, and that this justifies the shifting of the tense of *nunc* from the past of Horace's memory into the present of his speech to Thaliarchus; but this requires us to supply an awful lot of information from the 'subtext' of the interaction just to explain the time-reference. Ancona is more convincing when she invokes the sense of 'recall' as a shade of meaning in *repetantur* rather than its primary, 'literal' sense (Ancona 1994: 63).

[37] Shields 1958: 166–67 in fact interprets the *uides ut* clause in precisely this way, arguing that the poem takes the form of a parable on the model of the Biblical 'consider the lilies of the field'; thus, *uides ut…Soracte* would amount to 'Consider Soracte, how it stands…' Shields' proposed solution only serves to highlight the problem: that there is no such clear structural device in the poem, only a bare description.

[38] So, most notably, Pasquali 1920: 82.

[39] West 1995: 42–43; Pöschl 1966: 371. Vessey 1985: 32–33 argues that we should understand the *aequore feruido* not as the storm-tossed sea but as a flatland ravaged by a dust-storm, but his arguments are rather arbitrary, and in any case it is not clear what we stand to gain from such an interpretation.

apparently means to suggest that the imagery of the wind-battered trees is arbitrarily chosen, and any reminiscence of the pictorial details of the Soracte scene is incidental; but the reminiscence is there nonetheless, and to discount it would simply be irresponsible.

West's reading proceeds as though we can locate in the poem a decisive point of transition out of the realm of description — where trees are just trees and weather is just weather[40] — into a symbolic realm where those same things are transformed into vehicles for gnomic *sententiae*.[41] The fact that there is no such transitional point in the poem is not a problem that can or should be explained away, as West and Mayer try to do. Instead, we ought to take into consideration Nauta's suggestion that 'discussions about the interpretation of the "Soracte Ode" cannot be resolved simply by looking harder at the poem, but have to take into account the framework within which the text is read'.[42] As Nauta points out, West's interpretation is formulated within the framework of an interpretive strategy which involves reading the ode as a dramatic monologue, a strategy which itself was originally formulated as a critique of Heinze's theory of occasion.

3.4 The Soracte Ode as dramatic monologue

West points to the poem's opening word, *uides*, to corroborate his theory that the poem is best read as a dramatic monologue, going so far as to assert that this word directly instructs the reader to adopt this reading strategy.[43] He sets out what this entails as follows: 'In a dramatic monologue we read the words of a character speaking and we take pleasure in piecing the story together from the scraps of

---

[40] West goes so far as to assert that 'Horace's snow is primarily snow' (West 1967: 11); cf. Pöschl 1966: 369.

[41] West 1967: 10–11. Compare Pöschl: 'The winter in the Soracte ode is actually winter, but the storms are an analogy for life's hardships. [...] The first strophe depicts a real scene from nature, in the third an example is drawn from nature (Pöschl 1966: 369, 371).' This hard dichotomy between imagery and scene-setting causes problems further on, when he advances the argument that *et campus et areae* forms a unit distinct from *lenesque* sqq., and therefore that Horace is not advising Thaliarchus to run around outside by night in winter but rather to play sports in the fields by day and to pursue sex *indoors* by night (Pöschl 1966: 374–76). The question is, if we accept his premiss that stanza 3 makes a clean break from the '*Lebensnähe*' of the Soracte scene (Pöschl 1966: 368), what is there (besides a needlessly restrictive interpretation of *nunc*) to dictate that stanzas 5–6 must relate back to the concrete landscape which we supposedly left behind two stanzas ago?

[42] Nauta 1994: 227.

[43] West 1995: 40.

evidence we overhear'.⁴⁴ The 'story' that West envisions as emerging from this reading strategy is the story of the figures of speaker and addressee.⁴⁵ For him, the poem 'leaps into life' only once we start considering these figures as characters in a mini-drama and enquiring into the subtext of their interaction: 'Why is Horace comforting Thaliarchus? Why is Horace advising him to enjoy the love of girls?'.⁴⁶ Accordingly, he interprets the word *uides* as having a kind of expository function for the reader, establishing the *mise-en-scene* for Horace's speech to Thaliarchus. On this reading, the characters' viewing of Soracte is a figure of our own dramatic viewing of the characters (both signalled by the opening *uides*); through the poem, we observe these two characters in the process of reacting to the sight of the snow-covered mountain, transforming their particular experience into a piece of the universal human drama.⁴⁷

This interpretive strategy explains West's commitment to distinguishing scene-setting from poetic imagery in general; once we opt to read the poem as the drama of an interaction, it suddenly becomes important to accurately visualise the backdrop of this interaction. Once we have established our dramatic setting, other uses of imagery such as the stormy seas of stanza 3 can be understood as reflecting our speaker-figure's imagination at work as he responds in real time to some external stimulus within the scene: Catlow, for instance, imagines Horace settling back in his chair now that the fire is burning and the wine is poured and indulging in a bout of philosophising.⁴⁸ The strategy of reading poems as dramatic monologues in this manner is a hallmark of the modernist formalism of the New Critics.⁴⁹ West's application of this strategy to the *Odes* can be traced back to Quinn, one of the most influential proponents of New Critical methods in Latin literary scholarship,⁵⁰ who devotes a chapter in his *Latin explorations* to 'dramatic monologue in the odes of Horace'.⁵¹

---

44 West 1995: 40.
45 'The subtlest pleasure of dramatic monologue lies in the observation of character (West 1995: 43).'
46 West 1995: 43, supported by Günther 2013: 276.
47 This paraphrases the conclusion of Catlow 1976: 80. Cf. Quinn's description of Horace in this poem as a 'commentator [...] on the human comedy (Quinn 1980: 139).' Cf. Moskovit 1977.
48 Catlow 1976: 77.
49 For a critical account of the dramatic monologue reading strategy as applied to poems of all kinds, see Culler 2015: 109–19 and 271–74 (on the Soracte ode), with Tucker 1985. The latest application to the *Odes* of the dramatic monologue reading strategy can be found in Tarrant 2020: 47–65.
50 Quinn 1959 is something of a New Critical manifesto for Catullan studies; Wray 2004: 1–35 does an exemplary job of placing Quinn's 'Catullan revolution' in its historical context.
51 Quinn 1963. Cf. the opening remarks to his commentary on the ode (Quinn 1980: 139).

Quinn poses his dramatic monologue readings of a few[52] of the *Odes*, among them *c.* 1.9, as a direct challenge to Heinze's 'dialogic' conception of Horatian lyric. He demonstrates as the basis of this challenge the awkwardness that arises when one attempts to imagine certain odes as transcripts of real-world scenarioes in which Horace is actually speaking to his addressee; his example is the reproachful address to Lyce in *c.* 4.13.[53] His conclusion is that such a discourse makes more sense as a soliloquy, with the addressee necessarily out of earshot.[54] The difficulty with Quinn's discussion is that he seriously misrepresents Heinze's original proposals in the interest of developing his own arguments. He rebukes Heinze's theory on the failure of realism, but nowhere in his essay does Heinze imply that realism is a feature of the dialogic situations of the *Odes* as he sees them. On the contrary, Heinze envisions Horace as 'transporting' his readers to the romanticised world of the archaic bard, always ready to regale his audience with a song tailored to the occasion; fanciful anachronism is the entire point.

This brings us to a more fundamental discrepancy which Quinn fails to point out. As we have already seen, the main thrust of Heinze's argument is that Horace entertains the fiction that the *Odes* themselves are songs and that he is their performer. Quinn's conception of the guiding fiction of the *Odes* is radically different; for him, they are poetic representations of normal acts of speech.[55] Reading *c.* 1.9 according to this method means imagining the poem as representing the unpremeditated outpourings of an old man spontaneously driven to contemplation of life's brevity by the sight of the snow on Mt. Soracte.[56]

In order to set the stage properly for this dramatic reading according to Quinn's precepts, we must reconstruct a 'typical' real-world situation within which a 'typical' person might express the thoughts worked out through the poem. This implies an element of realism which Quinn sees as being at odds with the overt poetic form of Horace's Alcaic stanzas; our old man must not be imagined as expressing himself in verse.[57] In other words, the ode creates a fictional world within which it is no longer an ode. The departure from Heinze's model, where the poems' addressees are imagined as the audience to live performances, is absolute; the speaker and addressee are now identified as figures 'in' the poem

---

52 He distinguishes between 'obvious' dramatic monologues such as 1.27 and 3.13 and 'borderline cases' such as 4.13 and the Soracte Ode, but does not provide an exhaustive list.
53 Quinn 1963: 90–92.
54 Quinn 1963: 92.
55 Quinn 1963: 107–08. See Culler 2015.
56 Quinn 1963: 108–09.
57 Quinn 1963: 107–08.

rather than as participants in the (fictional) act of communication that *is* the poem.

We are now in a better position to evaluate, on the one hand, Quinn's dramatic monologue model as a revision of Heinze's theory of occasion in the *Odes*, and, on the other, West's application of this model to *c.* 1.9 as a solution to the problem of unity posed by Fraenkel. On both these fronts, I would argue, the dramatic monologue model creates more problems than it solves. This is not only because it is based on fatally outmoded New Critical theory.[58] On a more practical level, the dramatic monologue model fails to account for the problems of the Soracte Ode, and of the *Odes* in general, above all because it substitutes a rigid set of prescriptions for a method founded on critical enquiry.[59] It is telling that both Quinn and West open their respective commentaries on the poem by baldly stating that it *is* a dramatic monologue;[60] surely this is putting the cart before the horse.

The same criticism applies to their readings of the poem itself. They argue from the premiss that the parameters of the dramatic setting (sc. a realistic scene of a country house with a view of Soracte in winter) determine which of the poem's pictorial elements can be considered to form part of that setting (sc. *not* a tree-lined coast or a romp in the Campus), but they treat that dramatic setting as given in advance, as though it were somehow prior to the process of reading. Their positing of a predetermined dramatic setting is in fact predicated on removing the readerly experience of context-creation, which itself involves working through ambiguities such as the *nunc* of line 18, from the equation.

3.5 Setting limits

It should be clear at this point that the concept of 'setting' employed by proponents of the dramatic monologue approach relies on what is sometimes called the container theory of space. This setting is a space with rules of its own — rules based on commonsense perceptions of real spaces in the real world — which the poem (conceived somehow as a separate entity) is expected to uphold religiously. The setting thus serves to contain the poem itself, and to limit interpretation to a fixed set of parameters founded on the principle of unity of place. For West, who cautioned

---

[58] Culler 2015.
[59] See Culler 2015 on the pedagogical roots of the dramatic monologue model.
[60] Edmunds makes the same move early in his Jaussian 'reader-reception' account of the poem, implying that the 'dramatic' quality of the poem is a matter of course (Edmunds 1992: 4).

modern readers against being 'carried away by any feelings which are exclusively modern or inappropriate to the context',[61] the poem's definitive determination of its dramatic setting was also the determination of the context against which the 'appropriateness' of any given interpretation could be measured.

West's commitment to the unshakeable authority of a univocal text and a unitary context certainly belongs to a bygone era; his views on this particular front have already come under scathing attack by Edmunds.[62] This makes it all the more curious that the application of the dramatic monologue reading strategy to the *Odes* has never been critiqued with respect to the conception of setting and of space that it presupposes. Instead, scholars interested in this question with regard to the Soracte Ode have tended to restrict themselves to two alternatives: either the poem has a dramatic setting, or it does not.[63] Nisbet and Hubbard are representative of this tendency in their effort to downplay the role of setting in the ode as a criterion of artistic unity. Arguing that Horace in this poem 'is not describing a particular scene', nor 'professing to describe something that really happened, or represent his emotions on a particular occasion', they suggest that the poem exhibits only a loose commitment to depicting an internally consistent setting, and that its descriptions ought not to be considered as 'photographic' or 'representational'.[64] Their analysis is aimed at defending the ode against Fraenkel's condemnation, but as a contribution to the theory of occasion in the *Odes*, the substance of their comments is not much more than a recommendation to hold the setting at arm's length.

More recently, Davis and Schmidt have each independently reformulated this policy of indifference toward setting and occasion in the *Odes* into a full-blown theory. Their approach is directed against both Fraenkel and West, challenging the assumption that one ought to look for internally consistent and lifelike dramatic settings in any of the *Odes*, while at the same time rejecting Fraenkel's edict that we ought to expect a given *Ode* to be strictly unified even on the level of imagery. Schmidt adduces the numerous examples of sudden and unexplained shifts in the *Odes* from one addressee to another and from one setting to another to argue against what he regards as the *communis opinio* — which he traces to Heinze rather than to Quinn or West — that the *Odes* employ concrete,

---

61 West 1967: 9.
62 Edmunds 1992: 98–110.
63 Nauta, for instance, lumps Heinze's 'dialogic' approach together with the dramatic monologue approach, arguing that both 'are articulated within one and the same convention: that of reading lyric poetry as something spoken in the context of a situation. This convention may be powerful; it is not uncontested (Nauta 1994: 226).'
64 Nisbet and Hubbard 1970: 118.

'pragmatic' occasions or situations which are modelled mimetically on the performance occasions of archaic Greek lyric.[65] The unity of a given *Ode*, he argues, consists not in the dramatic setting of the discourse, but rather in 'the theme and in the lyric I, in their "continuous" speech.'[66] Speech in the *Odes*, according to Schmidt, is not speech uttered on a (real or fictional) occasion but 'absolute speech' (*absolute Rede*).[67]

Schmidt proposes that locating the unity in the speaking voice frees the reader's imagination to synthesise various aspects of the poem into new, emergent wholes, which he calls 'mental situations' (*geistliche Situationen*).[68] This would seem to suggest a slackening of the restrictions placed on interpretation by the dramatic monologue model; but Schmidt's approach carries strictures of its own. 'The mind's eye,' he insists, 'can see clearly without placing the body in the setting of the viewed object',[69] invoking a neo-Cartesian conception of the body and the senses as a straitjacket for the imagination. His objective is to break out of the '*Denkzwang*' ('rigid thinking') that demands from the *Odes* the scenic coherence of a photograph, but he ends up taking aim at the formal element of *mise-en-scene* in the poems themselves, as though this, rather than his opponents' theories, were the root of the problem.[70]

This attitude is in evidence in his reading of the Soracte Ode, which consists solely of the assertion that, after stanza 2, the fireplace scene becomes irrelevant; once 'the lyric I moves on from the prompting of the concrete occasion of viewing to the related philosophical topic of adolescence', he says, '[the] "occasion" of the appeal to enjoy youth is for its part no longer concretised in space and time.'[71] In this account, the 'concrete occasion of viewing' comes off as little more than a distraction for the reader to clear away in order to get at the real substance of the poem.

Davis' account of setting and occasion in the *Odes* similarly treats the whole topic as a pitfall which his interpretive method is designed to skirt. He advises us to conceive of 'unity' in the *Odes* in terms of 'internal consistency at the rhetorical and ideational levels', dismissing the search for unity at other (read: lower) levels

---

[65] Schmidt 2002: 299–301.
[66] Schmidt 2002: 304.
[67] Schmidt 2002: 305; this echoes Smith 1968: 16.
[68] Schmidt 2002: 299.
[69] 'Geistige Augen können offenbar sehen, ohne den Körper in die Szenerie des Geschauten zu versetzen (Schmidt 2002: 310).'
[70] Schmidt 2002: 299.
[71] Schmidt 2002: 308.

such as 'unity of "situation"' as misguided.[72] His defense of this stance is articulated in the form of a theory of the *Odes*' composition which treats *mise-en-scène* in the *Odes* as provisional 'scaffolding':

> [The] 'situation' or 'occasion' constructed by the lyrist in specific odes is itself one more counter in a larger argument. [...] [Such] fictionalized situations are aids to the construction of an ideational building, which it is part of the business of the critic to reconstruct. [...] [Parts] of the cognitive 'scaffolding' may be abandoned in the course of the poem once their rhetorical *raison d'être* has been fulfilled — as is the case with the Soracte ode [...].[73]

Davis' metaphor imposes a rigid hierarchy of interpretation which cannot stand on its own feet. It will surely be uncontroversial to claim against Davis that nothing in a poem ought to be reduced to a 'rhetorical *raison d'être*', and that 'abandoning' any part of it like so much 'scaffolding' is not a sound method of resolving difficulties. The idea of scaffolding works better as a metaphor for reading strategies like the dramatic monologue approach which fall apart once pushed beyond the heuristic stage; but Davis prefers to attribute the process of 'building' to Horace himself, while aligning the concerns of the critic with the end product of this authorial construction project. In this way Davis advances the tacit claim that his particular solution to the problem of occasion is sanctioned by the authority of the poet.

Davis' privileging of the 'ideational' aspect of Horace's poetic structures is thoroughly Platonic in pedigree, to the extent that occasion comes to resemble the 'matter' through which, and beyond which, the 'idea' of a given ode can at length be perceived.[74] Schmidt similarly gestures toward the transcendent realm of Ideas when, in the attempt to put an end to the search for 'concrete' and 'pragmatic' occasions in Horatian lyric, he ends up throwing out the concept of space in the *Odes* altogether:

> One does not get many impressions of space from Horatian odes, and even if we supply the sort of setpieces that presuppose a notion of space and conjure up for ourselves a mental picture of the odes to which those setpieces correspond, we still do not entirely succeed in spatialising Horatian lyric. And yet we continue to ask about the locations of the speech

---

72 Davis 1991: 9.
73 Davis 1991: 9.
74 See e.g. Davis 1991: 146–47 on *rapiamus amici* in *Ep.* 13.3: 'Though formally directed to the immediate community of assembled *amici*, the injunction is general in scope [...] The prescriptive apothegm, then, grows out of, but rapidly goes beyond, the particular occasion, which thereby functions as a kind of "scaffolding" [...] on which the ethical norms of the poem are constructed.' For a similar viewpoint as applied to the Soracte Ode, see Pöschl 1966: 377–78.

and of the occasions in Horatian odes, demanding the cohesion of the I, the speech, the setpieces, space and the placedness (*Ortseinheit*) proper to an occasion.[75]

As a critique of the dramatic monologue approach set out by Quinn, West, and others, Schmidt's argument here is salutary. However, he does a disservice to his subject by framing the question in terms of the spatiality of the *Odes tout court*. The blanket statement that '[one] does not get many impressions of space from Horatian odes' virtually refutes itself; space is not an arbitrary figure but an all-pervading metaconcept indispensable to thought, language, and life. Henri Lefebvre is surely right, therefore, in his observation that 'any search for space in literary texts will find it everywhere and in every guise: enclosed, described, projected, dreamt of, speculated about.'[76] To be sure, Schmidt is taking a rather narrower view of space and spatiality here, so that by 'impressions of space' he clearly means to refer to the kind of photographic scene-perception featured in West's readings; but it is precisely this narrow view of space which produces the approach that Schmidt is criticising, that is, the space of the *Odes* as the static, objectively determined container for the enunciative event.

However, overcoming the limitations of the dramatic monologue approach and the container theory of space does not require abstaining from asking questions about 'the locations of the speech and of the occasions in Horatian odes', as Schmidt suggests; rather, as I argued in chapter 1 in a related context, the key is to ask those questions while cognizant of the fact that the answers to them do not lie in a realm of pre-established facts which the text discloses. As I suggested there, we ought instead to attend to the ways in which space in all its various manifestations forms part of the whole experience with which the poem presents us. This means opening the narrowly defined space of enunciation which is typically referred to as the 'occasion' onto a broader conception of space as the ground of embodied experience and cognition, a conception which recognises a fundamental continuity, explored in chapter 2, between the use of space in figurative language and the orientation of space through the operations of literal reference such as deixis. The following section will present a reading of the Soracte Ode that leads in this direction. Its goal will be to provide an alternative to

---

[75] 'Man wird nicht viele Raumeindrücke von horazischen Oden in sich tragen, und selbst wenn wir solche Requisiten hinzunehmen, die Raumvorstellungen mit sich bringen, und uns die entsprechenden Oden vergegenwärtigen, machen wir uns die horazische Lyrik kaum insgesamt räumlich. Fragen wir dennoch nach den Orten des Sprechens und der Gelegenheiten in horazischen Oden, auch nach der Verbindung von Ich, Sprechen, Requisiten, Raum und der zu einer Gelegenheit gehörenden Ortseinheit (Schmidt 2002: 307).'
[76] Lefebvre 1991: 15.

the reductive conception of occasion as the staging ground for the enunciative event narrowly conceived.

3.6 The power of now

I suggested above that the interpretation of *nunc* in line 18 is primarily a question of frames of reference. We can now see that the prevailing approach to setting and occasion in the Ode involves an attempt to supply a predetermined frame of reference in the form of a concrete situation of utterance which will then decide problems such as the temporal reference of *nunc* for the reader. *Nunc* signals a present state of affairs, and in order to decide *which* present state of affairs is being referred to, we must turn to our available frames of reference. A dramatic monologue approach would dictate that the only pertinent frames of reference are those which are established as significant facts within the fictional world of the poem.[77] Horace has stated that it is cold outside and his addressee is a young man, so *nunc* must refer to one of those states of affairs; Mayer and West, as we have seen, argue that we must opt for the latter. If, however, we discard the assumption that the only relevant frames of reference stem from the concrete facts of the dramatic setting, *nunc* suddenly appears far more elastic than before.

Nunc is an adverb of time, and time is not only a mechanical determiner of the poem's dramatic setting; it is also one of the poem's central themes. In a classic study, Rudd demonstrates how the metaphorical structure of the ode is underpinned by the antitheses winter/spring and youth/age, with each of these antithetical pairs governing a philosophical sentiment: the passage from winter to spring brings to mind the *carpe diem* ('spring will come soon; do not be overcome by winter's worries'), while the passage from youth to age evokes the *memento mori* ('old age will come soon; do not squander your youth').[78] The winter/spring theme opposes present anxiety to future relief, while the youth/age theme sets present pleasure against future loss. In the first three stanzas, Thaliarchus is urged to attend to his present pleasure in the face of heavy weather because winter will soon turn into spring, and storm into calm. In the final three stanzas, he is advised to do the same thing, but for a different reason: because his opportunities for pleasure will expire with his youth. The objective in both cases is the cultivation of the present as the time for taking pleasure. When Horace refers to 'the now' in this poem, then, he presents it not only as an empty shifter but as an

---

[77] Moritz 1976: 169 dubs this rule 'the principle of autarky'.
[78] Rudd 1960.

object of desire. This has the effect of attaching a complex array of abstract and metaphorical predicates to 'now' which, in turn, expands the frame of reference within which *nunc* may be interpreted.

The passage from youth to age is linear, and ends in 'peevish gray' (*canities* [...] *morosa*, 17–18); the passage from winter to spring is more comforting because it is cyclical. It is fitting, then, that the actions which Horace prescribes to Thaliarchus are phrased in terms of restoration and renewal. As Nisbet and Hubbard note, the prefix to *reponens* (6) introduces the idea of 'return' or 'replacement', the relevance of which to the act of placing logs on the fire is not immediately obvious.[79] They suggest we should think of Thaliarchus as putting the logs 'back where they belong'; this is apt if we consider that, according to the moral standpoint developed in the poem, the logs 'belong' on the fire where they can be used, not stockpiled away for an unforeseeable future. But the re- prefix also dovetails with the comparative *benignius*, suggesting that Thaliarchus' generosity marks a return to an earlier state which had been somehow suspended. It is not only the heat from the fire which will allow him to 'thaw the cold' as Horace requests; rather the very act of freely dipping into his store of wine and fuel implies a return from a period of frugality to a period of largess which itself embodies the passage from winter to spring.

Paschalis observes in the poem an overarching dialectic between tension and restriction (the unyielding frost on Soracte) and dissolution or release (the free-flowing Sabine wine).[80] I would add that these abstract forces are themselves governed by a more fundamental metaphorical complex drawn from the realm of finance, based on the dichotomy of saving and spending.[81] In the fourth stanza, Horace shows that the advice he just gave about one's supply of firewood — don't spare it on a cold day — applies equally to the supply of time allotted to one's lifespan. Implementing the familiar conceptual metaphor TIME IS MONEY,[82] he recommends treating this allowance of days not as a wage to be saved up and carefully budgeted (tension), but as disposable income to be 'burned' like fuel in winter (release). Those who spend their time enquiring into their death-day (v. 14), by contrast, are implicitly likened to misers whose fear of losing their profits prevents them from making any use of them. Such people wrongly place a high

---

[79] Nisbet and Hubbard 1970: *ad loc.*
[80] Paschalis 2002; cf. Sullivan et al. 1981: 278. Cognitive linguistics would categorise these phenomena in the realm of 'force dynamics' (Talmy 2000: 409–70).
[81] On the financial metaphor, see Ancona 1994: 68.
[82] Johnson and Lakoff 1980.

value on knowledge of future events; the wise, according to Horace, know the intrinsic value of the present.

This leads directly into the final period, where Horace describes exactly how Thaliarchus is to gain a purchase on the present. 'Now is the time', he says,

> to reclaim/revisit [*repetantur*] the Campus and the playing fields, and soft whispers in the night at an appointed hour; now, too, the lovely laugh from a secluded nook that gives away the girl hiding there, and the love-token snatched from her arm or from a not-so-resistant finger.

A good deal of controversy has arisen around *repetantur*. Mayer sees in it a hyper-complex zeugma, arguing that the sense shifts with each of its subjects: 'With *Campus* and *areae* it means "return to" (*OLD* 1), with *susurri* "resort again to (an activity)" (*OLD* 3), with *risus* perhaps "recover" (*OLD* 5b), and with *pignus* "claim" (*OLD* 8).'[83] Not all commentators have been so comfortable with the semantic slippage, however. Nisbet and Hubbard aver that 'the prefix means "according to the compact" rather than "repeatedly"', but complain that '[the] force of the verb carries on into the next stanza, though there it is less appropriate.'[84] Surely we need an interpretation that accounts for the application of the full force of the verb, along with its prefix, to each of its subjects, while also acknowledging the polyvalence recognised by Mayer. I suggest therefore that the verb picks up both the financial metaphor from stanza 4 and the *re-* of *reponens* in v. 5.

In a financial context, *repetere* means to demand back what one is owed; the verb thus figures Thaliarchus as a creditor who now seeks repayment.[85] The ablative absolute phrase *composita* [...] *hora* which encloses the verb *repetantur* fleshes out the metaphor by introducing the idea that the playful and erotic activities described in stanzas 5 and 6 are stipulated by a contract of which Thaliarchus is the beneficiary. This idea attains literal realisation in the image of the *pignus* (token or pledge) 'snatched' from a reticent lover, permitting us to understand the *composita hora* as the hour appointed for the fulfilment of an oath betokened by the *pignus*. I would argue, however, that we ought to consider the financial metaphor as applying equally to all the subjects of *repetantur*. Horace here is expanding on his earlier advice to Thaliarchus to treat every day that comes to him as disposable income, i.e. as an opportunity for present pleasure. In order to accomplish this fully, he must also demand immediate return on his past investments.

---

[83] Mayer 2012: *ad loc.*
[84] Nisbet and Hubbard 1970: *ad loc.*
[85] *OLD*, *repetō* def. 8b.

Ancona points out that the act of snatching the love-token from the girl, as a figure for the act of sexual possession, enacts a 'symbolic rape' which is conceptually linked to the act of 'seizing the day' enjoined by the motto *carpe diem*.[86] As she further notes, the love-token is not only an arbitrary euphemism; it is chosen because it permits Horace to speak of sexual pleasure as something which is 'owed' to a male once he has 'put in the time', so to speak, with a female.[87] *Repetere* is apter in this respect than a bare *petere* would be since it incorporates the idea that Thaliarchus is reclaiming something which he had previously let out on loan. The girl of stanza 6 is thus parallel to the firewood of stanza 2: Thaliarchus' frigid, conservative worldview taught him to be content with the mere promise of future sexual pleasures just as it drove him to save up his fuel against blizzards yet to come.

It was argued above that the 'thawing' which Thaliarchus is urged to perform in v. 5 has both a metaphorical and a literal sense. Throwing more logs on the fire will warm him up, but at the same time the act of retrieving the logs is itself a token of the liberality which will 'melt' his former austerity. The 'cold' or 'frost' which is to be 'thawed' is thus, paradoxically, both the cause and the consequence of the abstemious ethic which is criticised in the ode. The third stanza evinces a similar duality. The truism that storms are always followed by calm justifies the advice to 'leave all else [sc. besides the requirements of present comfort] to the gods (9)'; but implicit here is the Epicurean sentiment, explicit in the previous stanza, that the very act of attending to one's present comfort can bring about the desired state of calm (ἀταραξία).[88] Just as in the first two stanzas, the weather is overdetermined. Inclement weather serves as the occasion for the exercise of an Epicurean ethic of attending to present pleasure which leads to a passage from anxiety to contentment; at the same time, this passage from anxiety to contentment is itself expressed metaphorically in terms of the weather.

This adds complexity to the *donec* clause of vv. 17–18, where seasonal change is employed as a metaphor for aging. With this stanza we have shifted into a new reckoning of time, turning from the cycle of the seasons to the cycle of human life, all the while remaining couched in the same symbolic logic. Spring is still linked to the possession of pleasure and winter to its lack, but the poles of present

---

86 Ancona 1994: 66.
87 Ancona 1994: 68.
88 Cf. Epicurus' *Letter to Menoeceus* 128: 'Everything we do is for the sake of removing pain and anxiety. As soon as this happens for us, all the storms of the soul die away' (τούτου γὰρ πάντα πράττομεν, ὅπως μήτε ἀλγῶμεν μήτε ταρβῶμεν. ὅταν δὲ ἅπαξ τοῦτο περὶ ἡμᾶς γένηται, λύεται πᾶς ὁ τῆς ψυχῆς χειμών).

and future have been reversed; the threat to present pleasure is no longer the concern for future threats but the very ephemerality of the present. Nevertheless, as argued above, we would be wrong to follow Mayer and West in taking the *donec* clause as introducing an entirely new problem or 'situation' which demands its own separate 'response'. *Nunc* at v. 18 indicates a mode of 'seizing the now' which is a response both to the ephemerality of pleasure which confronts us in spring and the vicissitudes of experience foregrounded by winter; it names both the promise of the present moment and its challenge. Accordingly, the subjunctive *repetantur* exhorts Thaliarchus both as to what this *now* holds in store and what is to be done in the face of this *now*; it indicates both an opportunity and an imperative.[89]

Just as the spatial metaphor implicit in *reponens* traces the movement from the frost that Thaliarchus sees and feels in stanza 1 to the warmth he experiences in stanza 2, I argue, the spatial metaphor implicit in *repetantur* helps 'explain' how Thaliarchus is to move from the frozen landscape of Soracte into the world of youthful pleasures set forth in stanzas 5 and 6. The echo of *reponens* in *repetantur* contaminates the frame of reference of *nunc* by reasserting the preliminary motif of the transience of winter's hardships directly athwart the new topic of the ephemerality of youth's pleasures. It shows that unredeemed debts like the love-token are frozen in the past just as stockpiled resources like the fuel and the Sabine wine are frozen in the future; both must be redeemed for the present, in the present. From this point of view, it is possible to see the *nunc* of v. 18 as simultaneously conjunctive and disjunctive: the state of affairs which it denotes is presented as both already in effect and contingent upon the act of reclamation signalled by *repetantur*. The second stanza reveals that, even in a world overcome by winter's chill, the means for 'thawing the cold' is close at hand, and this gives way to the realisation that the cold itself is a product of the parsimony that led Thaliarchus to stockpile his resources in the first place, rather than using them at his need. Like the fire which Horace urges Thaliarchus to feed in stanza 2, the pleasures of stanzas 5 and 6 are both there and not there for the taking; they exist in a now which stands both for the world as it is and the world as it could be if only Thaliarchus were to *seize* the now.

---

[89] This can be explained in terms of semantics as follows: If *repetantur* is jussive, then *nunc* is one of its predicates; if *repetantur* is potential, then *nunc* is part of the argument (this second interpretation is recommended by the initial position of *nunc*, but this does not rule out the first). The distinction can be clarified by parsing the sentence into a question-and-answer format: 1. (Jussive) Q: 'When can I reclaim [...]?' A: 'Now!' 2. (Potential) Q: 'What can I do now?' A: 'Reclaim [...]!'

Considered from this angle, the fundamental question addressed by Fraenkel's summary critique and all its various rebuttals — how can the activities described in stanzas 5 and 6 exist in the same time-space as the Soracte landscape? — emerges as the fundamental question to which the poem itself applies itself. The poem has been described as working out a 'meditation on time in the modality of being human' and even as waging a 'war on time',[90] but we can be more precise than this: the poem with its enigmatic, impossible *now* poses an imaginary solution to the problem of the relationship between the present — specifically the present as apprehended by the senses — and the attainment of pleasure. The 'trick' that the ode plays in order to produce this *now* is precisely the oddity of which Fraenkel complained, that is, the fact that the pleasures of stanzas 5 and 6 are not presented as an itemised list but rather as a cluster of images woven together into a densely-textured vignette, in such a way that we feel by the end of the poem as though we have been transported into a new world. It is precisely by presenting the snows on Soracte as a vision of the empirical world that Horace is able to bring this new world of pleasure into sensuous reality, and in showing us this new world, the poem performs the act of reclamation signalled by *repetantur*; that is, it enacts the reclaiming of pleasure for the present of the senses.[91]

3.7 Situation and response

In order to flesh out this argument, let us return once again to the structure of 'situation and response' that Mayer sees in the poem. The first word establishes the 'situation', i.e. the obstacles to the attainment of pleasure encountered in life, in terms of visual perception; Thaliarchus sees a world oppressed by ice and snow, and (we are to imagine) despairs of his own comfort and happiness. The 'frost' that Thaliarchus is said to feel in stanza 2, then, is brought about by a kind of sympathetic surrender to external circumstance which, Horace suggests, is

---

[90] Sullivan et al. 1981: 285.
[91] Suggestive here are the comments on temporality and the erotic in Carson 1986: 117: 'The lover's real desire [...] is to elude the certainties of physics and float in the ambiguities of a space-time where absent is present and "now" can include "then" without ceasing to be "now".' Cf. her account of Plato's fable of the men transformed into cicadas who sing themselves to death in *Phaedrus* 258e–269c: '[The cicadas] offer a new solution to the lover's paradox of "now" and "then." [They] simply enter the "now" of their desire and stay there. Abstracted from the processes of life, oblivious to time, they sustain the present indicative of pleasure from the instant they are born until [they die] (Carson 1986: 139).'

neither necessary nor wise: Thaliarchus can instead build up his own indoor world of easy luxury. Murray sees in the outdoors/indoors dichotomy worked out in the first two stanzas 'a conflict and a juncture between Earth and World',[92] but also in play here is a markedly Epicurean understanding of the border between the self and the outside world, characterised by the conception of the senses as the last bastion of defence against the anxieties produced by the vagaries of the imagination.

In this context, we can see the error of Thaliarchus which occasions the poem as essentially a visual misapprehension: viewing the bleak landscape of Soracte from a distance, he mistakes its affective content for an indication of the bleakness of his own condition, overlooking his more immediate environment and the amenities that lie within his reach. The *re-* of *reponens* would then signify, on top of everything else, a retreat from the natural world that is given to the 'bare' senses into the built world of human flourishing, whose sheltered enclosures act as an artificial extension of the faculty of reason which defends mind, body, and soul from harmful delusions.[93]

According to this reading, the initial *uides* opens up a dialogue with philosophical discourses on the theory of perception in relation to ethics and epistemology; but in order to keep from lapsing into pure philosophical allegory, we must bear in mind, as Schmidt, West, Pöschl and others take pains to underline, that in the context of the poem the perceptual act signalled by *uides* is something inescapably concrete, and secondly that through the use of the second person this act of perception attaches itself in its concreteness to the act of address which informs the whole of the ode. However, this does not mean we must follow West *et al.* in considering the viewing of Soracte solely as an event in a dramatic sequence to which we are detached spectators. Such an approach would sever the vital link between the perceptual act of seeing Soracte and the visual component in the reader's experience of the passage in which Soracte is described.[94] Thaliarchus as the poem's addressee is necessarily, among other things, a figure of the reader, and as such his viewing of the Soracte scene figures the reader's engagement with the visual dimension of Horace's poem.

It behoves us, therefore, to enquire into what Thaliarchus is doing when he looks at the frozen Soracte and what this act 'means', and to seek out points of contact between this and what the reader is doing — or rather what she might imagine herself as doing — when she reads the ode and processes its images. Here

---

92 Sullivan et al. 1981: 282.
93 Cf. Hardie 1993.
94 Moskovit 1977.

the philosophical dimension of *uides* comes back into play. The argument of the first two stanzas, according the interpretation presented above, makes Thaliarchus' viewing of Soracte into a figure for the act of surveying one's environment and assessing it as either hostile or hospitable. We can distil this argument into a logical sequence as per the following paraphrase: 'It may look grim out there, but don't take it to heart; everything you need to relieve your anxiety is in here.'

At the level of verse structure, this progression from 'out there' to 'in here' is formalised in the stanzaic architecture of the ode, so that each of the two spaces (outdoors and indoors) is contained within its own end-stopped unit of sound and sense. Each of these stanzaic units, moreover, is announced by a direct appeal to the senses: stanza 1 employs the distal sense-modality of sight (viewing Soracte from a distance), while the opening command of stanza 2 heralds a perceptual reorientation toward the proprioceptive sensation of body temperature ('thaw the cold'). The anchoring of this sensory reorientation to the metrical turning point between stanzas forms a sympathetic bond or graft between the perceptual experiences presented in the poem and the experience of reading the poem as an ordered sequence of words.

This observation permits us to perceive a performative and metareferential dimension in the stanza-initial expressions *uides ut* and *dissolue frigus*. Each of these expressions functions as a 'sense-suggestion' for the stanza which it governs (to employ the term introduced in chapter 1), providing a sensory frame which guides the reader's perceptual exploration of the respective spaces presented in each stanza. Here we can recognise a fundamental distinction between the perspective of the reader's experience and the perspective of the fictionalised experience of the dramatic setting by the characters who take part in it. If we imagine the world of the poem solely from the perspective of the fictional characters Thaliarchus and Horace, we are obliged to say with West that the indoor space of stanza 2 is already in place during the action of stanza 1, while our characters are looking out at the snowy landscape. Within the sequence of the poem, however, the indoor space does not appear until the command to 'thaw the cold' has been delivered. In this sense, the indoor space of stanza 2 is produced precisely in the turning away from the optical space of stanza 1 and toward a new sensory regime, populated by the tactile, ready-to-hand comforts of home.

The sensory reorientation thus enacted also brings about a change in the relation set up in stanza 1 between the bodied subject and the cold as an aspect of her environment. The second stanza 'reveals' that the cold is in fact not an elemental force exerted from outside the sphere of human control, but rather an elementary matter of self-care. In this respect, to 'thaw the cold' is also to 'break up' or 'dissolve' the mode of viewing instantiated in stanza 1, whereby marginal features of the environment such as the grim vista of the snow-covered mountain are misconstrued as imminent threats. The second stanza, again from the point of view of the reader's experience, does not simply list the benefits of turning from 'outside' concerns to 'inside' concerns; it creates the environment anew, performatively, as it appears to us when we take this turn for ourselves.

This effect is achieved simply by the sequential structure of the second stanza, in which the command to 'thaw the cold' is followed by a list of actions that may be performed within this indoor environment in order to achieve that goal. The command tells us how to feel our way through the indoor space before it is actually placed before our eyes as a concrete scene.[95] The room and the objects in it — the firewood, the hearth, the four-year-old wine in the Sabine jar — are thus all made to appear as if in answer to the impulse to thaw the cold, and in doing so to melt away the frozen landscape of Soracte.

The paradox of the fireside scene of stanza 2, then, is that it is at one and the same time a space of desire, produced by the act of seeking warmth which is performatively instantiated by the command *dissolue frigus*, and the concrete situation of utterance for Horace's speech to Thaliarchus. Everything in the stanza works to ground the scene in an immediate present; we have already seen that *reponens* and the comparative *benignius* locate Thaliarchus' newfound liberality in a decisive break from a parsimonious past, and the specification of the wine's age in *quadrimum* (6) reinforces the sense that taking down the bottle from the shelf marks a pivotal point of transition, the reassertion of the present moment in the face of the annual cycle. This stanza also incorporates the address to Thaliarchus (*O Thaliarche*, 8), a name whose etymology already contains the idea of new beginnings; its placement here draws a close link between the fireside scene with its associations of warmth and comfort and the intimacy implied by the address.

The invocation of Thaliarchus thus has the effect of creating what in chapter 1 was called a 'space of inclusion': the close, sheltered space which contains the necessary amenities for relief from winter's chill is also the sonic space of Horace's intimate address to Thaliarchus. This intimate space of the address excludes the distant spectacle of Soracte, and is not even allowed to appear in the poem until the present of viewing signalled by *uides* in line 1 is dispelled and fades away. In this way the poem affects in the present of the address to disclose a more immediate present *within* the present, or beyond it. This newly created present, a present mediated by the poem and attended by the newly inaugurated presence

---

95 See Scarry 1999: 9–20 on 'the specification of the material antecedents of the perception'.

of the poet's speaking voice, also necessarily coincides with the present of pleasure to which the philosophical argument of the poem exhorts us, and thus forms part of the horizon within which the *nunc* of v. 18 has meaning.

By the time we reach the fifth stanza, then, the 'situation' which serves as the background to the poem's enunciation has been subtly but decisively altered. We are no longer looking out at Soracte with Thaliarchus, not because we have somehow been transported to another concrete spatiotemporal setting, but because we have shifted into a new perceptual modality in line with the reorientation of self to world enjoined by the poem's philosophical argument. The argument is thus performative in the sense that it produces in Thaliarchus *qua* reader-figure an embodied subject who enacts in the poem the way of living recommended by the poem. Thaliarchus' enactment of this more perfect way of living, moreover, coincides directly with his presence 'here' with Horace (as opposed to dwelling on far-off anxieties), as well as with the presence to him of Horace's speaking voice. In heeding the command not to scorn love and dancing (*nec dulcis amores | sperne puer neque tu choreas*, 14–15), Thaliarchus enacts the content of his own name ('Party-starter'), making the dance of its etymology, initially held up as a distant memory or wish, come to life in a sensory present newly attuned to the present cadence of the ode's Alcaic stanzas. In this way the poet can testify to the validity of his philosophical proofs precisely by attesting to the perceptual presence of the voice in which he utters them.

3.8 *c.* 1.12: Following Orpheus

In this final section, I will attempt to pull together some of the arguments made so far in this chapter through a discussion of another ode, *c.* 1.12, which contains the first appearance of the 'merry echo' we encountered in *c.* 1.20. The readings of *cc.* 1.20 and 1.9 above traced a pattern in what we might call the 'dialectic of presence' in the *Odes* which can now be outlined explicitly. Both of these poems begin by setting a scene — the Socrate landscape in *c.* 1.9 and the ovation in *c.* 1.20 — which turns out upon closer inspection to be at some remove from the occasion of the poem's enunciation. In each poem, a rift is thus opened up between the position from which the poet speaks and the state of affairs about which he speaks. However, in the course of the 'argument' of the poem (in the loosest possible sense of this term), this rift is somehow bridged or, rather, undone: the 'merry echo' reasserts itself over the ovation as the better model for the aural dynamics of lyric performance, and the Soracte landscape recedes in favour of the indoor space of present pleasure. In each case, the poem divests itself of those aspects of experience which its own medium cannot compass.

C. 1.12 is less oblique, broaching the problem of occasion head-on by opening with a question: who should be the subject of my song, and what manner of being?

> Quem uirum aut heroa lyra uel acri
> tibia sumis celebrare, Clio?
> quem deum? cuius recinet iocosa
>   nomen imago
> aut in umbrosis Heliconis oris   5
> aut super Pindo gelidoue in Haemo,
> unde uocalem temere insecutae
>   Orphea siluae
> arte materna rapidos morantem
> fluminum lapsus celerisque uentos,   10
> blandum et auritas fidibus canoris
>   ducere quercus?
> quid prius dicam solitis parentis
> laudibus, qui res hominum ac deorum,
> qui mare et terras uariisque mundum
>   temperat horis,   15
> unde nil maius generatur ipso,
> nec uiget quicquam simile aut secundum?
> proximos illi tamen occupabit
>   Pallas honores,   20
> proeliis audax; neque te silebo,
> Liber, et saeuis inimica uirgo
> beluis, nec te, metuende certa
>   Phoebe sagitta.
> dicam et Alciden puerosque Ledae,   25
> hunc equis, illum superare pugnis
> nobilem; quorum simul alba nautis
>   stella refulsit,
> defluit saxis agitatus umor,
> concidunt uenti fugiuntque nubes,   30
> et minax, quod sic uoluere, ponto
>   unda recumbit.
> Romulum post hos prius an quietum
> Pompili regnum memorem an superbos
> Tarquini fascis, dubito, an Catonis   35
>   nobile letum.
> Regulum et Scauros animaeque magnae
> prodigum Paulum superante Poeno
> gratus insigni referam camena
>   Fabriciumque.   40
> hunc et incomptis Curium capillis
> utilem bello tulit et Camillum

saeua Paupertas et auitus apto
    cum lare fundus.
crescit occulto uelut arbor aeuo   45
fama Marcelli; micat inter omnis
Iulium sidus uelut inter ignis
    luna minores.
gentis humanae pater atque custos,
orte Saturno, tibi cura magni   50
Caesaris fatis data: tu secundo
    Caesare regnes.
ille, seu Parthos Latio imminentis
egerit iusto domitos triumpho,
siue subiectos Orientis orae   55
    Seras et Indos,
te minor laetum reget aequus orbem;
tu graui curru quaties Olympum,
tu parum castis inimica mittes
    fulmina lucis.   60

What man or hero do you elect to celebrate with the lyre or with the shrill pipe, Clio? What god? Whose name will the merry echo sing in response, either in the shady climes of Helicon or atop Pindus or on frost-bound Haemus, whence the forests blindly followed vocal Orpheus, who by his mother's art stayed the swift rush of rivers and blustery winds, and who had the charm to summon an audience of oak trees with his tuneful strings?

    What may I utter before the customary praises of the Father who governs the affairs of men and gods, who orders the sea, the earth, and the sky in accordance with the changing seasons, from whom nothing greater than himself is created and nothing thrives that is like to him or second to him? Nevertheless, Pallas bold in battle shall stand next to him in honour; nor will I pass over you, Liber, nor the maiden whom wild beasts call foe, nor you, Phoebus, dreaded for your sure arrow.

    I shall tell of Alcides too, and the sons of Leda, the one known for prevailing on horseback, the other in boxing; as soon as their star shines its fair light on sailors, rough water rolls off rocks, winds subside and clouds scatter, and the menacing wave at their command settles back into the sea. After these I am uncertain whether I should commemorate Romulus first or the peaceful reign of Pompilius, the haughty rods of Tarquin or the noble death of Cato.

    Regulus and Scaurus and Paulus, who gave freely of his great spirit when the Phoenician bested him, these will I gladly recall in glorious song, and Fabricius — he, like Curius of unshorn locks and battle-ready Camillus, was sustained by harsh frugality and a family farm with a good homestead. The fame of Marcellus burgeons treelike through the unseen lapse of time; the Julian star shines amid them all like the moon amid the lesser lights.

    Father and guardian of the human race, scion of Saturn, you have been appointed by fate to watch over Caesar: may you reign with Caesar as your second. As for him, whether he conducts in a rightful triumph subdued Parthians, the harriers of Latium, or defeated Seres and Indians of the far East, beneath you he will rule justly over a prosperous world; you will shake Olympus with your massive chariot, you will hurl vengeful thunderbolts on the groves of the impure.

The function of the 'merry echo' in this poem is to sound the name of Horace's prospective honorand, much as the echoed applause of *c.* 1.20 sings the praises of Maecenas for all to hear. Here, however, the transmissional function of the echo is ambivalent in its trajectory. The opening question establishes Horace in the traditional bardic role of the relayer of song that originates from a divine source, here the Muse Clio. The second sentence expands on this conception of the poet as the hearer rather than the deliverer of his song by introducing the figure of echo. One way of reading this sentence is to conceptualise the echo as the medium by which Clio will deliver the reply to the question asked by Horace in vv. 1–2. Thus Hardie suggests that we understand the question as 'an attempt to win [Clio's] favor by discovering that which is pleasing to her',[96] adducing as a parallel Callimachus *h.Dia.*4.183–86, where the poet asks the goddess to tell him which among a list of topics is most dear to her so that he can honour it in song.

At the same time, however, a convention inherited from Homer dictates that the song which Clio is about to begin will promptly be taken up by Horace as his own; according to this tradition, asking the Muse of whom she will sing is a dramatic way of announcing the topic immediately to follow, as for example with the prefatory question of *Il.* 1.8 which launches the reader directly into the narrative.[97] In this instance, Horace's question is followed by a catalogue of gods, heroes, and men whom he deems worthy of celebration in song (vv. 13–60), delivered *in propria persona* with frequent *verba dicendi* placing great emphasis on the act of delivery (*quid prius dicam*, 13; *neque te silebo*, 21; *dicam*, 25; *memorem*, 34; *referam*, 39).

Horace has thus decidedly shifted by v. 13 from the role of the recipient of song to that of its transmitter, a change which prompts us to rethink our initial conception of what function the Muse and her counterpart the 'merry echo' are performing in this poem. The poet's opening questions, we can now see, necessarily look forward not only to his imminent choice of subject, but also further on to the fame that will be bestowed on that subject by Horace's poem as it echoes in posterity. This is most apparent in v. 39, where the native Latin word for Muse, *Camena*, is employed as an ablative of means to specify the manner in which Horace will commemorate the heroes of republican Rome: the Muse has shifted from the poet's guide to a tool at his disposal.

Just as in *c.* 1.20, then, the echo serves as the sensory node which links two otherwise disparate experiences, namely, the fictive event of hearing Clio's re-

---

[96] A. Hardie 2002: 377.
[97] A. Hardie 2002: 381–82.

sponse and the aural effects of Horace's praise-giving poetry. The echo is simultaneously the channel through which Clio informs Horace of her subject of choice — by causing his name to echo from the mountaintops — and the medium through which Horace will sound abroad that same subject's praise. We have to do here with two distinct functions of names and naming: informative naming (the predication of identity, 'this is that') and naming as an act of praise and affirmation (cf. the figurative sense of *nomen* as 'reputation'). The shift from the first kind of naming to the second is attended by a shift in the balance of power between Clio and Horace. The echoing of the famous name which initially is entrusted to the agency of the Muse is finally enacted by the poem itself in the echoing of the name 'Caesar' in stanza 13 (*Caesaris*, 51; *Caesare*, 52).[98]

Hardie explains this transfer of authority by arguing that the poem draws on a traditional conception of the Muse as 'co-singer' with the poet,[99] for which he looks to Pindar and Stesichorus as models, suggesting that the voice that utters the catalogue is Horace's voice infused with the inspiring presence of Clio.[100] However, none of the parallels he adduces uses the metaphor of echo to illustrate this special relationship of 'voice-transmission'[101] between poet and Muse. In *N.* 3.10–12, for example, Pindar famously casts himself as an intermediary between the Muse and his chorus (and by extension his audience), leaving the roles of the various participants in the transaction rather well-defined and stable: the Muse is the primary source of the song, Pindar is her deputy, and the chorus and the lyre are the instruments by which he relays the song to the public.[102] The Muse is the source of knowledge for which Pindar is the privileged mouthpiece. A similar dynamic is in play in *Ol.* 2.1–2, the source of the Pindaric 'motto' which Horace employs in the first two lines of his own poem: here Pindar apostrophises 'songs, rulers of the lyre', and asks them 'which god, which hero, which man shall we celebrate'? The epithet ἀναξιφόρμιγγες ('rulers of the lyre') figures the relation between Pindar's songs and the instrument that plays them in terms of authority, an authority which is embodied in Pindar's own questioning of the songs, insofar as asking the songs to choose the subject for his lyre to celebrate entails submitting to their guidance.

---

98 A. Hardie 2002: 388.
99 A. Hardie 2002: 379.
100 A. Hardie 2002: 381–84.
101 A. Hardie 2002: 381.
102 ἄρχε δ' οὐρανοῦ πολυνεφέλα κρέοντι, θύγατερ, | δόκιμον ὕμνον· ἐγὼ δὲ κείνων τέ νιν ὀάροις λύρᾳ τε κοινάσομαι.

Horace's echo, on the other hand, functions according to a different communicative logic. His prefatory question, unlike Pindar's, will not be answered by a direct missive from the Muse herself, but will be transmitted to him second-hand through its echo. Just as in *c.* 1.20, where Horace transfers the agency for the act of praising Maecenas from the theatre audience to its echo by making *imago* the subject of the verb *redderet*, here the employment of *imago* as the subject of *recinet* transfers the agency for the production of Horace's Muse-inspired song from Clio herself to the echo of her reply. Unlike Pindar in *N.* 3, Horace does not claim to have exclusive access to the song of the Muse through a supernatural link with the goddess; instead, he simply claims for himself an ability to tune in to the reverberations of her heavenly music.[103]

This imperfect, mediate communion between poet and Muse can serve as an explanation of why the question which opens this poem, unlike Pindar's in *Ol.* 2.1–2, does not immediately receive a definite answer. Rather than sounding the name of a singular *laudandus* and expatiating on his achievements and noble lineage, Horace embarks on a sort of exploratory catalogue in which he tests out possible honorands for his song as if to find the right fit. With the *verba dicendi* cited above, Horace evinces a self-conscious attitude towards the construction of this catalogue of famous names in the very act of uttering it. The rhetorical question *quid prius dicam* (v. 13), which recalls many similar formulas employed whenever Jupiter/Zeus is invoked (refer back to Prop. 4.6.10, discussed in chapter 3, for a play on the convention),[104] draws attention to the act of ordering the song even as it rejects the possibility of any alternative order.

The formula *neque te silebo* (21), moreover, is not simply a redundant double negative: merely by mentioning the possibility of leaving any member of the pantheon out of the catalogue, Horace highlights the process of selection in his divine roll call. Finally, in stanza 9 (vv. 33–36), the poet professes aporia as to which name should take top billing among the glorious dead of Rome. Here, Horace's claim to be uncertain as to the ordering of these heroic names in the annals of history is belied by the neat chronological arrangement into which the names fall

---

[103] Various significances could be attached to the fact that the Greek word *heroa* divides v. 1 in a 'feminine' caesura, i.e. falling after the sixth (short) syllable, whereas every other hendecasyllabic line in the poem has a word-break after the fifth (long) syllable (the latter is the norm in Horace; see Becker 2010: 181–82 for statistics). One possibility is to hear the silence of Clio's reply reflected in the failure of the following verses to take up the Grecising cadence of the opening question. Morgan detects here the audible 'strain' that the weighty Pindaric material places on the delicate Sapphic metre, but this involves problematic assumptions about the inner meaning of metre as such (Morgan 2010: 270).

[104] See A. Hardie 2002: 384–85.

in the verse: first Rome's founder Romulus, then her second king Numa, followed by her last king Tarquin, and finally the elder Cato, a figurehead of the Republican era that succeeded the monarchy. An effect is achieved whereby the poet 'discovers' a kind of emergent order to the genealogy of gods, heroes, and great men in the very act of deliberating about this order.

The conceptual link between the ordering of Horace's catalogue-poem and the ordering of the cosmos is most overt in connexion with the subject of Jupiter, who first appears in stanza 4 (vv. 13–16). Here, as noted above, Horace states that Jupiter's status as progenitor of gods and men and prime mover of heaven and earth makes him the logical choice for the first mention in his catalogue, implying thereby that the catalogue must itself mirror the natural order over which Jupiter reigns supreme. It is in the context of this implicit directive that the argument of the following stanza (vv. 17–20) has relevance. Having set up the expectation of tracing a universal genealogy beginning from Jupiter, Horace runs into a conceptual stumbling block, namely, the realisation that Jupiter's absolute sovereignty precludes any of his offspring from superseding him in might (v. 17). This realisation poses a problem for Horace's choice of which being should take up the next place of honour in his catalogue (*proximos* [...] *honores*, 19–20), since, as he explains in v. 18, anyone descended from Jupiter cannot be placed in the same category as him and must be considered lesser than him not only in degree but in kind (*nec uiget quicquam simile aut secundum*, 18). By denying the possibility of anything *simile* or *secundum* to Jupiter ever arising, Horace casts doubt on the legitimacy of two of the logical principles by which his own catalogue may be ordered, i.e. categorisation and hierarchisation.

The next item in the catalogue is introduced only in spite of this proviso: '**Nevertheless**, Pallas bold in battle shall stand next to [Jupiter] in honour (19–21).'[105] The terminology of procreation and growth employed in *generatur* (16) and *uiget* (17) hints as to why Horace should turn at this juncture to Minerva of all gods: not only was she the first of all Jupiter's offspring to be born by Hesiod's account (Hes. *Th.* 894–96), but the manner of her birth — springing out of her father's head fully armoured — set her apart from all her siblings, and even, according to some sources, granted her a special share of her father's powers (Hes.

---

[105] For the reading *occupabit* in preference to the perfect *occupauit* of the MSS, see Brink 1969: 2, who proposes the emendation to accord with the future tenses of *dicam* (vv. 13, 25) and *referam* (39); the emendation is printed by Mayer and Shackleton-Bailey. Hardie dissents, opining that Horace is stating the fact of Minerva's status relative to Jupiter rather than announcing the next entry in his catalogue (A. Hardie 2002: 389–90 n. 71), but the perfect tense strikes me as unsuited to that purpose.

Th. 894–96; Call. *h.Min*.131–36; Pindar fr. 146). Minerva, neither *simile* nor *secundum* to Jupiter and yet closer to him in nature than any of his conventionally conceived offspring, would seem to have offered a loophole permitting Horace to continue his catalogue without qualifying the absolute incomparability of the king of the gods. Horace feeds the problematics of the Olympian family tree through the conventions of poetic composition in order to work through his (professed) authorial aporia. What results from the process is a lyric cosmogony which interrogates the problematic relation between its own organisational schemata and the principles that order the universe.[106]

Before the catalogue even gets started, however, Horace diverts his course by way of Mt. Haemus in Thrace to slip in another famous name: Orpheus (vv. 7–12). On the level of logical thought-progression, the story of Orpheus' music uprooting trees and staying the course of rivers and gales appears in the ode only as a bit of local colour appended to the mention of Mt. Haemus, which itself is only named as one of the possible mountaintops which might conduct Clio's echoed response to Horace's question. This should not dissuade us, however, from following Hardie in seeing Orpheus as in fact central to the poem's argument.

Hardie points out that the phrase *arte materna* (9) highlights Orpheus' parentage by the Muse Calliope as the source of his musical powers, and the epithet *uocalem* (7) locates those powers specifically in the voice, which can by extension be thought of as having been passed down genetically from mother to son.[107] He goes on to argue that Orpheus serves as a mythological template for the kind of Muse-inspiration which Horace professes to enjoy for the purposes of the catalogue that follows.[108] I would stress rather the notable disjunct between Orpheus' relationship to his own Muse mother and Horace's relationship to Clio as each is represented in this poem. As argued above, the implication that Horace will not receive the answer to his opening question directly from Clio but only from the echo of her reply suggests that his relationship to the goddess is of a different order than Orpheus' relationship to Calliope, and that he cannot directly channel her voice as his own.

---

106 Complementary to this reading are the discussions of Feeney and Henderson, who each dive into different aspects of this poem's engagement with the 'problem' of catalogue poetry: Feeney takes the poem as 'a systematic exploration and questioning of categories of divinity (Feeney 1998: 111)', while Henderson reads it as 'an exploration of the problematic of the specificity of praise (Henderson 1997: 97).' Feeney goes so far as to label the ode as 'a poem about the disruption of categories (Feeney 1998: 113 n. 127).'
107 A. Hardie 2002: 381.
108 A. Hardie 2002: 381.

I would argue instead for a different and somewhat subtler parallelism between Horace and Orpheus. The phrase *arte materna* (9) signifies a communion with the Muse that is out of Horace's reach, but it also serves to foreground the theme of filiation which, as argued above, serves as the central schema around which the catalogue is structured. An associative link is thus formed between the poet's access to Muse-inspiration and the capacity to order a cosmogonic song in harmony with the structures of the universe.[109]

The connexion between these two concepts is further cemented by the verbal echo of the word *unde* at the head of vv. 7 and 17. The antecedent in the first case is Mt. Haemus, the geographical starting point from which the forests of Thrace followed Orpheus' music, and in the second case Jupiter, who seems to be represented here as the genetic starting point from which everything in the cosmos proceeded.[110] If we set these two 'starting point – goal' schemata side by side, we can see the path of the trees following Orpheus down from Mt. Haemus as a literal instantiation of the path of song metaphor discussed in ch. 2 which mirrors the figurative path Horace is about to lead us down in embarking upon his catalogue, which will of course trace in verbal form the history of gods, heroes, and men beginning from Jupiter.

This gives new significance to Horace's characterisation of the trees that listen to Orpheus' music as 'following blindly' (*temere insecutae*, 7). It is apt to speak of the trees as 'following' Orpheus not only because he is himself in motion and would otherwise soon move out of earshot, but also because song is tied to temporality and must itself be 'followed' to its conclusion.[111] The trees' pursuit of Orpheus thus concretises in myth the desire for the resolution of rhythmic and harmonic movements that music engenders in its hearers. The adverb that qualifies this act of following, *temere* ('blindly', 'unadvisedly', 'pell-mell'), deepens the allegory of musical listening by characterising this very movement of auditory desire as unwitting and compulsory.[112] *Temere* implies not the absence of self-control and will but rather acting in spite of those faculties, and thus the word invests the trees with an entire psychology, a fact which leads Nisbet and Hubbard to remark that 'Horace is not taking the legend too seriously'.[113]

---

109 On harmony in this poem see A. Hardie 2002: 397–402.
110 See Norden 1913: 173.
111 Cf. Eur. *Iph. Aul.* 1211–15, where Orpheus' ability to cause stones to follow him is used to illustrate the power of verbal persuasion.
112 Cf. Fitzgerald 2010: 27–29.
113 Nisbet and Hubbard 1970: 148.

I would suggest rather that the attribution of human-like consciousness to the trees nuances the myth in accordance with Horace's purposes. In following Orpheus down the mountainside, the trees opt to follow not the edicts of nature (which presumably would have left them standing in place) but rather their ears, which, if we read *auritas* (11) as participial rather than adjectival, would seem to have only just appeared as a result of the same enchantment which lies on Orpheus' music. In essence, the trees are allowing themselves to be literally carried away by the music, without taking thought for the end point either of their journey or of the song which they are hearing. It is this blind pursuit of song, I suggest, that Horace holds up as the mythological model for the poetic journey on which he is about to embark.

Recall that Mt. Haemus is both the starting point of Orpheus' processional song and one of the vibrating bodies from which Horace hopes to catch Clio's echoed reply. In asking the Muse of whom she will sing and then listening for her response, the poet makes himself, like the trees, *auritus* ('all ears', if you will), so as to allow himself to be pulled along the thread of the cosmogonic song that will unravel before him. The haphazard meandering of Orpheus' train mirrors the uncertainty with which Horace orders his catalogue and thus provides an experiential anchor for the reader who hopes to discover through Horace's poem the answer to the question posed to Clio in the proem.

Now to return to the topic of presence with which we began. I suggested above that Horatian odes often begin by hypostasising a mode of presence which turns out to be unattainable or otherwise problematic. This desired mode of presence in 1.20 was represented by Maecenas' ovation, in 1.9 by the attainment of pleasure in the form of warmth and comfort. I propose that this ideal presence is linked in this poem to the presence of the Muse as the source of musical inspiration. Orpheus' maternal relationship to Calliope represents a maximal degree of Muse-presence, which shows forth in the use of his voice. Orpheus' familial closeness to Calliope is directly linked to the irresistible lure of his song, and hence of his ability to draw an audience and lead them down a path of his choosing. This ability to lead listeners unwittingly by the ear is in turn associated by extension with the capacity to compose poetic catalogues, which involves a form of 'leading' or 'guiding' on the part of the speaker and a kind of 'following' on the part of the audience. This capacity is itself tied to an understanding of the genealogical order of the universe (for *secundum* derives from *sequor*: to 'follow' is to 'come next' in a series, but to 'follow' a thread of discourse or song is to *know* what comes next). Horace's prefatory question is a bid to be allowed a share in this understanding. By the same token, the knowledge which the poet asks Clio to impart to him is the knowledge of a suitable subject for song. The song which

Horace asks to hear from Clio is thus a manifestation of her knowledge, and to be in the presence of her singing voice is to be in the presence of her knowledge, as an eye-witness.

As Goldhill notes, '[the] assumption, common throughout early Greek writing, that presence is a prerequisite of accurate knowledge, constitutes the poet as the instrument of the Muses, whose message is heard [...] and passed on through the poem.'[114] The voice of the Muse channelled through the voice of a poet thus enables the marriage of the two functions of naming specified above, the informative and the affirmative. The deferral of the Muse's reply to Horace's question signifies a momentary breakdown in this relationship. Despite having addressed this question to her directly as though in her presence, Horace must rely on the medium of echo to carry her reply to him. Unlike Orpheus, he is not linked to the Muse by a filial bond, and cannot channel her voice as his own. The intervention of echo deprives Horace's catalogue of the ring of truth, so to speak, that would be bestowed by the Muse's full presence, with the result that his catalogic utterances (represented in the poem by the *verba dicendi* listed above) can only advance a tentative claim to authenticity.

All this changes at stanza 12 (vv. 45–48), where a dramatic shift in the modality of the poet's speech takes place. Here, after cataloguing the champions of the Roman republic, Horace launches into a tribute to Marcellus (or to the Marcelli, depending on the reading of the text)[115] and to the 'Julian star' (*Iulium sidus*, 47), which points simultaneously to Caesar's comet, the icon of the deified Julius Caesar, and to the Julian *gens* currently headed by Octavian.[116] This pair of catalogue-entries stands out sharply from the rest for a number of reasons. Firstly, only here does Horace break the pattern of introducing each item in the catalogue with a *verbum dicendi* or another expression representing the act of placing that item in

---

114 Goldhill 1991: 70. See the famous invocation to the Muses in the Catalogue of Ships at Hom. *Il*. 2.484–7: ἔσπετε νῦν μοι Μοῦσαι Ὀλύμπια δώματ' ἔχουσαι· | ὑμεῖς γὰρ θεαί ἐστε πάρεστέ τε ἴστέ τε πάντα, | ἡμεῖς δὲ κλέος οἶον ἀκούομεν οὐδέ τι ἴδμεν· | οἵ τινες ἡγεμόνες Δαναῶν καὶ κοίρανοι ἦσαν ('Tell me now, Muses, who have your dwelling on Olympus — for you are goddesses, and you are present, and you know everything, but we hear only the report and do not know anything — which of the leaders and princes of the Danaans were there'). Cf. A. Hardie 2002: 4 ('The Muses, present always and everywhere, are called on to be present to the poet at the moment of composition; Muses and poet are in turn conduits of real presence to the reader, transforming memory of the past into an experience of being present at the time.')
115 See Mayer 2012: *ad loc*.
116 See Mayer 2012: *ad loc*. Cf. ch. 2 on Caesar's comet in Propertius 4.6.

the catalogue.¹¹⁷ Whereas in previous stanzas Horace first announces the intention to sing of a given subject and then relates the praiseworthy deeds or attributes of that subject, here he begins by simply remarking the greatness of his subject's *fama*. This detail alone intimates that a change has occurred in the poet's relation to the names in his catalogue. The remark that Marcellus' *fama* is on the rise makes a statement both about the praiseworthy deeds of Marcellus and the praise which those deeds have afforded him; it thus incorporates praise and the justification for that praise in a single utterance.

This contrasts markedly with the longer encomium of the Dioscuri at vv. 25–32, where the poet begins by verbally entering the demigods into the catalogue (25), then details the characteristic exploits for which each of them is *nobilem*, 'famous' (26–27), and concludes the period with a vivid description of their manifestation to mortals in the form of the phenomenon known as St. Elmo's fire (27–32). The sequence obeys a logic of assertion followed by proof: the enargeic exposition of the twin heroes' manifest influence on human life in vv. 27–32 offers palpable evidence of the legitimacy of the speech act by which the poet in v. 25 (*dicam*) inserts them into his catalogue. In vv. 45–46, by contrast, the 'proof' of the *fama* which justifies Marcellus' entry into the catalogue is nothing other than that *fama* itself, concretised through simile as an organic being growing with a tree's vertical trajectory.¹¹⁸ With the phrase *occulto [...] aeuo* (45), Horace emphasises the spontaneous and even miraculous nature of the flowering of Marcellus' reputation, which, like a tree, seems when observed to be stationary and yet shows evidence of impressive growth over time.¹¹⁹

The 'unseen lapse of time', as I have translated *occulto aeuo*,¹²⁰ thus points to the effects of the passage of time that are invisible to the naked eye, while also hinting at the darkness of oblivion to which those without renown are consigned. The force of the assertion made in vv. 45–46 is therefore that the magnitude of

---

117 See the list of *verba dicendi* above, p. 49. Though they do not include a *verbum dicendi*, vv. 19–20 do nevertheless foreground the act of ordering the names in the catalogue, provided that one accepts the reading *occupabit* and the interpretation advanced above.
118 The tree-simile recalls the account by Thetis of the rearing of Achilles at Hom. *Il.* 18.56 (ὃ δ' ἀνέδραμεν ἔρνεϊ ἶσος), which, among other things, seems to hint at Marcellus' heroic or quasi-heroic status.
119 Cf. *Epist.* 1.1.80, where similar language is applied to a financial context: *multis occulto crescit res faenore* ('many are those whose profit increases by the discreet accumulation of interest'). Mayer 1994 *ad loc.* translates *occulto* as 'imperceptible', which would also be apt for the use of the word in our passage.
120 Inspired by Rudd's translation 'silent lapse of time'.

Marcellus' fame remains in plain view despite the obscuring effects of time (contrast the vision of Marcellus in the underworld at Verg. *Aen.* 6.865–66: *qui strepitus circa comitum! quantum instar in ipso!* | *sed nox atra caput tristi circumuolat umbra*).[121] Marcellus' fame, that is, speaks for itself, and here the close etymological association of *fama* with speech is in full force.[122] For Horace to resume his earlier pattern, announcing, for instance, 'I will sing of the fame of Marcellus, which burgeons treelike, etc.', would be redundant, since the action of the voice on which that fame depends is already brought to bear by the word *fama* itself.[123] Horace does not need to *assert* that Marcellus would make a suitable entry for his catalogue because his *fama* is sensible without the mediation of Horace's voice.[124] The placement of the verb *crescit* in stanza-initial position foregrounds the palpable action of the *fama*-tree over the actual act of naming, which does not come until the following verse; the effect is that Marcellus' *fama* is made to outgrow the logic of the catalogue.

The exceptional status of Marcellus within Horace's catalogue, however, only complements the more radical exceptionality of Octavian and the Julian *gens*, which receives emphasis in the following lines of stanza 12 (46–48) and in the three stanzas that make up the poem's coda (53–60). Oliensis observes that the *princeps* often proves 'too strong a centre of gravity' for Horace, adding, 'Once introduced into a poem, he will tend to warp it into a shape that represents his own supreme authority';[125] and this is precisely what happens here. The unmatched brilliance of Caesar's comet attests self-evidently to the ascendancy of the Julian *gens* over all others, and here the metaphor of light gets its conceptual footing both from the preceding description of St. Elmo's fire (27–32), explicitly portrayed as originating from a star (*stella*, 28), and from the image of the shadow cast by the passage of time in *occulto* [...] *aeuo* (45).

The star's light does not only connote visibility and hence undying fame; it is posited specifically as the measure by which Octavian's family tree sets itself apart from its peers. Vv. 46–48 ('the Julian star shines amid them all like the moon amid the lesser lights') make the night sky itself into a diagram of prestigious names which allows the viewer to chart the relative *fama* of its subjects at a

---

[121] 'What a commotion from the entourage surrounding him! What a countenance in the man himself! But a dread darkness floats about his head, wreathing him with a shadow of grief.'
[122] On the etymological ties of *fama* see Bettini 2008: 352–57.
[123] See the invaluable discussion of the 'duplicities of *fama*', among them the troubled relationship between *fama* and *facta*, in Hardie 2012: 1–47.
[124] Relevant here is Quintilian's definition of *enargeia* as the term for discourse 'which seems not so much to say as to show (*quae non tam dicere uidetur quam ostendere*, *Inst.* 6.2.32).'
[125] Oliensis 1998: 127.

glance.[126] This visual schema of gazing at bright stars in the dark sky is itself prefigured by the neighbouring image of Marcellus' *fama* emerging out of the darkness of the passing years. The two conceits are bound together by the incantatory symmetry of the stanza, which traces the tripartite syntactic pattern of {initial verb — *uelut* | initial verb — *inter* | *uelut* — *inter*}:

> **crescit** occulto **uelut** arbor aeuo
> fama Marcelli; **micat inter** omnis
> Iulium sidus **uelut inter** ignis
>   luna minores.

The exceptionality of Marcellus' *fama* and the Julian *gens* is thus mirrored by the stylistic exceptionality of this stanza in Horace's poem. The cumulative syntactic patterning illustrated above has the effect of wrapping up the stanza into a self-contained unit, just as the omission of *uerba dicendi* exempts this passage from the linear progression of the catalogue. Caesar (along with those linked to him by family ties) is so far beyond comparison to his peers that his very presence demands that the universal order be reshuffled to accommodate it. This stanza, I suggest, enacts that cosmic reorientation within the context of Horace's catalogue.

From this point of view, we can reconceptualise the schema of light-in-darkness identified in stanza 12 as a figure of Horace's activity as catalogue-poet. As argued above, the Orpheus passage (7–12) set up an initial depiction of Horace's cosmogonic song as proceeding 'blindly' (*temere*, 7), i.e. without prior knowledge of the path that lies ahead. We can now refine this suggestion by positing that the image of the 'unseen lapse of time' in v. 45 refers back to the blind path of the uprooted trees following Orpheus' voice down Mt. Haemus.

Horace's opening question to Clio sets for his song the task of singling out one extraordinary individual out of a homogeneous mass. The darkness of the passing years which threatens to obscure Marcellus' *fama* and the vast field of constellations that surrounds the Julian star, competing for the attention of viewers, both stand for the challenges that beset this task of commemoration. Muse-inspired song, the proem suggests, can chart a cosmogonic course through the immense void of the past, but Horace's method of navigation has more in common with the oblivious wandering of the oak-trees than with the supernatural song of Orpheus. The verbal formulas that introduce each of the catalogue-entries up until stanza 12 frame each one of these entries as an attempt to answer the

---

126 Cf. ch. 2 on the 'eusynoptic' impulse in Propertius 4.6, which also makes use of Caesar's comet in this respect.

prefatory *quem uirum*, etc. by substituting Horace's own poetic voice for the absent response of Clio; but because of the deliberative, uncertain way in which they are expressed, they fall short of attesting to the inspiring presence of the Muse.

It is only in stanza 12, when Horace dispenses with the formulae of performative speech altogether, that the question with which the poem opened truly finds an answer. The treelike growth of Marcellus' *fama* and the unmatched radiance of Caesar's comet are simply self-evident in the manner of an epiphany, and do not need the testimony either of Horace or of Clio to vouch for them; their exceptionality disrupts the very logic of catalogic utterances, in quite the same way that Jupiter's status as the cosmic starting-point of all that is problematises the very notion of placing him in a list among other beings. The force exerted by the joint exceptionality of Jupiter and Caesar is such that, after stanza 12, their pairing prompts the articulation of a new universal order that directly contravenes the previous order set out in the catalogue, wherein Caesar, despite the express objection of v. 18 (*nec uiget quicquam simile aut secundum*), is to rule as Jupiter's second (*tu secundo | Caesare regnes*, 51–52).[127]

Horace hails this new world order, in which the fate of Caesar is the special preserve of Jupiter (50–51), by shifting the modality of his utterances from deliberative assertion to invocation and prayer, or from *Er-Stil* to *Du-Stil* (*tu* [...] *regnes*, 51–52; *te* [...] *reget*, 57; *tu* [...] *quaties*, 58; *tu* [...] *mittes*, 59).[128] To explain this shift in expression, it is not enough to say that Horace has found in the dyad Jupiter-Caesar the answer to the question originally put to Clio; he has also hit upon a solution to the dilemma of presence posed in the asking of that question. Relevant here is the invocation of Octavian as the earthly avatar of Mercury at *c.* 1.2.41–52,[129] as well as the opening stanza of *c.* 3.5, where Horace draws an explicit contrast between Jupiter and Octavian (now Augustus) with respect to their relative presence in human affairs:

---

[127] Cf. Johnson 2004: 125–26, with Feeney 1998: 113: 'Horace begins his poem by asking "Which man, hero, or god to celebrate?", and gradually reveals that those categories are now such that one name can be the answer in each case.' Morgan objects to Feeney that Horace stops short of explicitly making Caesar a god in this poem (Morgan 2010: 260–74), but he overstates his case when he characterises the poem's withholding of godhood as an 'intense surprise' (2010: 266), as if divinisation were an obvious and expected gesture (which it never is, even when Horace does extend it).

[128] Cf. Fraenkel 1957: 296: 'Surprisingly the poem returns to Jupiter, but this time he is approached, not as in the second triad with praise only, but with prayer.'

[129] *c.* 1.2.25–52 also mirrors the pattern we have observed in *c.* 1.12 of a deliberative catalogue culminating with the invocation of Caesar.

> caelo tonantem credidimus Iouem
> regnare: praesens diuus habebitur
>   Augustus adiectis Britannis
>   imperio grauibusque Persis (3.5.1–4)

Because Jove thunders in heaven, we believe in his sovereignty; Augustus will be regarded as a god incarnate when the Britons and the deadly Persians have been subsumed into our empire.

That is, Augustus' sovereignty over Roman territory parallels Jupiter's sway over heaven and earth, except for the fact that the evidence for Augustus' supremacy does not need to be sought in the distant rumble of thunder; his authority is *praesens*, present and palpable.[130] *c.* 1.12, I suggest, shows how this *praesentia* of Caesar translates into the kind of presence embodied by the inspiring voice of the Muse. More specifically, I argue, the epiphany of the Julian star in stanza 12 effects a paradigm shift in the problem of the performative efficacy of Horace's poetic voice which is foregrounded in the initial address to Clio.

Compare for instance stanza 4 (vv. 13–16), the opening stanza of the catalogue, with stanza 13 (vv. 49–52), which immediately follows the description of the star. Each stanza delineates Jupiter's role as the father of all life, but with an important difference. In stanza 4, as we have already seen, Jupiter's paternal status is posed as an existential problem for Horace's catalogic performance: by electing to 'utter the praises of the Father' (13–14) before all else, he creates the problem of who could possibly succeed the king of the gods. In stanza 13, by contrast, Jupiter's role as Father is broached in direct address when Horace invokes him as 'Father and guardian of the human race (*gentis humanae pater atque custos*, 49)'. Addressing the god directly as 'father' is not the same as merely stating that he is a father, even if he is the father of all human beings; the address embraces the epithet as the sign of a relationship between the speaker and the addressee.[131] The paternal relationship embodied in the poet's address to the god as Father harks back to the maternal relationship between Orpheus and Calliope

---

130 Cf. *c.* 4.14.43 *o tutela praesens*; *Epist*. 2.1.15 *praesenti tibi maturos largimur honores*. Augustus is given the epithet *praesens* also at Verg. *E*. 1.41 and Ov. *Trist*. 2.53–54 and *Ex P*. 1.2.105.
131 Cf. the prayer to Mercury/Octavian in *c.* 1.2.50 (*hic ames dici pater atque princeps*, 'Here may you adore to be called "Father" and "First Citizen"'): the divinised leader is imbued with a (quasi-)erotic desire to be invoked as 'Father and First Citizen' which itself binds him to the mortal realm (*hic*) and hence draws him into communion with the mortals who invoke him in this way.

profiled in v. 9, which, as argued above, acts as a foil for the more estranged relationship between Horace and Clio. In a sense, then, the invocation to Jupiter replaces or revises the unrequited invocation to Clio in the proem.[132]

The genealogical order of the universe, which is normally obscured by the 'unseen lapse of time', becomes clear as day once Caesar's place within that order is understood, and by invoking Jupiter as father of the human race and warden of Caesar's fate, Horace attests both to his possession of this understanding and to his own place within this order. As a result, the government of the Roman world in the present day by the twin forces of Caesar and Jupiter — the topic of the poem's final three stanzas (vv. 49–60) — can now be seen to have arisen in a process of organic development which can be traced to the origin of the cosmos.

The emblem of that organic development, finally, is the tree which symbolises the *fama* of Marcellus in v. 45. The *fama*-tree leaps forth epiphanically out of time's inexorable march to manifest to mortal eyes the cosmic order presided over by Jupiter, which is expressed in vv. 15–16 in terms of the subjection of natural forces to the law of seasonal change. As opposed to Orpheus' oak-trees, which follow the path of his song oblivious to their final destination, the tree of Marcellus follows a path whose orderly progression cannot be disrupted even by the deleterious effects of time. Horace's poem embraces this new path for his own song by turning away from the modality of utterance proper to cosmogonic catalogues and toward the mode of invocation and epiphany. To this extent, Horace obtains the echoed reply of Clio only when he ceases to regard her voice as a metaphysical authorising presence which must be petitioned and instead invokes it as a material presence, conjuring it thereby into the realm of the senses.

---

[132] The quaking of Olympus by Jupiter's chariot in v. 58 might be said to answer the echo from the mountaintops in vv. 3–6 in a kind of ring-composition.

4 Occasioning the Choral in Horace, *Odes* IV

4.1 Introduction

In the discussion of Horace *Odes* 1.9, 1.12, and 1.20 in the previous chapter, I established the premiss that the *Odes* use occasion as a conceptual tool for negotiating an array of poetic and philosophical problems which converge on the topic of presence. I focussed in particular on how these poems work out a dialectic between two competing conceptions of presence — metaphysical presence and material presence — suggesting that each of these poems admits of a reading whereby the metaphysical yields to the material. I tried to show, moreover, how this theoretical framework in turn permits us to develop an appreciation for the *Odes* as an experience addressed to the senses, capable of mobilising and engaging what was referred to in chapter 2, following Marco Caracciolo, as the reader's virtual body.

In this chapter I would like to refocus this discussion of the *Odes* with a look at the fourth book, paying particular attention to 4.1, 4.2, 4.5, 4.6, and 4.15. Horatian scholarship has taken this final collection of lyric poetry as either the fulfilment of lofty expectations set up in *Odes* 1–3[1] or as a kind of *reductio ad absurdum* — whether self-ironic or self-deluded — of the pretensions of the Roman *uates*.[2] Each of these positions originates from an attempt to narrativise the book's sudden swing from the 'private' to the 'public', which entails both a vested interest in the affairs of Augustus and those closest to him and the adoption of a stance as spokeperson for the whole Roman people. This shift of focus is attended by two significant modulations in Horace's lyric voice: the direct address of Augustus, which occurs first in 4.5 (thereafter in 4.14, 4.15, and *Epist.* 2.1), and the embrace of a collective, choral voice, which was latent in *Odes* 1–3 but was newly authenticated by the choral performance of Horace's *Carmen Saeculare* in 17 BCE.[3]

Scholarly narratives tend to frame these new developments in Horatian lyric in terms of the opposition between individual and state: the presence of Augustus leads critics to enquire about Horace's artistic independence from imperial pressure, while the sustained evocation of choral song and the ascendancy of the first

---

[1] Fraenkel 1957, Putnam 1986, Johnson 2004.
[2] Lyne 1995; Thomas 2011; Lowrie 2010b; La Penna 1963: 145–46.
[3] Feeney 1998: 102; Lowrie 2010b: 220–24; Barchiesi 2000: 178; Foster 2015: 628–29; Nagy 1994: 425 n. 45.

person plural[4] raise questions about the relation of Horace's individual voice to this new collective cry. I would like to pose a different question, however. Rather than ask what political stance is implied by Horace's embrace of the public and the communal, I will enquire into the idea of the choral voice as evoked and imagined by Horatian lyric. I will argue that, in *Odes* 4 in general and in particular in the 'choral moments' of *cc*. 4.1, 4.2, 4.5, 4.6, and 4.15, Horace develops a conception of the choral collective as an imagined locus of presence and as a privileged mode for the realisation of lyric occasion.

In order to trace the contours of this vision of choral collectivity, it is best to begin at the end, with the final period of the final ode of the collection (4.15), where Horace conjures an almost sentimental image of the Roman citizen body united in song (vv. 25–32). I print the ode in full:

>   Phoebus uolentem proelia me loqui
>   uictas et urbes increpuit lyra,
>   ne parua Tyrrhenum per aequor
>   uela darem. tua, Caesar, aetas
>   fruges et agris rettulit uberes   5
>   et signa nostro restituit Ioui
>   derepta Parthorum superbis
>   postibus et uacuum duellis
>   Ianum Quirini clausit et ordinem
>   rectum euaganti frena licentiae   10
>   iniecit emouitque culpas
>   et ueteres reuocauit artes
>   per quas Latinum nomen et Italae
>   creuere uires famaque et imperi
>   porrecta maiestas ad ortus   15
>   solis ab Hesperio cubili.
>   custode rerum Caesare non furor
>   ciuilis aut uis exiget otium,
>   non ira, quae procudit enses
>   et miseras inimicat urbes.   20
>   non qui profundum Danuuium bibunt
>   edicta rumpent Iulia, non Getae,

---

4 See esp. 1.25–28; 2.33–52; 5.37–40; 6.31–44; 15.25–32. Imagery of choruses or chorus-like congregations: 1.11; 3.14–15; 6.15; 7.6; 9.8; 14.21–22. The description of shepherds heralding spring with bucolic song in 4.12.9–12 is a generalisation, but the plural *dicunt* (9) groups the individual singers together into a notional chorus. The slave-boys and girls rushing to prepare the festivities for Maecenas in 4.11.9–10 can be thought of as analogous to the mixed-gender choruses of 4.1, 4.6, and the *CS*. Nagy points without further comment to the 'choral implications' of 10.6–8, where Ligurinus sees himself doubled in the mirror (Nagy 1994: 425 n. 45).

>   non Seres infidique Persae,
>   non Tanain prope flumen orti.
>   nosque et profestis lucibus et sacris   25
>   inter iocosi munera Liberi
>   cum prole matronisque nostris,
>   rite deos prius apprecati,
>   uirtute functos more patrum duces
>   Lydis remixto carmine tibiis   30
>   Troiamque et Anchisen et almae
>   progeniem Veneris canemus (4.15.25–32)

When I tried to speak of battles and conquered cities, Phoebus rang out a protest on the lyre against my setting sail in a small boat across the Tyrrhenian sea.[5] Your age, Caesar, has brought fertile crops back to our fields, restored to our native Jupiter the standards rescued from the proud door of the Parthians, sealed Janus Quirinus free from war, reined in the licentiousness that strayed out of line, expelled crime, and recalled the old arts by which the name of Latium and the strength of Italy blossomed, and by which the fame and greatness of our empire was extended to the land of the sun's rising from its western bed.

While Caesar watches over our common weal, neither civil strife nor violence will drive peace away, nor wrath which hammers swords and makes enemies of ill-fated cities. The Julian edicts shall not be broken by those who drink from the deep Danube, not the Getae, not the Seres or the faithless Persians, not those born beside the river Tanais. As for us, on both working days and holy days, surrounded by the gifts of merry Liber and in the company of our children and our wives, after first paying due veneration to the gods, we will sing, mingling our hymn with Lydian pipes, of leaders who lived virtuously in the tradition of our fathers, of Troy and Anchises and the progeny of bountiful Venus.

Nestled between the first-person plural pronoun (*nos*, 25) and its corresponding verb, 'we will sing' (*canemus*, 32) are two stanzas shot through with images of social integration and communal solidarity. Fraenkel sees the 'we' of this passage as an imaginary society into which Horace can graduate now that he has come to

---

[5] Thomas 2011: 261 follows Ps.-Acro and Porphyry in taking *lyra* (2) with *loqui* (1) rather than *increpuit* (2), designating Horace's lyre rather than Apollo's, while Fedeli and Ciccarelli 2008: 609 argue that 'Apollo accompagni le sue parole di biasimo col suono della lira, che è il suo strumento'. The distinction becomes less important if we consider that the lyre is Apollo's instrument by definition, and the lyric poet 'borrows' its music to accompany his words, which it might do either favourably or unfavourably in accordance with the god's attitude (Prop. 4.1[B].73–74; Tib. 2.5.1–4; Ov. *A.A.* 2.493–94, *Rem.* 705–06; cf., with other gods, Hor. *c.* 1.29–34 and Ov. *F.* 6.812). As well as fitting better with the word order, taking *increpuit* with *lyra* brings out the literal, sonic sense of the verb alongside the figurative sense of 'protest': Apollo makes the lyre accompanying Horace sound a jarring note which derails his warlike song.

fully embrace Augustus.⁶ Oliensis looks instead to the terminal silence that follows the future-tense *canemus*, arguing that Horace's singular 'I' disappears amid the crowd in a strategic withdrawal from a political scene now completely dominated by Augustus;⁷ Lowrie goes further, finding in this passage the eclipse not only of the poet's *ego* but of the aesthetic realm itself in the face of an authoritarian regime.⁸

At the heart of these two opposing views is a fundamental ambivalence about the value of collectivity, which can represent to the individual both the possibility of a transcendent unity and the threat of dissolution and disintegration. The question of whether the community which Horace's *canemus* brings into being entails a loss of self or an integration into a greater whole depends largely on the value we place on the future society that we imagine to lie beyond that final word.⁹ But we can also take the lyric silence that follows this call to song as an invitation to suspend our verdict momentarily and linger in the space opened by the lacuna of 'we will sing…'. In this liminal space, the passage into the collectivity remains not-yet-accomplished, and the collectivity itself still in the process of emerging.¹⁰ Not only is the future reality posed by the tense of *canemus* not yet in effect, but the parameters of inclusion for the 'we' designated by the first-person plural of *canemus* are themselves not yet determined — this is a hortatory rather

---

6 Fraenkel 1957: 448–40, 452–43.
7 Oliensis 1998: 151–53; cf. Breed 2004: 250–51: 'the lyric *me* of line 1 becomes the communal *nos* of the conclusion. As the chorus [...] sings the praises of Augustus, the lyric *ego* of Horace slips quietly from the scene.' He goes on to argue that Horace here symbolically bows to the *Aeneid* as a better vehicle for the praise of Augustus (Breed 2004: 249–52). Thomas similarly interprets the silence following *canemus* as 'the ultimate *recusatio* (Thomas 2011: 270).'
8 Lowrie 1997: 351.
9 Griffin is oversimplifying the issue when he attributes Oliensis' misgivings to a 'Romantic' dichotomy of public and private (Griffin 2002: 331–32); the difference between *canam* and *canemus* is still meaningful. Putnam sidesteps the dilemma by downplaying Horace's choral fade-out as a feint: 'Horace's speaker apparent[ly] yields his individuality to a communal celebration of the Augustan age, but in reality his inventiveness in the telling is what will preserve his subject matter (Putnam 1986: 274).' Murray pronounces the placement of the future *canemus* at the end of the book 'impossible' and would transpose *c*. 4.15 to the beginning (Murray 1985: 41).
10 Along similar lines, Johnson makes the 'we' of this passage into a symbol for his 'sympotic' (i.e. dialogic) conception of praise in *Odes* 4: 'Here is the model for Horatian praise: [...] a praise that lacks a definitive resolution and therefore requires an interpretive community to actively engage the song and negotiate its meaning through their voices (Johnson 2004: 201).' Cf. Johnson 2011: 183. I am suggesting here that it is not only the 'meaning' of the song as an act of praise but its very phenomenality as a vocal production that is indeterminate and open to negotiation. Johnson's argument that Horace is not 'retreating into community' but rather 'inviting to community' (Johnson 2004: 211) is more in concert with what I am proposing here.

than an indicative 'we'.¹¹ The inclusion/exclusion of Horace's singular 'I' and (by extension) the inclusion/exclusion of the reader's singular 'I' remain radically undecided, in suspense. I propose that we read *Odes* 4 as dwelling, throughout, in this liminal space of transition into the communal 'we' of choral song.¹²

4.2 Fantasising the choral

A crucial step here is bringing out the element of fantasy in this and other evocations of the choral in Horatian lyric. The fantastic finds its way into the above-cited passage in the transition between the two stanzas, turning from the collective subject of the song ('us' and our wives and children, at a banquet) to its collective object (great Romans of the past and their Trojan ancestors). At the pivot point between stanzas, wedged between two lines detailing the procedure of the song to be performed (28, 30), we find the duplicitous phrase *more patrum* ('in the tradition of our fathers', 29), which can either be taken with the adjacent *functos* or projected forward onto *canemus*.¹³ The ambiguity of the language reflects an ambiguity in the song: in singing the praises of 'our' virtuous ancestors, 'we' participate in the same ancestral tradition that 'our' song affirms. This ambiguity is functional, promoting a wishful fiction of continuity between the 'we' who sing and the *mos patrum* which informs the song. The *mos patrum* is the axis on which past and present, the subject and the object of communal praise, converge in performance, forming an imaginary projection of what Benedict Anderson would call the 'imagined community' of the Roman citizen body under the Principate.¹⁴

---

11 See Barber 2014 on the centrality of the future tense in the *Odes*. He remarks on p. 355: 'A thrilling note of spontaneity and incompletion sounds when the speaker of an ode announces and anticipates a future song.' In the same vein, Fedeli suggests that '[f]orse il *canemus* con cui il libro si conclude sottintende un progetto, che però non verrà mai realizzato' (Fedeli and Ciccarelli 2008: 55); I would propose that we read this lack of realisation back into *canemus* itself. Barchiesi has yet another take: he argues that the poem 'ends by looking forward, self-reflexively, to reperformance (Barchiesi 2009: 428)'.
12 See Porter 1975: 223–24 on the 'motif of music and dancing' in *Odes* 4.
13 Putnam 1986: 271–72 and n. 13; Griffin 2002: 329–30; Thomas 2011: *ad loc*. Fedeli and Ciccarelli 2008: 627–28 among others argue that word order dictates that *more patrum* must be taken only with *functos* [...] *duces*, but this does not rule out the possibility of functional ambiguity.
14 Anderson 2006. Quintilian gestures toward the same convergence of noble song and noble singer when he recommends that students learn 'the music [...] with which the praises of brave men were sung, and with which the brave themselves sang (*musice* [...] *qua laudes fortium canebantur, quaque ipsi fortes canebant, Inst.* 1.10.31).'

If we follow the lead of Steven Connor's brief but illuminating essay 'Choralities', we can attribute the imaginative power that this imaginary song exerts to the choral voice itself. Connor argues that the assembly of voices into a choral aggregate always conjures up 'the fantasy of a collective voice-body that is not to be identified with any of the individuals who compose it.'[15] In the case of the civic-sympotic hymn of c. 4.15.25–32, the 'collective voice-body' which is made the subject of the song expands to exceed the bounds not only of the individual voice, but of the individual occasion of singing, so that an entire calendar of holidays and workdays is synthesised into a phantasmal vocal unity.[16]

Lowrie would attribute this supernatural expansiveness to Horace's idealisation of choral lyric as the bearer of a lost plenitude for which his own lyric voice strives in vain.[17] She sees in this passage a Horatian fantasy about an Augustan restoration of an archaic song-culture such as that described in Cic. *Tusc.* 4.3 and *Brut.* 75,[18] arguing that here Horace 'forwards the image of a communal, foundational song that is greater than his own individual poetry can ever be.'[19] But if, as Connor argues, the choral voice is always itself a fantasy — 'the sonorous actualising of the otherwise abstract or merely attributive idea of a collectivity'[20] — then to fantasise the choral, as Horace does in this poem, is already to participate in chorality. The 'collective voice-body' imaged forth by Horace's *canemus* does not preexist the act of singing, but instead comes into being by exerting on bodies a gravitational pull that wills their identification and draws them into itself.[21] In uttering *canemus*, Horace emits a voice which is poised at the threshold of assimilation into this collective 'we', an in-between space in which the fantasy of the

---

15 Connor 2015: 3.
16 Differently, Lowrie 2009a: 59.
17 '[Horace's] theoretical interest in choral lyric and drama stems from a desire to reconstitute through displacement a social function for his own poetry he perceives as lost (Lowrie 2009a: 235).'
18 Lowrie 2009a: 48–60, esp. 58–59; cf. Johnson 2004: 203. See Zorzetti 1991 on the question of an archaic Roman song-culture in view of these passages. I cannot agree with Lowrie in seeing in Cicero's *utinam* (*Brut.* 75) a nostalgic desire for song-culture *per se*; he laments the loss of the specific convivial songs which Cato describes, not of a wider tradition of *carmina convivalia* to which they belong.
19 Lowrie 2010b: 227.
20 Connor 2015: 3.
21 'Just as choric utterance is a giving of a body to the event of speech, so it aims to draw its constituent speakers into identity with this voice-body; in giving a body to utterance, it draws utterance into the body (Connor 2015: 3).'

choral, of 'the voice as pure amplitude', remains intact because the 'hyper-body' it sets out to create is still embryonic, still an emergent virtuality.[22]

Seeing choral utterances as enactments of a fantasy of communal voicing allows us to emphasise points of continuity between 'real' choral performances, such as that of the *Carmen Saeculare*, and 'fictional' chorality such as we find throughout *Odes* 4. There is a tendency in the scholarship to treat the *Carmen Saeculare* as exceptional and without parallel in Horace's work, and indeed in Augustan poetry generally, based principally on the fact that we have documentary evidence of its performance. Representative of this is an influential paper by Rossi which looks to the prosody of the *CS* for evidence of a formal distinction between performance poetry and book-poetry.[23] Rossi argues that the metrical peculiarities of the *CS*, which he claims are tailored to better suit choral performance, negatively confirm that the musical thematics of the *Odes* belong instead to 'the mimesis of a musical event.'[24] His central example is *c.* 4.6, which he labels the 'literary counterpart' of the *CS*, i.e. a poem about the *CS* and its performance which is not itself intended for performance.[25] In vv. 31–44 of this poem, Horace delivers what look like stage-directions for the *CS* or a similar performance, with vivid detail evoking the action of the chorus:

>uirginum primae puerique claris
>>patribus orti,
>
>Deliae tutela deae, fugacis
>lyncas et ceruos cohibentis arcu,
>Lesbium seruate pedem meique   35
>>pollicis ictum,
>
>rite Latonae puerum canentes,
>rite crescentem face Noctilucam,
>prosperam frugum celeremque pronos
>>uoluere mensis.   40
>
>nupta iam dices 'ego dis amicum
>saeculo festas referente luces
>reddidi carmen docilis modorum
>>uatis Horati.'

---

[22] '[If] my voice is that which goes beyond me, then the choral voice is the voice that goes beyond itself. It is the voice as pure amplitude, having the power both to adhere to other voices and to swell excitably like a kind of inflammation. It is not just the body's power of emanation, it is emanation's power to grow into a kind of hyper-body (Connor 2015: 8).'
[23] Rossi 2009.
[24] Rossi 2009: 363.
[25] Rossi 2009: 373.

You, first among maidens, and you boys born of noble fathers, charges of the Delian goddess who stays with her bow the flight of lynxes and stags, observe the Lesbian foot and the striking of my thumb, duly hymning Latona's child, duly hymning the Night-gloamer who waxes in light, who blesses crops and speeds the careening cycle of the months. Now when you are married you will say, 'When the new age brought the feast-days back around, I discharged a song beloved of the gods, obedient to the measures of Horace the bard.'

Rossi classes the directions for singing and dancing in this ode as instances of 'musical mimesis', arguing that the presence of such elements itself proves that this poem was never intended to actually be sung.[26] He contrasts the final stanza of the *CS*, where the chorus comments self-reflexively on its performance as follows:

> haec Iouem sentire deosque cunctos
> spem bonam certamque domum reporto
> doctus et Phoebi chorus et Dianae
>   dicere laudes. (*CS* 73–76)

> I bring back home a good and certain hope that Jupiter and all the gods hear these words, I, the chorus instructed to sing the praises of both Phoebus and Diana.

For Rossi, the critical distinction between the evocations of choral performance in *c.* 4.6 and the *CS*, is that, in the latter, 'the performance is *acted* and not imitated, in the form of a final invocation'.[27] This implies that, when Horace commands his chorus to sing in *c.* 4.6.37, he is performing a 'mimetic' rendition of what the chorus enacts directly in the *CS*. It is worth asking, however, what exactly is being enacted in the *CS*. At no point does the chorus of the *CS* ever declare performatively 'I sing', or even 'I will sing', as we might reasonably expect from a hymn. Instead, the emphasis is laid on the prayer which is conveyed to the gods by means of the song (but also by means of the sacrifices it accompanies):

> Phoebe siluarumque potens Diana,
> lucidum caeli decus, o colendi
> semper et culti, date quae precamur
>   tempore sacro,
> quo Sibyllini monuere uersus,   5
> uirgines lectas puerosque castos
> dis, quibus septem placuere colles,
>   dicere carmen (1–8)

---

26 Rossi 2009: 373.
27 Rossi 2009: 373.

> O Phoebus and wood-mistress Diana, shining glory of heaven, whose worship shall always continue and always has, grant what we pray for in this sacred time, when the Sibyl's verses counselled that a select group of virgins and chaste boys should sing a hymn for the gods who favoured the seven hills.

There are two layers of divine propitiation at work here: the prayer sung by the chorus is intended to prevail upon Phoebus and Diana, while the assembly of the chorus on this occasion is intended to fulfil the prophecy laid out in the Sibylline Books. The second stanza contributes nothing to the prayer strictly speaking; it simply presents the body of the chorus, justifying its existence and lending legitimacy to its requests. The final stanza (quoted above) reflects this: the chorus calls upon itself to vouch for the efficacy of the prayer it has just performed. In the last stanza as in the second the chorus utters an outwardly redundant formula that does no more than state its identity: virtually, 'I am the chorus chosen to sing this hymn'. Implicit in these formulae is the idea that the function of the chorus, what it is here to *do*, is no more than to be present, to be here on this occasion singing and dancing in chorus.

The purpose of the chorus' self-presencing, as expressed in the final stanza, is not just to convey the content of the prayer but to convey 'back home' the *hope* that the gods have heard and accepted the prayer (*spem bonam certamque domum reporto*, 74). 'Home', as Thomas notes, means the individual homes of each of the twenty-seven boys and twenty-seven girls from families with two living parents decreed by the Sibylline verses.[28] The idea that hope is something that the choreuts will 'carry back home' is motivated by the fact that they were separated from their families in being chosen to participate in the chorus and will return to them when their duty is done.

This very act of returning to rejoin a healthy and prosperous family (cf. the Sibyl's word ἀμφιθαλής in v. 278, 'of two living parents' or lit. 'blooming on both sides') thus confirms that the hope which the prayer conveys has already been answered in part: the chorus asks the gods to bless child-rearing in vv. 13–20 and 47 and the education of young people in v. 45. The boys and girls in the chorus do not only convey this hope; they themselves stand for it, and by appearing in the choral assembly they lend corporeal form to this hope for the course of the ceremony. From this perspective, the rhetoric of the chorus is shown to be entirely self-referential: the chorus assembles to make manifest the idea of choral assembly. The chorus 'enacts' nothing outside of itself, nothing beyond the fantasy of a collective voice-body.

---

28 Thomas 2011: *ad loc.*; vv. 151–52 in Thomas' printing (Thomas 2011: 277–78).

The 'fictional' chorality of *c.* 4.6 does the same thing in a different way. When Horace in *c.* 4.6.35–36 commands the chosen boys and girls to 'observe the Lesbian foot and the striking of my thumb' (*Lesbium seruate pedem meique | pollicis ictum*), he is in one sense, as Rossi assumes, simply commanding them 'perform the *Carmen Saeculare* in accordance with the metre'; but if we bring out the shades of meaning in *seruate,* we can draw a conceptual link between the rhythmic correctness of the chorus' performance and the propitiatory function of their hymn. Just as he previously asked Apollo to 'defend the glory of the Daunian (i.e. his own) Muse' (*Dauniae defende decus Camenae*, 27), he now asks his chorus to use their performance to 'preserve' the hymn entrusted to them, and, by extension, to help cultivate the hope for Rome's future which the hymn represents.

In the final stanza (41–44), it is revealed that this act of preservation must extend beyond the occasion of the *Carmen Saeculare* itself: Horace envisions a child of the chorus now grown to adulthood and married looking back on the hymn she once sang and commemorating her experience. As part of her account, she notes that the hymn was *dis amicum* (41), 'beloved of the gods' or 'friendly to the gods.' By affirming the hymn's success in this way, she effectively reperforms the closing act of the chorus in the *CS*, whereby the members bring back to their families the hope that their collective prayer has reached the ears of the gods. Simply by growing up and accomplishing marriage, the former choreut proves that this hope is still alive, and in this way she embodies the dream of the chorus in her own person. The fantasy of the collective voice-body of the chorus is thus not the fantasy of the 'liveness' that may be achieved in a singular event of performance, but rather the fantasy of a self-prolonging and self-extending presence which overflows the individual and surpasses the mortal moment.

4.3 Choral presence and the future tense

Reading Horace's evocations of choral song in this way as not only fantasies of collective song but as actual participations in the lived fantasy of chorality loops us back to the master-trope of presence. Connor's proposition of a choral 'hyperbody' resonates with ancient accounts of choral song as effecting a kind of 'hyperpresence', as instanced by the space of inclusion created by the chorus in Callimachus' *Hymn to Apollo.* Here, as discussed at length in chapter 1, the epiphanic presence of Apollo is predicated upon and inseparable from the god's participation in the collective body of the chorus. Another example which I have already had occasion to cite is the lyric fragment Call. fr. 227.1 Pf., where the god epiphanically appears already 'in' the chorus at the striking of the lyre.[29] In these two Callimachean poems, the embodiment of collective identity that is the chorus acts both as a locus of presence and as the catalyst for the production of a presence beyond itself. Horace offers his own take on the chorus' powers of presence as part of his 'apology for poetry' in the *Epistle to Augustus*:

> castis cum pueris ignara puella mariti
> disceret unde preces, uatem ni Musa dedisset?
> poscit opem chorus et praesentia numina sentit,
> caelestis implorat aquas docta prece blandus,   135
> auertit morbos, metuenda pericula pellit,
> impetrat et pacem et locupletem frugibus annum;
> carmine di superi placantur, carmine Manes   (*Epist.* 2.1.132–38)

> How would the girl who knows no husband learn to pray in the company of chaste boys if the Muse had not provided a bard? The chorus asks for help and feels divine presences [or feels the gods as present]; it begs enticingly for water from heaven with studied prayer; it averts disease, wards off grave threats, secures both peace and a harvest abundant with crops; with song the gods above are appeased, with song the gods below.

The phrase *praesentia numina sentit*, 'feels divine presences/feels the gods as present', does not permit us to distinguish between the act of collective prayer and its fulfilment, nor between the 'presence' of divine beings as the indication of their benevolence and their presence to the senses.[30] The *et* of v. 134 is ambivalent regarding the logical relation between the act of 'asking' (*poscit*) and the act of 'feeling' (*sentit*) which it links, so that we can readily imagine the two as forming a continuum, and thus as bearing witness to the special power of choruses to produce in their own audiovisual spectacle the divine presences which they themselves invoke.[31]

And yet it is hard to miss how this passage subtly conflates the specific practice of prayer through public communal hymns like Horace's own *Carmen Saeculare* with prayer in general by lumping them together under the catchall term *carmen* (138), which of course also embraces the whole realm of poetry. Horace thus seems to advance the notion that the hyper-presences of chorality are a special case of the universal power of poetry and prayer. The anaphora of *carmine* in

---

29 ἔνεστ' Ἀπόλλων τῷ χορῷ· τῆς λύρης ἀκούω ('Apollo is in the chorus; I hear the lyre'). Cf. Ov. *Rem.* 703–06.
30 The near-rhyme *praesentia sentit* strengthens the affinity between presence and the senses.
31 On the thaumastic powers of choruses see *HH* 3.156–61.

v. 138 drives this home by mimicking the formulaic refrains of prayer, as if to produce within the present hexameter discourse a prayerful song capable of reaching the numinous presence to which the *Epistle* is addressed, Augustus (who appears as *praesens* to his worshippers at v. 15).[32]

To return, then, to our initial opposition between metaphysical presence and material presence, we can say that, if Horace gestures toward a mystificatory fantasy of the power of the chorus in v. 134, then the anaphora of *carmine* in v. 138 brings us back down to earth by exposing this power-fantasy as itself the product of *carmen*. The *numina* which Horace's imaginary chorus calls into presence through versified prayer are no more — or less — real than the chorus which Horace calls into presence through his own versified prayer to plead his case for him.[33] In this sense we can see Horace as participating in the fantasy of chorality already in the incantation *carmine...carmine*, which substitutes verbal repetition for the plurality of the choral collective. Here we may recognise the influence of the 'imperative or enjoining force' that Connor perceives in choric modes of expression:[34] in the act of invoking the chorus as his mouthpiece, Horace finds himself pulled into its collective voice-body, drawn into their communal task of summoning *praesentia numina*.[35]

The pull of the choral voice can be detected in each of the numerous occasions in *Odes* 4 in which Horace either voices a community or else invokes the idea of communal voicing;[36] but, if we are to follow Connor in understanding chorality as a fantasy of collectivity which nevertheless originates with the individual voice, we must also look for its influence where the idea of a plural subject of voicing is latent or only tacitly implied. Chanting and singing are two modes of individual voicing which enjoin chorality by bringing out the qualities of rhythm and sonority in the voice. 'To chant', Connor says, 'is to spread the individual

---

[32] On Augustus as *praesens diuus* see above, chapter 3 n. 130.

[33] The phrase *praesentia numina* borrows a prooemial apostrophe from Verg. G. 1.10 (*et uos, agrestum praesentia numina, Fauni*; 'and you Fauns, present gods of country folk...') which Ovid uses to invoke the Muses at *Met*. 15.622 and *Ex P*. 1.2.105; also [Verg.] *Ciris* 245. That is, in every other instance of the phrase, it coincides immediately with the act of invocation it implies.

[34] Connor 2015: 3; he catalogues phrases from contemporary hymns which classicists would recognise as 'self-fulfilling commands'.

[35] The evocation in this passage of the repetitiveness of prayer extends even to the word for 'prayer' itself (*preces*, 133; *prece*, 135).

[36] Alongside the passages collected in n. 4 above, see for example the evocation of the *uox populi* of Rome at 4.3.13–16, 21–22, 4.4.27–44 (with the remarkable *o Roma* at v. 37), 4.5 *passim*, and 4.14.1–6; the vision of the collective experience of Rome's enemies at 4.4.1–28 and 4.14.7–9; Hannibal's speech on behalf of his entire people at 4.4.50–76; and the expression of 'our' (mankind's) common fate at 4.7.14–16.

voice out into a kind of imaginary amplitude which corresponds to the spreading of sound to occupy space'; likewise, 'song may itself be seen as pushing the individual voice in the direction of the collective'.³⁷ So the verbal repetition in the near-chant *carmine…carmine* (*Epist.* 2.1.138) approximates not only the ritual insistence of prayer but also the drone of multiple voices sounding as one. Horace makes the spaciousness of the choral voice extend even into the temporal dimension of utterance, so that song fills the hexameter line just as the choral voice-body fills space with its sonic amplitude.

Another aspect of the expansive power of the choral voice is its heightened capacity to produce effects of resonance and synchronicity with non-vocal media such as dancing bodies and musical instruments. In the example of *c.* 4.15.25–32, the mention of Lydian pipes 'mingled' with the choral song (*Lydis remixto carmine tibiis*, 30) almost anthropomorphises the instruments, figuring their harmonic contribution as equivalent to the corporeal augmentation of the choral collective effected by the adding of each human voice to the subject of *canemus*.³⁸ At the same time, the 'mingling' of human voice and *tibia* which this passage attributes to the collective voice-body of the chorus is also an apt expression for the act of blending Horace performs by evoking the sonic texture of flute-accompanied song in his poetry. The reader will not have to wait for this promised song to become a reality in order to experience this miraculous blending of the human voice with its nonhuman others, since the ode already enacts the coming-together into the choral by producing it as a fantasy.³⁹

The fantasy of the choral voice in *Odes* 4 is also intimately bound up with the idea of ritual as a means of ordering time.⁴⁰ The time-expression *et profestis lucibus et sacris* ('on both working days and holy days', 25) ties the song to the temporal order of the calendar, while the stipulation *rite deos prius apprecati* ('after

---

37 Connor 2015: 6.
38 The harmonious mingling of the chorus with the pipes contrasts with the dissonance between Horace's *loqui* and Apollo's *increpuit* in vv. 1–2. Thomas suggests that *Lydis* may hint at the Lydian mode as well as the provenance of the instrument (on which see Fedeli and Ciccarelli 2008: 628), citing Plato *Rep.* 398e (Thomas 2011: *ad loc.*). Harrison detects a nod to the association of the Lydians with the Etruscans (Harrison 2007: 205–06). He suggests this points us to the *Aeneid* (where the link is made several times) and hence to the convergence of lyric and epic, but 'Etruscan pipes' is also reminiscent of Roman stories of archaic Italian musical practices such as Liv. 7.2.3–8. Cf. also Pin. *O.* 5.19, ἱκέτας σέθεν ἔρχομαι Λυδίοις ἀπύων ἐν αὐλοῖς ('I come as your suppliant, calling on you among Lydian pipes').
39 Cf. Holzberg's playful suggestion that Horace's final *canemus* challenges the reader 'die Lektüre der vier Gedichtbücher erneut zu beginnen, dabei laut zu lesen und uns vorzustellen, wir würden von lydischen Flöten begleitet (Holzberg 2009: 186).'
40 See Barchiesi 2000.

first paying due veneration to the gods', 29) inscribes the performance within the smaller-scale temporal order of ritual procedure. The word *rite* in this context signifies not only general ritual correctness but also the observance through ritual practices of the temporal structures in which those practices are embedded: to perform this prayer *rite* is to perform it once each day before the song, and to perform this song *rite* is to perform it once each day after the prayer, and so on.

The temporal structure of the ritual thus exerts a regulating force on bodies which is instrumental to the consolidation of the collective subject of *canemus*.[41] This regulating force is bidirectional: the regular and coordinated assembly of bodies for daily prayer and song also has the effect of imposing order and meaning on the lived experience of time.[42] In this case, the eternally renewed song-performance repeatedly heralds the unabated flourishing of what Horace here calls *tua, Caesar, aetas* (4): the Augustan age.[43] The assembly of the chorus day after day to sing of the ancestry of Aeneas and the Julian *gens* makes tangible through ritual the continuance of the Augustan age and the stability of the Augustan peace.

The overlaying of the time-scheme of the ritual onto the historical time-scheme introduced by the term *tua, Caesar, aetas* produces two distinct temporal perspectives which correspond to the frames of experience-report and performed speech. From the vantage point of Horace's poem, looking hopefully from the early years of this new era and into its uncertain future, *canemus* represents a prophecy of peace and prosperity to come, like the predictions of stanzas 5–6.[44] This vantage point belongs to the frame of experience-report, since within this frame the description of the daily song-performance is presented as a vision of the tranquility of the Roman people. Within this frame, the time-expression *et profestis lucibus et sacris* (25) is a generalisation equivalent to 'every day as long as the Augustan peace lasts', and accordingly the future tense of *canemus* carries an imperfective aspect (virtually, 'we will be singing').

In v. 28, however, the time-expression *rite deos prius apprecati* shifts the temporal perspective to the sequence of actions in the rite, which consequently allows us to reconceptualise the future *canemus* as iterative, detailing the actions to be performed on each successive ritual occasion. This makes available the

---

41 Cf. the 'sacred time' of the *Carmen Saeculare* (*tempore sacro*, 4). See Bell 1992: 94–117 on the concept of the 'ritual body', with Kurke 2005 on choral lyric as a ritual practice.
42 On ritual and lived time see e.g. Rappaport 1999: 177–81.
43 Breed 2004.
44 Breed 2004: 249.

frame of performed speech, within which the future of *canemus* takes on an enjoining force, willing the consolidation of the collective voice-body of the chorus ('we shall sing'). We might attribute this speech act of injunction to song to Horace, acting individually as the founder of the tradition; but such an injunction would be equally apt if uttered as part of the song on each successive occasion, affirming the solidarity of the choral assembly and pledging to carry on the ritual of song on each following day. In this sense, *canemus* can be heard as an instantiation of the repeated song it enjoins.[45]

Thus the individual utterance of Horace is swept up in a collective voice-body which spreads itself not only in space through the accumulation of bodies but also in time through repetition. By weaving the song into an unbroken chain of repetitions stretching into the far horizon of the Augustan age, the choral assembly proffers itself as the body of proof for the continued vitality of the *res Romana*, secured by the still-unbroken Julian edicts (*non* [...] | *edicta rumpent Iulia*, 21–22). As Breed notes, the ablative absolute *custode rerum Caesare* in v. 17 implies at first that this era of peace will end with Augustus' mortal lifespan, but the song of the final two stanzas tells a different story.[46] The choral assembly is specified in v. 27 as a constellation of household groups — the *paterfamilias*, the *matrona*, and their offspring — and the subject of their song is men who carry on the *mos patrum* (29) and the divine lineage of both Aeneas and Augustus from Venus (31–32), who appears here in her aspect as fertility goddess, the *alma Venus* of Lucretius who brings all things to flower.[47] The song includes within itself, both as subject and object, the generative principle that ensures the continuity both of the *pax Augusta* and the collective voice-body of the chorus that utters it, reminding us that Caesars can be reproduced as readily as songs can be reperformed.[48] On each occasion that the chorus 'sings the progeny of bountiful Venus' and pledges to sing it again, it sings the endurance of that bloodline up to (and beyond) the

---

45 Lowrie takes issue with the fact that *canemus* 'cannot literally be fulfilled by the ode itself; it cannot be its own future (Lowrie 2009: 91–92).' This is only a problem if we attempt to read *canemus* as a future referring to the present (as does Harrison 2007: 205; see p. 17 for the argument against this conception of the 'Pindaric future'). In my reading, *canemus* opens up onto multiple futures of singing, but never ceases to be futuric.
46 Breed 2004: 247–49.
47 *DRN* 1.1–61; Putnam 1986: 295–96; Fedeli and Ciccarelli 2008: 628. See Feeney 1998: 101–04 on the many faces of Venus in *Odes* 4.
48 Breed sees an opposition here between the boundedness of human life and the immortalising powers of poetry, specifically of Vergil's *Aeneid* (Breed 2004: 249), but this strikes me as rather arbitrary; I see Horace rather as figuring the memorialising function of poetry and song in terms of the principle of procreation which also sustains the Julian *gens*.

present of singing, attested both by the presence of a governing Caesar and the presence of the chorus itself as living proof of the legacy of Troy.[49]

From this we can conclude that repetition exerts a power on the voice which is structurally equivalent to the multiplication of voice that constitutes the choral.[50] Through repetition, the collective voice-body attains a diachronic as well as a synchronic dimension. The fantasy of the choral voice in Horace's *canemus* as the incarnation of the progeny of Venus gestures towards the blending of these two dimensions, so that the 'we' of singing is assimilated into the totality of all instantiations of that 'we' on each occasion of singing. These two dimensions of the choral voice's self-extension, repetition and multiplication, correspond to the sonic phenomena of rhythm and resonance. The recurrence of the song in regular daily intervals produces a rhythm which complements the effect of resonance produced by the coordination of voices in the rhythmic-harmonic unit that is the song itself.

This self-extension of the choral voice through rhythm and resonance makes itself heard in the sonic texture of Horace's Alcaic verses. The topic phrase of the final period, 'we will sing', is stretched over the span of two whole stanzas, with the subject *nos* in v. 25 and the verb *canemus* delayed by hyperbaton to v. 32.[51] Everything in between is there only to fill in the details of place, time, participants, and sung content for this one act of singing. This semantic stretching slows the pace of the verse down to a crawl.[52] Each line, moreover, represents a self-contained unit of sense, until the tricolon of vv. 31–32. No action transpires; there is no movement of thought, no parenthesis, no enjambment to break up the flow. The interval between *nos* to *canemus* is not a path of song, because we have not progressed anywhere; we end up right back where we started. This is not a journey, but a construction project. Horace builds up the song brick by brick, each segment of verse adding to the total mass without altering its substance. Each successive line forms a unit of sound rather than of sense, chiming in rhythmically with the sustained tonic note sounded by the hyperbaton of *nos...canemus*. Curtailing the forward momentum of goal-directed discourse (*logos*) turns up the

---

49 Putnam 1986: 290.
50 Cf. Burnett 1983: 6.
51 Fraenkel aptly praises '[t]he splendour which is spread over these two stanzas (Frankel 1957: 452).'
52 For Johnson, by contrast, the hyperbaton expresses Horace's 'retreat' into 'the anonymous Roman crowd' (Johnson 2004: 200). This interpretation implies a purely graphic conception of word order, and does not take into account the effect of hyperbaton and related devices on rhythm and pacing.

volume on the sonority of language, heightening its receptivity to harmonic resonances and rhythmic patternings and thereby pushing it in the direction of the choral (cf. Connor's argument that 'any distension or lengthening out of the voice may simultaneously tend to the univocity of the choric').[53]

Yet however close the ode may come to collapsing the distinction between itself and the choral song it enjoins, it never overcomes the phantasmal quality of the choral voice. Chorality remains the 'beyond' of lyric, the fantasy of a realm of pure consonance and communion through song which lyric itself dreams up. The collective subject of *canemus* may go on extending itself through an indefinite series of repetitions, but Horace's poem ends as soon as the word is out. The full stop after *canemus* constitutes what Oliensis calls an act of enclosure,[54] marking the border between Horace's lyric utterance and the potentially unlimited expansiveness of the choral voice. Oliensis seems to regard this particular act of enclosure as a largely successful one: Horace cuts his losses by beating a hasty retreat from lyric.[55] But borders are always also lines of contact. Horace marks here not only the point where his own lyric ends and the choral begins, but the point at which his lyric borders on the choral.

A small chorus of commentators has argued that the 'beyond' of lyric to which *canemus* points is the realm of epic, specifically the new epic terrain carved out by Vergil's *Aeneid*.[56] But the Vergilian allusion of vv. 1–2 leads by a more direct route to the sixth Eclogue, where Apollo nudges the poet away from the theme of war and back into the fold of pastoral (1–8). Vergil obliges by recounting the song of Silenus, which proves less high-flown than martial epic but much more ambitious than the pastoral norm, on a par with the *paulo maiora* of Eclogue 4. Apollo's rebuke is the occasion for Vergil to test the boundaries of pastoral, not to cross over into another genre entirely.[57] The pull of epic does not seduce the bucolic poet away from his *deductum carmen*, but rather stretches it to capacity until it collides with Hesiodic cosmogony. I would suggest that *c.* 4.15 follows a similar pattern: so far from pronouncing the eclipse of lyric by epic, Horace is taking lyric right up to its limit point, the point at which the singular 'I' explodes

---

53 Connor 2015: 6.
54 Oliensis 1998: 102.
55 Oliensis 1998: 153.
56 Breed 2004; Harrison 2007: 205–06; Zarecki 2010; Johnson 2011: 183; Thomas 2011: 270. Zarecki's argument, that the subject of *canemus* is the duo of Horace and a resurrected Vergil and no one else, is neither convincing nor productive in my view; however, the voice of Vergil can certainly be heard *within* the chorus.
57 See the excellent discussion of Harrison 2007: 30–44.

into a choric 'we'.⁵⁸ This poem may stage a confrontation with epic, but the battleground is still that of lyric.⁵⁹

In the remaining sections of this chapter, I will explore how poems 1, 2, and 5 of *Odes* 4 prefigure the climactic encounter with the collective voice-body that utters the final word of the collection. At a pivotal moment in each of these poems, Horace stages an event of choral singing, collective prayer, or group dance which, like the genealogical song of *c*. 4.15.25–32, is situated in a liminal position relative to the occasion of his own lyric utterance, neither coinciding with it directly nor entirely separable from it. The result is that he is always poised precariously between fantasising the choral voice and becoming one with it. This in turn means that the collective voice-body of the chorus remains always nebulous and indistinct, not because it is insubstantial but rather because it is forever in the process of emerging. Wherever it appears, it signals its relation to the idea of lyric presence, but its value in relation to this idea oscillates between positive (a greater communion)⁶⁰ and negative (a crowd to disappear into).⁶¹ Chorality is the *Ur*-occasion, the stage on which Horace performs both the becoming-present and the becoming-absent of his lyric voice, playing out a dialectic of presence which culminates in the final presence/absence of *canemus*.

4.4 Rhythm and repetition: *c.* 4.1

The first poem of the collection, like the initial poems of each previous book, begins by introducing the poet in his latest incarnation and setting out a kind of prospectus for the odes that follow. The opening word, *intermissa* ('deferred'),

---

58 The advantage of this reading, in my view, is that it has Horace engaging with Vergil as a complex and nuanced model rather than as a one-note poster boy for military epic. We could even see Horace as tracing in the three parts of this poem — the bucolic *recusatio* of war poetry (1–4), the hymn to Italian peace (5–24), and the choral celebration of Rome's Trojan ancestry (25–32) — a progression parallel to the three stages of Vergil's career, marked by the *Eclogues*, the *Georgics*, and the *Aeneid*, all within the scope of Horatian lyric.
59 The same can be said of other poems in which Horace plays with the boundaries of his genre, such as *cc.* 1.6, 2.1, 3.3, and 3.25.
60 The chorus represents Horace's communion with the patron gods of lyric poetry at *cc.* 1.1.29–34 and 3.4.25–28.
61 For the chorus as a place to conceal oneself, see c. 2.5.20–24: Cnidiusue Gyges, | quem si puellarum insereres choro, | mire sagacis falleret hospites | discrimen obscurum solutis | crinibus ambiguoque uultu ('or Cnidian Gyges, whom, if you placed him in a chorus of girls, the sharpest of strangers would find themselves amazingly unable to pick out, hidden behind his flowing locks and ambiguous face').

nods self-reflexively at the long hiatus which separated this work from Horace's previous lyric output.⁶² Venus has come back after all this time to trouble the poet again, but he protests that he is too old for her games:

> Intermissa, Venus, diu
> rursus bella moues? parce, precor, precor.
>   non sum qualis eram bonae
> sub regno Cinarae. desine, dulcium
>   mater saeua Cupidinum,   5
> circa lustra decem flectere mollibus
>   iam durum imperiis: abi,
> quo blandae iuuenum te reuocant preces. (4.1.1–8)

Are you starting up long-deferred wars again, Venus? Pray, pray, forbear. I am not as I was under kind Cinara's reign. Inveigle no longer, fell mother of sweet Desires, one who, close to his fiftieth year, is now hardened against the soft touch of your authority; off with you to wherever the fawning prayers of youths summon you.

Horace here produces an inversion of the cletic hymn, dismissing the goddess in an audacious ἀποπομπή rather than willing her into presence.⁶³ Commentators have seen this poem as a direct response to the invocation of Aphrodite in Sappho fr. 1,⁶⁴ which probably would have opened Sappho's collected poems in Hellenistic editions,⁶⁵ as well as to two earlier invocations of Venus in Horace's own book 1 (1.19 and 1.30).⁶⁶ Sappho prays for the love-goddess to release her from the pain of unrequited love by helping her to capture the object of her desire. She pleads her case using the *da quia dedisti* argument ('grant my prayer because you have done so in the past'), citing previous occasions on which Aphrodite has come to her aid, and in the process even quotes the goddess directly:

---

62 Suetonius refers to a *longum interuallum* (Suet. *Vit. Hor.*). Thomas argues that '[there] is no particular reason to assume that [Horace] stopped writing lyric in 23 BCE and started again around 19 or 18', suggesting that the poems that make up the final book might have been written individually throughout this period (Thomas 2011: 5–7). However, even if Suetonius' account of a return to lyric *ex longo interuallo* does not correspond with the actual chronology of Horace's individual lyric compositions, it does at least cohere with the *narrative* of the reappearance of the lyric Horace in book-form hinted at by the opening word *intermissa*. See further Hills 2001 on the connexions between this proem and that of Ennius *Annals* 16.
63 Fraenkel 1957: 410; Kiessling and Heinze 1930: 386; Fedeli and Ciccarelli 2008: 83–84.
64 Barchiesi 2000: 172–73; Feeney 1998: 101–02; Nagy 1994: 417–21; Putnam 1986: 39–41; Fedeli and Ciccarelli 2008: 87. Thomas 2011: 86 also compares Ibycus 286 *PMG*.
65 See Barchiesi 2009: 424–27.
66 Putnam 1986: 44.

σὺ δ', ὦ μάκαιρα,
μειδιαίσαισ' ἀθανάτῳ προσώπῳ
ἤρε' ὄττι δηὖτε πέπονθα κὤττι 15
    δηὖτε κάλημμι,
κὤττι μοι μάλιστα θέλω γένεσθαι
μαινόλᾳ θύμῳ· τίνα δηὖτε πείθω
ἄψ σ' ἄγην ἐς Fὰν φιλότατα; τίς σ', ὦ
    Ψάπφ', ἀδικήει; 20
καὶ γὰρ αἰ φεύγει, ταχέως διώξει·
αἰ δὲ δῶρα μὴ δέκετ', ἀλλὰ δώσει·
αἰ δὲ μὴ φίλει, ταχέως φιλήσει
    κωὐκ ἐθέλοισα. (fr. 1.13–24)

And you, O blessed one, with a smile on your immortal face, asked what was happening to me once again and why I was calling you once again, and what I wished to happen most of all in my mad heart: 'Whom shall I persuade once again to come back into your affections? Who is it who wrongs you, Sappho? If she flees you, she will soon pursue; if she refuses gifts, she will give them instead; if she does not love you, she will love you soon, even against her will.'

The speech of Aphrodite is remarkable for its split temporality.[67] For the purposes of Sappho's prayer, the speech serves to remind the goddess of the preexisting relationship between the two by recalling a previous instance of prayer and fulfilment (which, as indicated by ποτα in v. 5, is not unique but representative of a trend). The logic of the appeal hinges on the notion that the request will be more attractive to the goddess if it is framed as a ritualistic repetition of a previous divine intervention. This principle of repetition in turn governs the form of the quoted response, which is universal rather than specific — this could be any of Sappho's old flames — and alludes to previous occasions of prayer with the repeated word δηὖτε, 'now again' (15, 16, 18).[68]

In the next and final stanza, this rule of repetition spills back over into Sappho's present request with the command 'Now too, come to me' (ἔλθε μοι καὶ νῦν, 25). But Sappho's poem has already enacted this desired repetition by rehearsing it in advance through the medium of quotation. The quotation repeats from a past occasion the response which Sappho hopes to hear again on the present occasion; her repetition arises out of a desire for further repetitions. Sappho thus invents in the ritual of poetry a homeopathic cure for the endless δηὖτε...δηὖτε...δηὖτε of

---

[67] My discussion of this poem draws extensively on Nagy 1994: 417–19.
[68] Cf. Mace 1993: 355–61.

erotic suffering.⁶⁹ The potency of this poetic ritual derives finally from the temporal split effected by the quotation of Aphrodite's words in direct discourse, which pulls them out of the past of Sappho's narration and into the present of the poem's enunciation, so that the striking use of the poet's proper name in the vocative (20) can be felt as heralding a new occasion of address, and so that the forecast of erotic victory in vv. 21–24 can be felt as performatively enacting its content in the moment of utterance.

With the opening complaint of *Odes* 4, Horace writes himself into the legacy of the ritualised rapport between Sappho and Aphrodite by presenting his own take on the problem of love's recurrence posed by Sappho fr. 1.⁷⁰ Venus is coming again (*rursus*, 2), but too much has changed between this visit and the last; the poet has grown old and is no longer at the mercy of the beguiling goddess. Horace is in effect attempting to ward off Venus by asserting a new temporal order in opposition to the order of desirous repetition initiated by Sappho. Whereas Sappho emphasises the continuity between each individual occasion of her lovesick prayers, Horace's weighty word *intermissa* points to the intervening space between Venus' comings and goings as a token of the limit set on love's cyclical self-renewal by mortality. He claims that he is 'now hardened [*durum*] against the soft [*mollibus*] touch' of Venus' authority (6–7), but the only cause of this newfound intractability is his age, which he measures out with relative precision to 'around ten *lustra* (*circa lustra decem*, 6)', or fifty years. I would suggest that the act of measuring involved in the enumeration of the poet's lifespan is itself a defense against the erotic temporality imposed by the Sapphic Venus.⁷¹

---

69 See Carson 1986: 118–20 on the erotic temporality instigated by δηὖτε, with Mace 1993 on its use in Greek lyric (Barchiesi 2009: 426 dubs it 'a password of lyric ideology'). My use of the term 'ritual' in connexion with Sappho is informed by Yatromanolakis 2004, who recognises that ritual modes of signification such as prayer should not be taken as determining contexts or 'backgrounds' for Lesbian lyric but rather as multivalent nexus of meaning which Sappho and others were more than capable of using creatively (hence my term 'invention'). See also the discussion in ch. 3 of the not-so-simple relation between Adonic poetry and the various documented ritual practices that formed part of the worship of Adonis, and cf. Culler 2015: 122–24 on Roland Greene's concept of the 'ritualistic' dimension of lyric poetry (Greene 1991).
70 Putnam 1986: 39–40. His ambitious interpretation — that Horace prays for a 'reritualization' of the goddess whom Sappho had refashioned into a desacralised poetic icon — depends on the division of literature and religion into too-neat 'spheres' (against which see Feeney 1998).
71 On temporality and desire in this poem see Ancona 1994: 85–93, who notes that time poses much less of a threat to Horace's own sexual identity than it does to figures of the beloved such as Lyce (4.13) and Barine (2.8).

Hardie notes that the verb *moues* (2) endows Venus with a property of 'mobility and lability' which is the source of her power.⁷² We can add that this property in turn determines the 'soft' (*mollibus*, 6) and 'beguiling' (suggested by *flectere*, 6) quality of her overtures, to which Horace opposes the 'hardness' of old age (*durum*, 7). This hardness implies both immobility and resistance to change, but it is precisely because Horace *has* undergone a change that he is able to withstand Venus. 'I am not as I was under kind Cinara's reign', he insists (3–4), partly restating *Epist.* 1.1.4: 'I'm not the same man, not in age, not at heart (*non eadem est aetas, non mens*)'.⁷³ Venus' error is that she expected to come back after a long absence and find the same Horace as always, just as Sappho's Aphrodite treats each of her visitations as a repeat performance of each previous occasion. She has failed to take account of the fact that, as she has been dutifully observing the ceremony of eternally reflowering desire, Rome's sacral calendar has not stopped marking out its territory in the finite lives of human beings.⁷⁴

The unit of time with which Horace counts his years is the *lustrum*, a five-year period which takes its name from a sacrificial rite (*lustratio*) which traditionally attended the completion of the census⁷⁵ — itself a highly valorised ritual of enumeration. The *lustrum* as a timekeeping device appears in *c.* 2.4.22–24, where Horace has only passed his fortieth year — already too old for love's games⁷⁶ — and in the *Carmen Saeculare*, which includes a prayer to Apollo to 'prolong the Roman state and bountiful Latium into another *lustrum* and an ever-brightening future (*remque Romanam Latiumque felix | alterum in lustrum meliusque semper | prorogat aeuum*, *CS* 66–68)'. It also appears later in book 4 (4.14.34–40) to measure

---

72 Hardie 1993: 131.
73 These two passages contrast suggestively with *Sat.* 2.1.57–60: 'To be brief: whether peaceful old age awaits me or death hovers about me with sable wings, rich, poor, at Rome, or — if fortune so demands — in exile, I will write, whatever the colour of my life shall be (*ne longum faciam: seu me tranquilla senectus | exspectat seu mors atris circumuolat alis, | diues, inops, Romae, seu fors ita iusserit, exsul, | quisquis erit uitae scribam color*).'
74 See Feeney 2009: 27–31 on the paradigm shift in lyric temporality brought about by Horace's importation of the Julian calendar and modern Roman conceptions of time into the world of Greek lyric. The metaphor of the kind 'reign' of Cinara, besides playing off the conceit of Venus' 'wars' (*bella*, 2), also makes Horace into a sovereign state that has a dynastic history of its own; Venus fails to respect the proper periodisation of Horace's love life.
75 See Liv. 1.44, 3.24.
76 *fuge suspicari | cuius octauum trepidauit aetas | claudere lustrum* ('Let go of all suspicion for one whose age has hurried his eighth *lustrum* to a close'). Ov. *Tr.* 4.10.77–78 and Mart. 10.38.9 also measure lifespans in *lustra*. Contrast the quite different measuring system employed in *Epist.* 1.20.26–28 ('four times eleven Decembers' = 44). It is worth noting that Horace records his age in a concluding *sphragis* to that book, but in the opening of *Odes* 4.

the time between Actium and the favourable outcome (*secundos* [...] *exitus*, 37) of Octavian's campaign in the civil war. That is, the *lustrum* only appears in Horace as a yardstick either of the poet's sexual vivacity or of the vitality of the *res Romana*.

However, in none of these other instances of Horatian self-dating is the *lustrum* employed as an *approximate* measure, as it is here. The remark that Venus' appearance takes place only 'around' Horace's fiftieth year (*circa lustra decem*, 4) does not only serve to foster an *effet de réel*; instead, we can see Horace here as positing the lustral cycle, and hence the Julian calendar,[77] as an alternate metric for his lifetime with which Venus' visits fail to coincide evenly. It is this reckoning of time, Horace intimates, that governs the qualitative changes in his own being (*non sum qualis eram*; *iam durum*), and not the erotic temporality determined by the frequency of Venus' apparitions. Horace wards off the latest of these uncalled-for epiphanies by checking his calendar, and the act of measuring implied therein can be read as a direct response to the entrainment of ritualistic repetition performed by Sappho's poem. According this new poetic almanac erected by Horace, Venus is not only too late; she is tragically out of sync.[78]

We have already met, in chapters 2 and 3, the opposition between cyclical and linear conceptions of time as negotiated in and through poetry. It was argued that both Horace *c*. 1.9 and Bion's *Lament for Adonis* work out poetic strategies for combatting the linear span of mortality by (re)asserting against it a principle of cyclical renewal on the model of the annual round of the seasons. The power-struggle with time in each of these poems is waged not merely through philosophical reflection in the poems but through poetry as a time-bound medium; thus we saw Horace inventing in the course of his poetic speech to Thaliarchus an impossible meaning for the word 'now' (*nunc*) which begets a new time-space of present pleasure, and Aphrodite attempting to recapture Adonis' dying kiss by obsessively repeating the fragments of a broken refrain.

It might seem at first blush as though the Horace of *c*. 4.1 is working in the opposite direction, affirming the annalistic conception of time expressed in 3.30.4–5 as a vast totality formed out of 'the innumerable succession of years and

---

[77] Cf. Feeney's remark that with the calendar reforms that transpired in Horace's lifetime, 'Julian and natural time [were] now one (Feeney 2009: 228)'.
[78] Horace reminds us of Venus' intimate association with the Roman calendar in 4.11.13–20, commemorating Maecenas' birthday on the Ides of April, 'the month of seaborn Venus' (*mensem Veneris marinae*, 15). See Putnam 1986: 191.

the fleeing of ages (*innumerabilis | annorum series et fuga temporum*).⁷⁹ Calendrical reckonings of time such as *circa lustra decem* imply by their very use of numbered units of measurement the possibility of extending the sum total of those units into an infinite, homogeneous series. The impossibility of returning to any previous point in the series is the harsh lesson of such reckonings, a lesson which Horace recites to the aging Lyce in 4.13.13–16 with the help of an imaginary public calendar which records her passing years.⁸⁰ There is no room here for the continual reawakening of desire associated with the Sapphic love-goddess.

Yet Horace's verses exhibit on the level of form a sliding into refrain-like repetition. First there is the plaintive epizeuxis (immediate repetition of a single word) *precor, precor* in v. 1, which Thomas finds to be unparalleled in Latin,⁸¹ reduplicating Sappho's λίσσομαί σε (2). Secondly, v. 5, in which Venus is addressed as (*dulcium |*) *mater saeua Cupidinum*, duplicates *c.* 1.19.1, the opening line of a poem in which Horace girds himself with prayer and propitiatory sacrifice against an unstoppable onslaught of passion by the goddess. The power wielded by Venus in that poem extended even to the point of controlling Horace's speech:

> in me tota ruens Venus
> Cyprum deseruit, nec patitur Scythas
>   aut uersis animosum equis
> Parthum dicere nec quae nihil attinent. (1.19.9–13)

> Venus has abandoned Cyprus and descends upon me with all her might, and does not permit me to [speak/sing] of Scythians or of the Parthian emboldened by his cavalry's retreat or of matters of no importance.

The fact that Horace not only repeats the metre and subject-matter of this poem in 4.1 but actually reproduces its first line exactly shows that Venus still exercises this power over the poet's speech, not only constraining him to sing of love but compelling him, like Sappho before him, to repeat himself.⁸²

The clash between the erotic temporality of Venus' visits and the linear span of Horace's life foregrounds the relation between poetic utterance and occasion

---

79 Feeney 2009: 228–29.
80 *Nec Coae referunt iam tibi purpurae | nec cari lapides tempora, quae semel | notis condita fastis | inclusit uolucris dies* ('Neither your Coan dyes nor your precious stones restore to you the years which winged time has set down in the chronicle of public knowledge').
81 Thomas 2011: *ad loc.*
82 'Thus Horace is repeating his words of love poetry, repeating himself, repeating his *self*, at the very moment when he prays never again to be a love poet: he is up to his old tricks of poetic reversal (Nagy 1994: 420).'

as an existential problem for Horatian lyric. Horace dismisses Venus because she has come at the wrong time for love, and hence at the wrong time for love poetry; and yet at the same time it is this unwanted visit which occasions the poem, and hence the entire book. The intervening space (*intermissa*) between this latest visitation and the last coincides with the long silence of Horace's lyric voice, a silence which he permits us to measure with precision by comparing the lustral dating of v. 6 with that of *c.* 2.4.22–24. Like Venus, we were not witness to the transformation he claims to have undergone, into an old and hardened creature. Even in his most recent work, the first book of *Epistles*, he appeared to have been lately 'under kind Cinara's reign (3–4)';[83] in 4.13 this love-affair is suddenly long dead, along with Cinara herself (vv. 18–28). We are no more privy than Venus is to these intervening events which apparently brought about Horace's sexual recalcitrance.

To this extent, Horace has Venus act out the expectation for venereal poetry which he projects onto his audience, a ploy which reverses the usual order of epiphanic experience. This time, it is not the visitant who is the source of mortal wonder, delivering a moment of profound clarity (like Diespiter/Jupiter in 1.34) or sublime ecstasy (like Calliope in 3.4 or Bacchus in 3.25); rather, the epiphany of the ever-recurring Venus only serves to throw into relief the epiphany of the calcified Horace.[84] Unfit to channel the erotic energy of the love-goddess' presence, Horace attempts to turn our gaze elsewhere, to a location 'more in keeping with the season' (*tempestiuius*, 9), namely the house of Paullus Fabius Maximus, who was soon to enter Augustus' household by way of marriage to the *princeps*' cousin Marcia:[85]

>   tempestiuius in domum
> Paulli purpureis ales oloribus   10
>   comissabere Maximi,
> si torrere iecur quaeris idoneum.
>   namque et nobilis et decens
> et pro sollicitis non tacitus reis
>   et centum puer artium   15

---

[83] Cinara appears only at *Epist.* 1.7.25–28, 1.14.33, and *cc.* 4.1.3–4 and 4.13.18–28. See Thomas 2011: *ad* 4.1.3–4 on the question of Cinara's name and the possibility of identifying her with the Glycera of *Odes* 1 (*c.* 1.19.5–8, 1.30.3, 1.33.2); cf. Nagy 1994: 421–23.

[84] A kind of parallel for this dynamic can be seen in Propertius 4.7, where the beloved Cynthia, suddenly and surprisingly dead (much like Cinara in *c.* 4.13), visits the poet as a ghost and recounts all the injustices he has committed against her, showing us through her eyes a very different Propertius from the one we thought we knew.

[85] See Habinek 1985, who reads this poem as an oblique epithalamium.

late signa feret militiae tuae,
  et, quandoque potentior
largi muneribus riserit aemuli,
  Albanos prope te lacus
ponet marmoream sub trabe citrea.   20
  illic plurima naribus
duces tura lyraque et Berecyntia
  delectabere tibia,[86]
mixtis carminibus non sine fistula;
  illic bis pueri die   25
numen cum teneris uirginibus tuum
  laudantes pede candido
in morem Salium ter quatient humum.
  me nec femina nec puer
iam nec spes animi credula mutui   30
  nec certare iuuat mero
nec uincire nouis tempora floribus. (9–32)

The time is riper for you to lead a carouse on the wings of bright-feathered swans to the house of Paullus Maximus, if you seek a suitable liver to fire. Noble and gracious, unafraid to speak up for anxious defendants, a youth of a hundred talents, he will surely carry your banners in far-reaching campaigns, and when he laughs in victory over the gifts of a big-spending rival, he will set you up in marble beneath a citrus roof by the Alban lake.

There you will flood your nostrils with copious incense and be entertained by the lyre and the Berecyntian pipe, interspersed with songs accompanied by the reed; there twice each day boys and tender maidens will venerate your godhead, rocking the ground with their fair feet in triple measure after the Salian custom. I no longer take pleasure in women or boys, in the wishful longing for a kindred spirit, in drunken contests or in wreathing my temples with early-blooming flowers.

It was argued in the discussion of Sappho fr. 2 (chapter 1 above) that this poem, a cletic hymn calling on Aphrodite to join a gathering of worshippers in a grove, does not so much summon the goddess to a place as call into being a space in which her presence is possible. The poem achieves this effect through the medium of description, which is delivered with the stanza-initial anaphora of ἐν δέ

---

[86] The MSS have both *lyraque, Berecyntia, tibia* (abl.) and *lyraeque, Berecyntiae, tibiae* (gen. or dat.) Thomas 2011: *ad loc.* prefers the genitive (which would produce 'the combined strains of lyre and Berecyntian pipe with the pan flute too'), conjecturing that the passage is describing only instrumental music; but Fedeli and Ciccarelli 2008: 105–06 provide good parallels for ablative absolutes with *mixto/mixtis* being used to add an item to a list (q.v.), and my translation reflects their interpretation. On this reading, however, the reader can still opt to take *lyra* and *tibia* as ablatives with *mixtis*, which is recommended by the Horatian parallels at 4.15.30 (*Lydis remixto carmine tibiis*) and *Ep.* 9.5 (*sonante mixtum tibiis carmen lyra*).

('Within...', 5, 9) introducing the pleasing contents of the grove to which the goddess is summoned, followed by a climactic ἔνθα δή ('Once there', 12) which introduces the pleasurable activities she will enjoy once she has arrived. The *enargeia* or evocative power of the description stems from a sense of immediacy which is itself an extension of the immediacy of direct address; the 'here and now' of the epiphany is also the 'here and now' of the poet's speech to the goddess.

Horace follows this pattern in *c.* 1.30, where he asks Venus to relocate 'into the house of Glycera who is calling you, graced with plenty of incense (*uocantis | ture te multo Glycerae decoram | transfer in aedem* (2–4).' The house of Glycera (or her 'room', or 'temple'?) is the place on which the desires of poet, beloved, and goddess converge; by entering the house, Venus will fulfil her own desire to receive aromatic tribute, Glycera's desire for her prayers to be heard, and Horace's desire for sex. The house is a triple orifice — nostril, ear, and vagina — and the poem offers a means of filling it with sensory presence, creating in its own 'here and now' an epiphanic space capable of housing Venus and her entourage. In *c.* 4.1, Horace paints Paullus' house as an attractive place of worship similar to Sappho's grove and the house of Glycera in *c.* 1.30, even echoing Sappho's repeated ἐν δέ with the anaphora of *illic* (21, 25);[87] but the fact that the poet explicitly absents himself from the party severs the vital link between the epiphanic space to which the goddess is summoned and the enunciative space of the invocation. This is an inversion of the cletic hymn, not only in that the goddess is dismissed instead of summoned, but also in that the poet is banished from the epiphanic space his own poem creates.[88]

The qualities that make Paullus' house an ideal destination for Venus are expressed as a product of the character of its master, which is already hinted at by the cognomen *Maximus*: this is the 'host with the most'.[89] The catalogue in vv. 13–20 depicts a man teeming with exemplary traits (note the polysyndeton)[90] which are all conveyed in terms of quantity and extent: he can always spare a few words for his (plural) clients (14), he will bear Venus' standards over great distances (16), he is prepared to outspend rival lovers many times over (17–18), and, most

---

[87] Putnam 1986: 36–37.
[88] Fedeli and Ciccarelli 2008: 83–84 note that the expulsion of Venus is patterned on scapegoating prayers; but the 'twist' is that the new target is not an enemy, but someone who will benefit from the goddess' attentions.
[89] Of course, in playing on the literal meaning of the *cognomen Maximus*, Horace also draws our attention to the *praenomen Paullus*, which literally means 'small' (used as such in 4.9.29); a playful irony?
[90] Thomas 2011: *ad* 13–16.

impressively at his age,[91] he has twice as many talents as Horace has years (15). The appellation *centum puer artium* balances and mirrors the epithet of Venus in vv. 4–5, *dulcium | mater saeua Cupidinum*; this 'boy' is as rich in marketable skills as this 'mother' is rich in offspring — offspring who themselves embody the desire for procreation. This theme of fecundity culminates at vv. 19–20, when Horace vows a statue to Venus on Paullus' behalf in thanks for a victory over a rival lover. The passage not only promotes the younger man as *maximus* in both financial prosperity and sexual potency, but also ascribes to him the reproductive power of plastic art: if Venus favours him, she will be rewarded with a new version of herself in marble.[92]

The imagined reception in vv. 21–28 exudes an aesthetic of exuberance and profusion which reflects the youthful fecundity of its host. This is adumbrated in vv. 9–11, where Venus is urged to come not alone, but leading a festive procession (*comissabere* from Gk. κωμάζω) carried by a bevy of swans. In v. 10, the phrase *purpureis ales oloribus* (literally, 'winged with purple swans') — a variation on the team of doves that conveys Aphrodite in Sappho fr. 1.9–12 — almost melds goddess and birds into a composite body, as the adjective *purpureis* can be thought of as describing either Venus' attire[93] or the sheen of the swans' feathers.[94] In vv. 21–22, the *ture* [...] *multo* with which Glycera fills her house in *c.* 1.30.3 is upgraded to the superlative *plurima* [...] *tura* as if to better accord with the superlative Maximus. The near-rhyme *tura lyraque* (22) effects a smooth fade from olfactory to auditory stimulation, conveying a sense of simultaneity and flow which is carried over to the musical performance itself, distributed among a variety of instruments

---

91 Johnson 2004: 45 finds humour in the use of the word *puer* for Maximus, who was probably around 30 in 16 BCE; but the comparatively ancient Horace is as much the butt of the joke as anyone.

92 The doubling of Venus also entails the production of a new place of worship (the Alban lake) in addition to the house. This creates an interesting ambiguity in *illic* (21, 25); are we back at the house, or is this a congregation centred on the lakeside shrine with its marble icon? Hardie assumes the latter, arguing that this sculpted goddess is a 'supernaturally animated statue, able to inhale the sweet smell of incense and to enjoy the hymns sung in her honour (Hardie 1993: 131).' But the two are not mutually exclusive, and we can certainly imagine the festivities at either or even both of these locations (or are they perhaps contiguous?).

93 As in Bion *Adonis* 3.

94 Thomas 2011: *ad loc.*; Putnam 1986: 45 ('for the first time in literature not only are her swans purple but she herself is winged, akin to the creatures who bear her aloft').

which may be thought of as either playing in concert or alternating in a medley (22–24).⁹⁵

The choral song-dance of vv. 25–28 brings the period to a climax in a multi-sensory banquet of sound (the hymns to Venus), touch (the 'tender' bodies of the girls and the beating of their feet), and colour (the youthful white of the feet in v. 26 reflecting the brilliant hue of Venus' swans and the glistening marble of her promised statue). The characterisation of their performance as 'Salian' (*in morem Salium*, 27) suggests a dance that involves leaping up and down (hinting at the derivation *Salius* from *salio*),⁹⁶ which would make this an especially animated spectacle.⁹⁷ The passage is bookended by two numerals, *bis* (24) and *ter* (27), which count out two interlocking rhythms for the chorus to follow: the three-beat measure that regulates the movement of their feet and the solar rhythm which determines the timing of their assembly twice each day (anticipated by the double *illic* in 21 and 25). By overlaying the *one-two-three* of the dance-moves on the *one-two* of the chorus' daily reconvening, Horace allows us to see how the dance orders time by folding cycles into sequences. When the morning dance has come and gone, the evening dance is still in the offing; when the evening dance has gone through all its steps, a new day and its dances are still on the horizon.

The chorus' dance of time resumes the preoccupation with number and counting that we observe in vv. 6 and 15, where Horace's ten hard-hearted *lustra* are measured against the 'one hundred talents' of the *puer* Maximus. The contrast between the two men comes back into view in the three lines immediately following the choral flourish of vv. 25–28, where the temporal adverb *iam* marks the return from the *tempestiuius* of Paullus' lusty youth (9) to the 'now' of the poet's sedentary old age (*iam*, 7). This *iam* marks the death in Horace of sexual pleasure and desire as contemporaneous with the beginning of the cycle of dances for Venus in Paullus' house. Each of the erotic activities which Horace swears off here —

---

95 A musical jingle can be heard in the playful repetition of the two short syllables *-be-re-* in vv. 22–23 (*Berecyntia* | *delectabere tibia*), which also forms a kind of 'rhyme' with v. 11 (*comissabere Maximi*).
96 Varro *L.L.* 5.85.
97 At 1.36.12 the phrase *morem in Salium* describes unrestrained festive dancing, while in 1.37.1–4 'Salian banquets' (*Saliaribus* [...] *dapibus*) are attended by similarly lively foot-thumping (*nunc pede libero* | *pulsanda tellus*, 1–2). Foster 2015 discusses the ties of the choral performance to Greek and Roman song and dance traditions, arguing that Horace effects an innovative blend of the Roman Salian hymn with the Greek paean, building on his appropriation of the paean genre in the *Carmen Saeculare*. I would expand the genealogy of Paullus' chorus to encompass the hymeneal assembly of Cat. 62 and Tibullus' erotic vision of the Elysian fields at 1.3.59–64.

uniting his heart with another's (30), engaging in drinking contests (31), fastening a garland on his temples (32) — involves a form of joining or linking which simulates both sexual union and the supreme togetherness of chorality.[98] Horace is disqualified from this choral congress not only because he is *durum* ('hardened') but because he is *iam durum*: *now*-hardened, congealed into a temporal inertia which makes him perennially out of step with the dance of youthful promiscuity (and which makes his *tempora* ill-suited for garlands).

Anathema to this state of *duritia* is the 'wishful longing for a kindred spirit (*spes animi credula mutui*, 30)' that attends erotic desire, hopelessly oriented toward the other rather than the self; the lover deludes himself into trusting in fantasy rather than fact — i.e. the future rather than the present[99] — and only attains his desire at the expense of lending out his psyche to be shared with another (the etymological sense of *mutuus*).[100] Horace's *duritia* is thus both the inertia which shackles him to the irreversible 'now' of old age and a protective membrane which shields his singular selfhood from merging with others.[101] The assertion 'I am not as I was under kind Cinara's reign (3–4)' expresses this ethic of stable self-identity with powerful concision. Being ruled by love made him a different person, the kind of person who could be ruled by love. But he is not that person any more, cannot be. The finality of the transition into old age precludes any backsliding. The temporal span of life sets natural limits on the self's capacity for qualitative change. Love is just a phase; it has no power to move, affect, or transform once its time is up. And yet...

>   sed cur heu, Ligurine, cur
> manat rara meas lacrima per genas?
>   cur facunda parum decoro   35
> inter uerba cadit lingua silentio?
>   nocturnis ego somniis
> iam captum teneo, iam uolucrem sequor
>   te per gramina Martii
> Campi, te per aquas, dure, uolubilis.   40

---

98 Oliensis also sees in the garland an 'emblem of the closed circle of ring-composition', and hence a symbol of the closure which will be unceremoniously breached in vv. 33–40 (Oliensis 1998: 119).
99 For the thought, cf. the third Glycera ode, *c*. 1.33, as well as 4.11.21–36 (*auaras | spes*, 25–26).
100 Cf. Callimachus *Ep*. 42, with Hor. *cc*. 1.3.8 (*animae dimidium meae*) and 2.17.5 (*te meae* [...] *partem animae*), both referring to *amici* rather than lovers.
101 The idea of love as a threat to the stability of identity is explored further in *c*. 4.13.13–22, where Lyce's transformation into an old woman, unrecognisable as the young woman who once ensnared Horace, strips her of her power to sabotage Horace's own sense of selfhood.

> But why, ah, Ligurinus, why does the odd tear course along my cheeks? Why does my articulate tongue falter between words in a silence that breaks decorum? At night in my dreams, now I hold you clasped tight, now I chase you, flying over the grass of the field of Mars, flying, cruel boy, through rolling waters.

This is an apostrophe in the strongest sense of the term (lit. 'turning away'); the surprise appearance of Ligurinus as interlocutor not only disrupts the thread of the discourse but also suddenly throws into question everything that has come before.[102] The two questions in vv. 33–36, borrowing as they do from the so-called 'symptoms of love' motif of Sappho fr. 31 and Catullus 51 (already adapted by Horace in *c.* 1.13.1–12), have an obvious answer: because, despite all he has said, he is in fact still touched by desire.[103] But when the tongues of Sappho and Catullus went limp, they at least knew the cause, namely, the sight of their beloved with someone else. Similarly, the chemical reaction Horace experiences in *c.* 1.13.1–12 is in response to his Lydia's fawning over one Telephus. In *c.* 4.1.33–36, by contrast, Horace claims not to know what makes his eyes water and his tongue fail. There is therefore no logical connexion between the vocative *Ligurine* and the questions asked unless we supply the all-too-obvious subtext, which is then made explicit in the following four lines. This is an ironic apostrophe: the uttering of Ligurinus' name supplies the reader with information about Horace which he himself claims not to have.[104]

This involves an interesting variation on *c.* 1.13.5–7, in which a jealous Horace complains that 'moisture drips surreptitiously onto my cheeks, proving how deeply I am tormented by slow-burning flames (*umor* [...] *in genas | furtim labitur, arguens | quam lentis penitus macerer ignibus*).' That passage plays on the idea

---

[102] Walsh 1990 discusses some similar instances in Greek poetry. Thomas sees continuity in discontinuity, noting that 'the frames (1–8, 33–40) could serve as self-standing epigrams of eight lines each (Thomas 2011: 87).'

[103] Thomas follows Bradshaw in arguing that Ligurinus is a memory from Horace's past rather than a current love-interest (Thomas 2011: *ad* 33–40; Bradshaw 1970: 153), but their rationale is unconvincing. They remark that running and swimming are more appropriate for a young man, but dreams are not reality, and in any case Horace's inadequacy is precisely the point. Furthermore, Bradshaw's comment that Roman men were expected to 'outgrow' homosexuality at a certain age (not mentioned by Thomas) reflects an attitude that most of us have hopefully outgrown ourselves. Finally, if we understand the tears of vv. 33–36 as occasioned only by the memory of lost youth and not by a previously unacknowledged passion, as Thomas and Bradshaw argue, then the repeated *cur* is all but pointless, since the question has already been answered. Putnam's observation that 'Ligurinus is very much the speaker-poet's former self (Putnam 1986: 45)' is still valid if Ligurinus is also an object of sexual desire.

[104] The vocative *Ligurine* (33) at the beginning of the period is balanced by the vocative *dure* (40) at its end, which sustains the mode of apostrophe throughout the passage.

that the symptoms of love can be diagnosed by others, which marks a significant departure from Sappho and Catullus. In the Sapphic model, the symptoms of love culminate in a deathlike obliteration of the senses (τεθνάκην δ' ὀλίγω 'πιδεύης | φαίνομ' ἔμ' αὔτᾳ, Sappho 31.15–16; *misero quod omnis | eripit sensus mihi*, Cat. 51.5–6). In Horace, on the other hand, the emphasis is on the symptoms of love as intelligible signs which communicate information about their sufferer against his will.[105] Whereas lovesickness robs Sappho and Catullus of both their senses and their powers of expression, Horace shifts into a state of hypercommunicativity.[106] The present poem (which incidentally shares its metre with *c.* 1.13) combines these two conceits into a new whole: with the thought of Ligurinus, Horace's tears become more eloquent (*facunda*, 35) than his tongue.

For Oliensis, this passage is a masterpiece of poetic artifice: 'In a beautifully scripted outbreak of spontaneous desire, Horace simulates the tones of an authentic lyric voice'.[107] She says 'scripted' and 'simulates' in order to stress the point that the power of this passage does not derive from any insights it might afford us into the true, inner self of the poet behind the textual veneer, but rather from its ability to fool us into thinking that lyric poetry can in fact do such things. I think we can cover more ground by simply throwing out the problematic concept of an 'authentic lyric voice' along with the concomitant notion of the poet's inner self instead of trying to co-opt it as Oliensis does. If we allow that the final two stanzas of the poem may contain nothing more or less 'authentic' — or mock-authentic — than anything else in Horace, then there is nothing to be fooled by and no curtain to peek behind.[108] On this reading, there is no 'outbreak of spontaneous desire', scripted or otherwise, because there is no textual 'inside' for desire to break out of.

The relevant matrix of inside-outside relations is provided instead by Horace's *body*, as we can already see in *c.* 1.13.5–7, where moisture glistening on the surface of the skin attests outwardly to the passions that burn on the inside.[109] External perspiration and internal 'boiling' are placed in a signifying relation, but

---

105 Nisbet and Hubbard 1970: 169; on the 'symptoms of love' motif in Hellenistic poetry, see Fantuzzi and Hunter 2004: 338–41.
106 See also *Ep.* 11.7–10, where Horace is betrayed as a lover not only by his sighs and sluggish demeanour, but by his silence (*silentium*, 9). Close intertexts are Call. *Ep.* 44 Pf. = *AP* 12.134 and *AP* 12.135 Asclepiades. See further Fedeli and Ciccarelli 2008: 110–11.
107 Oliensis 1998: 120.
108 See Freudenburg 2010 on the limitations of the concept of Horatian 'personae'.
109 We are afforded a glimpse of Paullus' 'insides' in vv. 9–12 in contrast to Horace's own: an attractive liver (the seat of the passions) housed by a noble domicile ('into' which Venus will come).

not such that the one becomes a symbol or substitute for the other: both are equally part of the same body, even the same bodily process. Likewise, the events that transpire in *c.* 4.1.33–37 — the leaking of suppressed tears, the stammering of the tongue, the involuntary gasp of *heu Ligurine* — are all bodily performances, each of which is readily perceptible to an external audience through the medium of the voice. Moreover, these performances need not be referred to anything 'beyond', 'beneath', or 'behind' the text if we remember that the reader, unlike Horace, is always *there* in body to supply the experiential gap between poem and living voice.[110]

The process is helped along by the sonic effects of the verse. The rapid monosyllables of v. 33 make audible the distracted 'fall' of the voice between words described in vv. 35–36.[111] V. 34 stands agape with the sustained *a-a-a* of mourning (*manat rara meas lacrima per genas*). Liquid consonants form a sympathetic bond between *Ligurine, lacrima*, and *lingua*.[112] Finally, the synaphea of v. 35, where the hypermetric *-o* of *decoro* oversteps its bounds to collide with the *i-* of *inter* in v. 36, produces what Bradshaw hears as an 'audible sob'.[113] The reader who sounds out the *-o* performs the break in decorum to which the word refers, only to be promptly 'corrected' by the next line's initial vowel. Whether we scan the line aloud or silently, we are forced to attend to our own activity of dwelling on syllables or cutting them short, foregrounding in our act of reading the presence of the same ebb and flow of sound and interruptive silence thematised in the poem. The danger of falling into the spaces between words (*inter uerba cadit lingua*, 37) to which erotic desire exposes Horace impinges no less on the reader in her efforts to string together his lines into ordered verse.[114]

The apostrophe performed in v. 33, then, is not only a 'turning away' from Venus to Ligurinus, but also an introspective turning from the external and exteriorising powers of speech (casting the goddess out, finding her a new place to dwell apart from the space of the poem) to the internal workings of the voice and the bodily processes that threaten to interfere with the functioning of the vocal

---

110 Stewart 1990 makes a powerful case from a post-structuralist standpoint for the immanence of voice in literary texts.
111 Thomas 2011: *ad loc.*; Fedeli and Ciccarelli 2008: 109.
112 Oliensis 1998: 121 n. 42.
113 Bradshaw 1970: 153.
114 Quint. Inst. 1.8.1 provides a good outline of the physically demanding task of reading (superest lectio, in qua puer ut sciat ubi suspendere spiritum debeat, quo loco uersum distinguere, ubi claudatur sensus, unde incipiat, quando attollenda uel summittenda sit uox, quid quoque flexu, quid lentius celerius concitatius lenius dicendum, demonstrari nisi in opere ipso non potest).

organs. The voice as physical emanation outpaces and overflows the faculty of ordered speech (*facunditas*). We do not have to entertain the notion of an 'authentic lyric voice' to appreciate this, because what happens to the voice in this passage does not happen only to Horace, the subject of a particular erotic experience, but also to the reader as she produces (out loud or silently) the sound of the text. If the repeated *cur* of vv. 33–35 is Horace listening to the sound of the idiosyncratic stammer in his own individual voice, the elided *-o* of *decoro* is the juncture at which the idiosyncracies of Horace's individual voice meet the embodied act of vocal production which is the present occasion of reading. Whereas in *c.* 1.13.5–7 it was perspiration that attested to the inner feeling of jealousy, here it is the emotionally-tinged sound of a voice broken by intermittent sobs — *rara* can denote frequency as well as density — that exposes the hidden meaning of the non-sequiturial utterance *Ligurine*. By making the sound of that voice with the elided *-o* of *decoro*, the reader reproduces the vocal evidence for Horace's passion anew.

What is discovered in vv. 33–40 is therefore not so much the continuity of sexual desire as the affectivity of the voice.[115] In vv. 4–9, Horace attempts to dissociate his newly 'hardened' (*iam durum*) self from the *mollitia* ('softness', 'wantonness') of Venus' commands (*imperiis*) and the *blanditia* ('coaxingness', 'caressingness') of young lovers' prayers (*preces*). *Mollitia* and *blanditia* are affects of the voice which belong to lovers, not to the aging Horace. This negative characterisation of erotic speech throws into relief the character of Horace's own speech act, which is profiled by the epizeuxis in v. 2 as an urgent prayer: *parce precor, precor*. The coda of the poem brings our focus back from the content of the prayer to the act of uttering it, allowing us to retrospectively read that initial *precor* as a stutter, an affective disturbance in the voice. But the doubling of the word for 'pray' also recalls Sappho's expansion of the time for prayer to Aphrodite into an unending litany. Repeating the word that gives voice to erotic desire prophesies the inevitable recurrence of that desire on future occasions.

The final quatrain in which Horace relives his recurring dream of Ligurinus bears this out. V. 38 employs an emphatic mid-verse sense-break, the only one of its kind in the poem besides v. 2:

---

115 This interpretation fits well with an etymology of the name Ligurinus from λιγυρός: the 'clear-voiced one' demands Horace's undivided attention and drains the powers of his own voice. Cf. Putnam 1986: 43–47, who links Ligurinus to the Ligurian Cupavo, son of Cycnus (the swan), in Verg. *Aen.* 10.185–93. Thomas 2011: *ad* 33–34 prefers a derviation from *ligurrire*, appropriate for someone associated with *conuiuia*.

> rursus bella moues? || parce precor, precor
> iam captum teneo, || iam uolucrem sequor

In both cases, the syntactical fracture of the line coincides with verbal gemination (*precor, precor*; *iam, iam*). Verbal repetition denotes urgency because it implies failure. The continuous cycle of capture and pursuit in Horace's dreams (and perhaps the dreams themselves) would come to an end if either of these dream-acts were decisive. The fumbling after Ligurinus in the dream mirrors the 'falling' of the tongue in v. 36 (*cadit*), and the boy's mercurial motility, allowing him to soar over open fields and glide through whirling eddies, corresponds to the eloquent 'flow' of effective speech[116] which Horace's tongue fails to keep up with.[117] The verbal repetitions and hard stops of vv. 2 and 38, together with the anaphora of vv. 39–40 (**te per** gramina Martii | Campi, **te per** aquas, dure, uolubilis), work to break up the prosodic flow of the verse, signalling the breakdown of linguistic composure and the failure of speech to encompass its objects.[118]

The double *iam* in v. 38, meanwhile, answers directly to the singular *iam* of Horace's hardened old age in vv. 7 and 30. In waking, Horace can define himself by the irreversible 'now' of the stage of life he inhabits; in dreaming, he sees himself split between two irreconcilable presents which open onto one another in an infinite loop. The two events of capture and pursuit are not causally related. There is no mention of Ligurinus slipping from Horace's grasp only to be caught again. The two 'nows' are rather two separate dream-scenes which the dreaming Horace experiences in alternating sequence. In the waking world, these two scenes might correspond to periods in Horace's love life like the one referred to in vv. 3–4, 'kind Cinara's reign': once Horace possessed Ligurinus, then he lost him, and may have continued to pursue him for a while. But real-world causality has no place in the dream world; here, there are no events of possession and loss,

---

116 The metaphor of the 'flow' of words is of central importance for the next poem in the book (4.2.5–8, picked up in Quint. *Inst.* 10.1.61, discussed below, extolling Pindar's *eloquentiae flumen*); it is also present in the Greek word ῥυθμός (from ῥέω).
117 In v. 40, it is now Ligurinus rather than Horace who is *durus*; with the vocative *dure*, Horace reappropriates the *mollia imperia* with which Venus attempted to cajole him. See Hardie 1993: 131 on the interplay between mobility and immobility in Horace's relationships to Venus and Ligurinus.
118 The simile at Hom. *Il.* 22.199–201 on which this passage is based, likening Achilles' pursuit of Hector to an endless dream-chase, also makes heavy use of verbal repetition: ὡς δ' ἐν ὀνείρῳ οὐ δύναται φεύγοντα διώκειν· | οὔτ' ἄρ' ὃ τὸν δύναται ὑποφεύγειν οὔθ' ὃ διώκειν· | ὣς ὃ τὸν οὐ δύνατο μάρψαι ποσίν, οὐδ' ὃς ἀλύξαι.

only a vision of a self in possession which gives way to a vision of a self in loss.[119] The dream narrative obliterates the notion of identity over time. There is no singular self moving from past to future, only a succession of 'nows' which mould the self into a series of poses. In the dream world, Horace becomes plural.[120]

This dream of the dissolution of the self into a cycle of repetitions is itself tied to the cyclic recurrence of nighttime, as indicated by the otherwise redundant *nocturnis* (37). Since nightfall is an inevitability and sleep is a necessity, the dream of Ligurinus is as inescapable as the desire it reawakens. The daily compulsion to sleep, exposing the unconscious mind to unasked-for dreams, is therefore equivalent to the involuntary silences into which Horace's tongue falls at the thought of Ligurinus. Desire makes speech stutter with emotive silences and punctuates consciousness with nightmares of impotence.[121] The stutter and the dream both take the form of periodical interruptions to what would otherwise flow in a steady stream: the flow of eloquent speech and the flow of subjective time in the journey from birth to death.[122]

The first of these streams is set in motion at the beginning of the poem by the prayer, *parce precor, precor*; the second, by the identity statements that form part of that prayer, *non sum qualis eram* etc. and *circa lustra decem [...] iam durum imperiis*. The prayer is itself a gesture of resistance to the interruptive force of Venus, who has come to resume a thread of erotic experience which should already have been cut (*intermissa*).[123] But the final proof of the prayer's futility is not an abstract *omnia uincit amor*; rather, the delusion of old age as love's terminal boundary stone is shattered by the realisation that life is not so much a linear span as a network of rhythmic cycles. Horace may have passed the threshold of old age once and for all, but each day still ends in sleep and dreaming, another

---

119 'Ligurinus always enters and always eludes Horace's enclosing embrace (Oliensis 1998: 120).'
120 In c. 4.10, in which Horace returns to Ligurinus to warn him of the transience of youth, the tables are turned: this time it is the aging Ligurinus, seeing his changed appearance in a mirror, who is doomed to recognise the other in himself (*te speculo uideris alterum*, 6).
121 Cf. Cicero's theory that dreams are caused by the mind's desire for constant activity to offset the paralytic state of sleep (*Div*. 2.62.128, 139–40).
122 Dido's love for Aeneas also leads to halting and repetitive speech which breaks up the flow of everyday life: nunc media Aenean secum per moenia ducit | Sidoniasque ostentat opes urbemque paratam, | incipit effari mediaque in uoce resistit; | nunc eadem labente die conuiuia quaerit, | Iliacosque iterum demens audire labores | exposcit pendetque iterum narrantis ab ore (Verg. Aen. 4.74–89).
123 Northrop Frye writes that personal lyric poetry 'often takes off from something that blocks normal activity, something a poet has to write poetry about instead of carrying on with ordinary experience (Frye 1985: 32).' For Horace, poetry itself is the block.

occasion for the renewal of desire. The serenity of the face is disfigured by the sporadic rhythm of tears coursing along its surface. Broken by emotive stammers, speech takes on the enforced rhythmicity of verse.[124]

We are allowed to hear the sound of this rhythm before Horace hears it in his own tear-choked voice. We hear it in the twice-a-day, three-beat song-and-dance of the chorus in vv. 25–28. The chorus exemplifies a mode of being in step with the rhythms of life from which Horace mistakenly disqualifies himself. He cannot join the chorus, he protests, because his age determines his identity, and his life no longer has the rhythm of a dance. The stutter and the dream which return to overwhelm him in vv. 33–40 are relics of that youthful rhythm which persists in him despite himself.[125] The dream is coordinated with nightfall (*nocturnis*, 37) just as the choral assembly is coordinated with the daily round (*die*, 25), and in the nightly spectre of the dream, Horace undergoes a doubling of the self in desire which approximates the collectivity of the chorus.[126]

We have seen how Venus and Paullus Maximus embody this property of collectivity through their shared association with number and plurality and with the capacity to multiply and extend oneself through procreation.[127] Horace on the other hand presents himself as a monad, a self-contained unit impervious to change and resistant to extension in both time and space. The opening petition to Venus is a bid for a perfect self-sufficiency; in a radical reversal of the Sapphic model, Horace prays that this may be his last prayer to the goddess, the final speech of unfulfilled desire to pass his lips. But the stutter and the dream betray the presence of desire even in this wish for the annihilation of desire, intimating that this prayer cannot be the end of all such prayers: it must itself be repeated. Horace's prayer to be spared Venus' attentions is no less futile than his endless pursuit of Ligurinus; both acts continually reproduce the longing they attempt to assuage, reconstituting the desiring subject in a new form on each successive occasion. What starts as an ἀποπομπή to the goddess ends, ironically, as a hymn to

---

124 '[It] is desire that creates the abrupt stops and starts that distinguish poetry from prose and lyric from more expansive verse-forms such as the hexameter (Oliensis 1998: 121)'. Cf. Habinek 1985: 414.

125 Cf. the Ciceronian theory that dreams originate 'from the remnants, as Aristotle says, left behind from things which one has done or thought while awake (*ex reliquiis, ut ait Aristoteles, inhaerentibus earum rerum quas uigilans gesserit aut cogitauerit, Div. 2.62.128*).'

126 Note how (as pointed out by Habinek 1985: 415) the musical performance of 22–24 (*lyraque et Berecyntia | delectabere tibia | mixtis carminibus non sine fistula*) is echoed by 4.15.30 (*Lydis remixto carmine tibiis*).

127 As we learn in v. 14 (*pro sollicitis non tacitus reis*), Paullus also possesses the fluency of speech which escapes Horace (Habinek 1985: 413).

her power, and Horace adds his newly deindividuated voice to the chorus' song of praise (*numen* [...] *tuum* | *laudantes*, 25–26). The failure of the voice in vv. 33–36 is thus also the failure of the *individual* voice, the subsumption of the singular subject of voicing into the collective voice-body of the chorus.

4.5 *c.* 4.5: Return and recognition

The second and fifth poems of book 4 both revolve around a single occasion, the anticipated return of Augustus from Gaul which would fall on 4 July, 13 BCE.[128] In both poems, this occasion is marked out by ritual as a momentous event in the public life of the SPQR: at 4.5.3–4, Horace represents the *princeps* as having formally promised a timely homecoming to the Senate, while at 4.2.41–60, he speaks of a period of festival during which the Roman people will pay vows made in both public and private capacities for Augustus' safe return. In the remaining sections of this chapter, I would like to consider the way in which Horace in these two poems gives voice to this event and to the relation between Augustus and the Roman citizen body which subtends it. This act of voicing comes about through a formal idiosyncracy which sets these two odes apart from all the rest: they each use quoted speech to represent an instance of collective worship in which Horace himself is implicated (4.2.45–52, 4.5.37–40). I will address these poems in reverse order, turning to 4.5 first and concluding the chapter with the longer and more difficult 4.2.

> Diuis orte bonis, optime Romulae
> custos gentis, abes iam nimium diu;
> maturum reditum pollicitus partum
>   sancto concilio, redi.
> lucem redde tuae, dux bone, patriae;   5
> instar ueris enim uultus ubi tuus
> adfulsit populo, gratior it dies
>   et soles melius nitent.
> ut mater iuuenem, quem Notus inuido
> flatu Carpathii trans maris aequora   10
> cunctantem spatio longius annuo
>   dulci distinet a domo,
> uotis ominibusque et precibus uocat
> curuo nec faciem litore dimouet,
> sic desideriis icta fidelibus   15
>   quaerit patria Caesarem.

---

[128] See Du Quesnay 1995, Hardie 2015 and Harrison 1995: 115–17.

tutus bos etenim rura perambulat,
nutrit rura Ceres almaque Faustitas,
pacatum uolitant per mare nauitae,
    culpari metuit fides,   20
nullis polluitur casta domus stupris,
mos et lex maculosum edomuit nefas,
laudantur simili prole puerperae,
    culpam poena premit comes.
quis Parthum paueat, quis gelidum Scythen,   25
quis Germania quos horrida parturit
fetus incolumi Caesare? quis ferae
    bellum curet Hiberiae?
condit quisque diem collibus in suis
et uitem uiduas ducit ad arbores;   30
hinc ad uina redit laetus et alteris
    te mensis adhibet deum;
te multa prece, te prosequitur mero
defuso pateris et Laribus tuum
miscet numen, uti Graecia Castoris   35
    et magni memor Herculis.
'longas o utinam, dux bone, ferias
praestes Hesperiae!' dicimus integro
sicci mane die, dicimus uuidi,
    cum sol Oceano subest.   40

Progeny of kindly gods, most excellent guardian of Romulus' tribe, you are too long absent now: since you promised a timely return to the sacred assembly of elders, return. Restore light to your country, dear leader; for once your face has come to shine on the people with the look of spring, the day's passing is happier and the sun's glow is kinder.

    As a mother whose son is kept away from sweet home, detained by the south wind's jealous blowing across the vast Carpathian sea longer than the space of a year, calls to him with vows and prayers and words of omen, never turning her face away from the crescent shore, so our country looks for Caesar, smitten with faithful longing. For indeed the ox roams the fields in safety; the fields are nourished by Ceres and bountiful Prosperity; sailors glide over the placid sea; faith dreads reproach; no scandals besmirch the virtuous household; good conduct and the law have subdued foul sin; new mothers are dignified by like offspring; punishment keeps close company with crime.

    The Parthian, the frozen Scythian, the spawn that rugged Germany brings forth — who would fear these while Caesar is alive and well? Who would concern himself with the war in wild Iberia? Each man brings the day to a close in his own hills and marries the vine-stalk to uncoupled trees; from here he comes home happily to a drink of wine and receives you as a god at the second table-setting; he showers you with much prayer, showers you with libations of unmixed wine, coupling your godhead with his household gods, as Greece does in memory of Castor and mighty Hercules. 'Dear leader, would that you might bring long holidays to Hesperia!': this we say in early sobriety when the day is full; this we say in drink when the sun is beneath the Ocean.

Each of the choral moments in these two poems involves a layered and dynamic movement between individual and collective utterances. In 4.2.33–52, Horace imagines himself in the midst of a public celebration for Augustus' triumphant return, where Octavian's nephew Iullus Antonius leads a song of praise. Between stanzas 9 and 13, both the song and Horace's presentation of it in the poem weave through three different voicings: first Antonius' song is paraphrased through a catalogue of its subjects, introduced by the repeated *concines* at the head of stanzas 9 and 11 (33–44), then Horace in stanza 12 presents his own individual contribution in quoted speech, introduced by *canam* (47), and finally in stanza 13 Horace is now part of the 'we' of the crowd as they chant (*dicemus*, 50) the triumphal cry *io Triumphe*, which is repeated in the text just as the imagined crowd will repeat it in the procession (49–50).

The final four stanzas of 4.5 (vv. 25–40) likewise move almost imperceptibly from the individual to the collective in a sweeping view of the Roman populace under Augustus' rule. What begins as an indefinite, rhetorical 'who?' (*quis*, 25) morphs into a generalising 'each one' (*quisque*, 29) as we follow a typical farmer home after a long day, but no sooner is the mealtime prayer to Augustus uttered than this singular representative figure coalesces into an all-encompassing 'we', and Horace inserts himself into the enunciative space of the prayer by quoting it in direct speech (37–38). At v. 37, the quoted prayer repeats the same honorific address paid to Augustus in v. 5 (*dux bone*), forming a ring-composition and uniting Horace's own opening request to the collective petition of the whole Roman people.

What is the use of this redundant re-petition? The second time *dux bone* appears, the message it delivers is practically unchanged from the first. The repetition of the greeting signals a new occasion of address rather than a change in content. In fact, the structure of the entire poem reveals itself on reflection to be circular. The tranquil atmosphere of the final prayer for Augustus' return is adduced as an example of the peace Rome enjoys under his rule, which in turn is the cause for the 'faithful longing (*desideriis* [...] *fidelibus*, 15)' felt by the people for Augustus, which is only mentioned in the first place as the reason why Augustus should make a speedy return. The '*dux bone*' prayer rebounds on itself, miming the return which it repeatedly requests and circling us back to the beginning of the poem.

We have already discussed the effects of distributing verbatim repetitions among various quotational frames in the section on Bion's *Adonis* in chapter 2. It was argued there that quotation works on repetition like an amplifier, allowing it to approach the condition of echo. One possible explanation for this effect is that quotation is already a mode of repetition, and overtly marked as such. A quotation combines two (or more) separate instances of an identical utterance into a single occasion of speech. When one speaker quotes the words of another speaker, those words are extended over time and space and the two speakers are brought into a kind of identity with one another by way of mimesis. In the case of self-quotation, both utterance and speaker are *a priori* identical, and repetition takes its most basic form: we become aware of the power of the same person saying the same thing in different situations, and thereby of the power of repetition in itself.

The quotation of *c.* 4.5.37–40 both is and is not a self-quotation. The subject of the repeated *dicimus* [...] *dicimus* includes Horace by definition, but the quotational frame is a marker of difference, gesturing toward a point of origin outside the space of its enunciation. The device of quotation thus allows us to experience Horace's passage from the singular (the speaker of the word *dicimus*) to the plural (the collective subject of the quoted prayer) as a shift in subjectivity, an assimilation of the other into the same. This transition comes about by a gradual process which begins in stanza 8 (vv. 29–32). Here, we are introduced to the everyman figure of the farmer whose evening meal incorporates the worship of Augustus. The first sentence of the passage (29–30) initially appears to follow the pattern of stanzas 5–6, a series of general statements about the tranquility of the *patria*, but in v. 31, the deictic pronoun *hinc* draws a narrative thread from one scene to another and establishes this everyman as our focalisor-character. Focalisation fosters a sense of involvement in the narrated action, and this involvement is intensified in vv. 31–36, when Horace narrates the worship paid to Augustus by our farmer, employing the second-person pronoun (*te* [...] *te* [...] *te* [...] *tuum*, 32–34) as though he were himself a participant in the prayerful offerings which he narrates.

Horace's interweaving of second-person address and third-person narration here constitutes an act of imaginative identification which informs the logic of the poem on a fundamental level. By addressing Augustus in the act of narrating a prayer which addresses Augustus, Horace identifies himself with the speaker of the prayer and places himself and his reader within the scene, but the speaker with whom Horace asks us to identify is himself merely a representative proxy, and the scene of his dinnertime prayer is not a particular event but an abstraction derived from a generalisation about the typical behaviour of typical members of a populace. The prayer therefore inhabits a time-space which is not actual but virtual, formed by the collapse of separate but analogous items into a notional unity. With the repeated *te* and *tuum* of vv. 32–34, Horace gives voice to this virtual event of prayer through the medium of the poem, producing thereby the fantasy of collectivity that is the choral voice.

When our farmer 'brings the day to a close in his own hills' in v. 29, he has not yet joined this new collectivity. The pronoun *quisque*, as opposed to other collective pronouns such as *omnis* or *totus*, preserves the individuality of each member within the set to which it refers, and the mention of private property in the same line (*collibus in suis*) furthers the sense of each *quisque* as a separate entity. The mode of identification which *quisque* signals is thus one predicated on analogy rather than partitivity. The table, the wine, the libation-bowls, and the household gods which form the *mise-en-scène* of the prayer, as well as the prayer itself, are all the belongings of that particular household and the private possessions of that particular individual. No one of these scenes of domestic worship is identifiable with any other except insofar as they are mutually interchangeable on the basis of their similarities. In the final stanza, by contrast, the first person plural of *dicimus* signals a mode of identification which goes beyond mere analogy: in the act of prayer to Augustus, the people of Rome are as one.

This shift in subjectivity is mirrored by the shift in the temporal frame of reference that occurs in the transition from stanza 9 to stanza 10. The *mise-en-scène* of v. 29 ('Each man brings the day to a close in his own hills') places us at a particular time of day, with the idea of habitual activity and recurrence present but backgrounded. The repeated *te* of vv. 31–36 lends a sense of internal time to the ritual, ordering it into a sequence of words and gestures. In stanza 10, by contrast, the sun replaces the day as the yardstick of time, and we zoom out from the internal time of the ritual to the calendrical reckoning in which it figures. The repeated word this time is not *te* but *dicimus*, signalling the repetition of speech acts as opposed to the repetitions within speech.

In vv. 39–40, we hear that, while the prayer itself remains the same, its performers cycle through two diametrically opposed bodily states, 'dryness' or sobriety (*sicci*, 39) and 'wetness' or inebriation (*uuidi*, 39), corresponding respectively to morning and evening. The dichotomy 'dry' and 'wet' thus recognises difference at the corporeal level between individual performances of the prayer and thereby foregrounds the possibility of differentiating its individual performers from one another. By the same token, however, the cycle of 'dry' and 'wet' mirrors the movement of the sun, emerging to parch the earth with its heat by day and submerging itself in the ocean at night, as described in v. 40. Here, the word for sun (*sol*) is in the singular, whereas in v. 8 above it appears in the plural (*soles melius nitent*). Unlike *soles*, which come and go with each passing day, the singular *sol* survives the passage of time intact (cf. *integro* [...] *die*, 39), moving along its course while remaining itself.[129]

The formulaic expression *dicimus sicci, dicimus uuidi* represents the performance of the prayer as a symbolic enactment of this property of identity-within-difference transferred from the sun to the Roman people. The prayer represents a strand of continuity within the mutability and contingency of the mortal lifespan. Dry turns to wet and wet to dry, but the prayer remains the same, not only the same on each occasion of prayer but also the same for each individual. The prayer, then, serves as a means by which the individual farmer-citizen, returning to his private life at the end of the day, may performatively *recognise* himself as part of a larger whole, part of a continuum of prayers, workdays, mealtimes, properties and property holders, sunrises and sunsets.

The theme of recognition makes an appearance in v. 23, where Horace lists it as one of the tokens of Rome's prosperity under Augustus that 'new mothers are praised for like offspring (*laudantur simili prole puerperae*).' The line alludes to Augustus' policies relating to sexual morality and illustrates the ideal of the *casta domus* mentioned in v. 21. The adjective *simili* is a remarkably concise means of invoking the moment of the newborn's presentation to the outside world, when the recognition of the father's likeness in its features confirms the child as legitimate. This miniature drama of the infant's arrival and acceptance into the family echoes the extended simile in stanzas 3–4 comparing Rome's longing for the absent Augustus to a mother's pining for her young son away on a military campaign.[130] Here Horace tells us that Rome misses the sight of Augustus' face (*uultus*, 6), which 'shines on the people with the look of spring (6–7),' just as a mother misses a son removed from 'sweet home (12),' and 'never turns her face away from the crescent shore (14)' in anticipation of his return.

The perfect tense of *affulsit* (7), which I have rendered 'has come to shine,' places the emphasis on the dramatic moment of Augustus' arrival before the *populus*, which encourages a conceptual link between the luminous quality attributed to his face in stanza 2 and the spectacle of his return. The sustained imagery of light and the comparison of Augustus to the sun in this passage can therefore be referred to a particular act of viewing, the viewing of Augustus by

---

129 Cf. 4.7.13–16, of the moon: 'But moons quickly recover their losses in the sky; once we fall down where Father Aeneas, where rich Tullus and Ancus fell, we are dust and shadow (*damna tamen celeres reparant caelestia lunae: | nos ubi decidimus | quo pater Aeneas, quo diues Tullus et Ancus, | puluis et umbra sumus*).'
130 For Augustus as *iuuenis*, cf. *c*. 1.2.41–44.

the people on his homecoming. By centring our viewpoint on the face, Horace picks out as the dramatic highlight of this act of viewing the moment of recognition, i.e. the moment at which the people witness the fact of Augustus' safe return for themselves by observing him in the flesh. The return for which Horace petitions in the opening stanza is thus more precisely the return of Augustus into visible presence.

Stanza 7 (vv. 25–28) makes explicit the power of this visible presence: as long as they can trust that Caesar is alive and well (*incolumi Caesare*, 27), Romans can put to rest the fear of external military threats. A homecoming spectacle would be an occasion for the Roman people to communally verify Caesar's *incolumitas* and thereby to ease collective anxieties about the continued wellbeing of the state.[131] The light which Augustus' hoped-for return will bring with it is thus a property of the event of the homecoming itself as much as it is of Augustus' person in isolation from the event.

This moment of recognition when Augustus' familiar face returns to brighten his homeland is directly paralleled, in v. 23, by the moment of recognition when a newborn is confirmed to bear a resemblance to the father, thereby ensuring the continuation of the *casta domus*. Just as Augustus passes through the dangers of war and returns home unscathed (*incolumis*, 27, connoting 'wholeness'), the likeness of a male parent, token of the paternal bloodline, 'returns' to the household when a legitimate child is born, 'unscathed' by adultery. The farmer of vv. 29–40 who returns home after a long day and recites the prayer to Augustus performs the same drama of recognition, recognising himself as part of a prayer's collective subject, the imagined community of the *patria*.

4.6 *c.* 4.2: Imitation and identification

What I hope to have shown thus far is that the collective voice-body appears in each of these poems in a way that wills Horace's identification with it, but also that Horace positions himself in relation to the chorus in different ways in each poem. In each case, the chorus manifests a powerful form of presence, but that presence is qualified differently in each of Horace's successive encounters with it. I would like to conclude with a look at *c.* 4.2, which treats the same occasion

---

131 The series of rhetorical questions in vv. 25–28 ('Who would fear...?'), although they belong in a more immediate sense to the argument of vv. 17–24 (viz., 'Rome is at peace'), can thus also be referred back to the overarching argument established in the first stanza (viz., 'Come back soon, Augustus'): his return will strengthen his people's resolve.

as *c.* 4.5 — the homecoming of Augustus in 13 BCE — with a focus on the grand collective triumph-song to be led by Iullus Antonius (nephew of Marcus Antonius). Horace contributes to this song by joining his voice to that of the crowd, chanting the refrain *io Triumphe* (49–50) and offering a small snatch of verse (*o sol pulcher, o laudande*, 46–47), which, as Fraenkel notes, approximates the *uersus quadratus* traditionally sung by the soldiers accompanying the triumphing general in the victory procession.[132]

This passage represents one of Horace's most concerted studies of the choral voice, but my focus in this concluding section of the chapter will be on what leads up to this final choral moment. The entire first half of the ode, up to v. 32, is taken up by a discourse on the hubris of attempting to rival Pindar in poetry. I will argue that Horace here draws a functional contrast between *aemulatio* and *imitatio*, or competitive and non-competitive imitation, which lends legitimacy to his choice to play the role of 'chorus member' to Antonius' triumph-song. This reading rests upon an analogy between the organisation of choral voices and the relations between rival poets: by singing along with Antonius' song rather than trying to upstage him, Horace becomes part of something larger than himself, just as the poet who imitates without envy joins himself to the company of his peers rather than usurping the place of another. This analogy is brought to the fore in another poem, *c.* 4.3.13–16, where Horace thanks the Roman people for placing him 'among the lovely choruses of the bards' (*inter amabilis | uatum [...] choros*, 14–15) and thereby freeing him from the sting of Envy (*iam dente minus mordeor inuido*, 16).

> Pindarum quisquis studet aemulari,
> Iulle, ceratis ope Daedalea
> nititur pinnis, uitreo daturus
>   nomina ponto.
> monte decurrens uelut amnis, imbres   5
> quem super notas aluere ripas,
> feruet immensusque ruit profundo
>   Pindarus ore,
> laurea donandus Apollinari,
> seu per audacis noua dithyrambos   10
> uerba deuoluit numerisque fertur
>   lege solutis,
> seu deos regesque canit, deorum
> sanguinem, per quos cecidere iusta
> morte Centauri, cecidit tremendae   15

---

[132] Fraenkel 1957: 439.

flamma Chimaerae,
siue quos Elea domum reducit
palma caelestis pugilemue equumue
dicit et centum potiore signis
    munere donat, 20
flebili sponsae iuuenemue raptum
plorat et uiris animumque moresque
aureos educit in astra nigroque
    inuidet Orco.
multa Dircaeum leuat aura cycnum, 25
tendit, Antoni, quotiens in altos
nubium tractus; ego apis Matinae
    more modoque
grata carpentis thyma per laborem
plurimum circa nemus uuidique 30
Tiburis ripas operosa paruus
    carmina fingo.
concines maiore poeta plectro
Caesarem, quandoque trahet ferocis
per sacrum cliuum merita decorus 35
    fronde Sygambros;
quo nihil maius meliusue terris
fata donauere bonique diui
nec dabunt, quamuis redeant in aurum
    tempora priscum. 40
concines laetosque dies et urbis
publicum ludum super impetrato
fortis Augusti reditu forumque
    litibus orbum.
tum meae, si quid loquar audiendum, 45
uocis accedet bona pars, et: 'o sol
pulcher, o laudande!' canam recepto
    Caesare felix;
tuque dum procedis,[133] io Triumphe!
non semel dicemus, io Triumphe! 50
ciuitas omnis, dabimusque diuis
    tura benignis.
te decem tauri totidemque uaccae,
me tener soluet uitulus, relicta
matre qui largis iuuenescit herbis 55
    in mea uota,
fronte curuatos imitatus ignis
tertium lunae referentis ortum,

---

133 See Thomas 2011: *ad loc.* on this reading and the textual difficulties of the passage.

qua notam duxit niueus uideri,
   cetera fuluus.   60

Whoever aspires to rival Pindar, Iullus, flies on waxen wings of Daedalean make, only to give up his name to the glassy sea. Like a river cascading from a mountaintop, fed by rain until it spills over its accustomed banks, Pindar seethes, flowing in immense streams from a fathomless mouth. He earns the prize of Apollo's laurel when he unravels novel words in bold dithyrambs, carried along by unruly measures; he earns it when he sings of gods and kings, the blood of the gods, at whose hands the Centaurs suffered their death sentence and the flame of the dread Chimaera fell; he earns it when he tells of a boxer or a racer conducted homeward by the celestial palm of Elis and awards him a prize greater than a hundred statues; he earns it when he mourns a young man who was snatched away from his weeping bride and lifts up to the stars his strength, his courage, and his golden character, scorning black Orcus.

A mighty wind carries the Dircaean swan aloft, Iullus, whenever he aims for the high course of the clouds. Slight as I am, I fashion my painstaking songs in the mode and manner of the Matine bee that toils in grove after grove and all along the riverbanks of well-watered Tibur picking sweet thyme-buds.[134] You, a poet of a grander plectrum, will hymn Caesar once he drags the fierce Sygambri up the sacred hill, decorated with a well-earned garland; none greater or better than him have the fates and the kind gods granted the earth, nor will again, even if time comes back around to the ancient gold. You will sing of merry days, of public rejoicing in the city over the prayed-for return of brave Augustus, and of the banishing of legal disputes from the Forum.

Then, if anything I say will be heard, the better part of my voice will join in, and 'O fair sun, O praiseworthy!' I will sing, joyful at Caesar's reception. And as you march in procession, we citizens will cry *io Triumphe!* all together, not just once — *io Triumphe!* — and offer frankincense to the generous gods. Ten bulls and as many heifers will fulfil your pledge; my debt will be paid with a tender calf which is growing ripe for my vow on rich pasturage apart from his mother, mimicking with his brow the fiery arc of the moon as it restores its third rising: though he is tawny all over, here you can see he has drawn a mark of snowy white.

Quintilian cites this poem as an authority for his assertion that Pindar is the 'foremost' (*princeps*) of the nine lyric poets, interpreting Horace as arguing that the Theban poet is 'imitable by none' (*nemini imitabilem*).[135] If we accept this interpretation, we must still ask ourselves what would be the point of Horace saying

---

134 For *plurimus* in the singular with countable nouns, cf. c. 1.7.8–9. Thomas 2011: *ad loc.* and Fedeli and Ciccarelli 2008: 152–54 take the adjective with *laborem*, Harrison 1995: 114 with *nemus*; but both sense and syntax are arranged in such a way as not to militate a decision in favour of one or the other. Whether we read 'much labour' or 'many a grove', the topic remains the large scope of the honeybee's task relative to its size. I have opted for the latter because it fits the English idiom of my translation somewhat better.
135 'Of the nine lyric poets, Pindar is the foremost by a long way, in inspiration, in sublimity, in aphorisms, in figures, in the bountiful wealth of his subjects and vocabulary and in the unique

this in a poem, and secondarily what would be the point of his saying it to Iullus Antonius, who, as we learn in vv. 33–52, has been chosen to celebrate Augustus' anticipated return from Gaul in triumphal song. This question is crucial for our understanding of the relationship between the two halves of the poem, the excursus on Pindar (1–32) and the comparison of Horace and Antonius as poets in the context of the anticipated performance (33–60). I will argue that the poem's central themes of emulation and imitation need to be understood in light of the fact that this anticipated performance will be 'choral' in nature, i.e., relying on the conjunction of many voices. I suggest that, in this poem, literary imitation is represented as a form of identification which is analogous to the identification with the collective that occurs in choral song.

Thomas, following Harrison, Fraenkel, and others, interprets the poem as a *recusatio* on the model of *cc*. 1.6 and 2.12: Horace turns down a request to compose a Pindaric victory ode for the occasion of Augustus' return and suggests that Antonius take up the task in his stead.[136] However, as Fedeli and Ciccarelli point out, no such request is ever mentioned in the poem.[137] The *recusatio* interpretation asks us to infer that the statements of vv. 1–32 ('no one can emulate Pindar') are a means of opting out of the enterprise of celebrating Augustus' return, insofar as this task represents a potential occasion for emulating Pindar. The difficulty is that nothing is said about a specific occasion for poetry until v. 33, when Horace finally gets around to the topic of the triumph-song for Caesar. The 'natural' assumption would be that this second topic is occasioned by the first, not the other way around.[138]

This interpretation also requires us to take *concines* (33) as a future of invitation, inviting Antonius to do what Horace himself cannot (like *scriberis* in 1.6.1 and *dices* in 2.12.10), but the fact that this supposed request for a triumph-poem

---

flow, as it were, of his eloquence. It is for these reasons that Horace rightly believes him imitable by none (*nouem uero lyricorum longe Pindarus princeps spiritu, magnificentia, sententiis, figuris, beatissima rerum uerborumque copia et uelut quodam eloquentiae flumine: propter quae Horatius eum merito nemini credit imitabilem*, Quint. *Inst.* 10.1.61).'

136 Hardie 2015 critiques the *recusatio* interpretation, and some of my own arguments are based on his, but his alternative — to turn the poem into a dramatic dialogue with vv. 33–52 in the mouth of Antonius — is extreme, and creates more problems than it solves.

137 Fedeli and Ciccarelli 2008: 119. In 1.6 and 2.12, by contrast, Horace explicitly refers to both his own potential lyric contribution and the preferable contribution of another writer on the same topic in a different genre.

138 So Ps.-Acro's commentary has it that the anticipated imitator of Pindar is Antonius rather than Horace, and vv. 33ff. are an alternative suggestion.

has not been mentioned until now makes this problematic.[139] The idea that *concines* is Horace's way of deflecting the request to Antonius is also hard to reconcile with the opening warning that *anyone* who strives to emulate Pindar is doomed to failure.[140] Harrison's solution to this dilemma is to propose that Antonius' version will be epic instead of lyric, and therefore not Pindarising,[141] but this is begging the question; if we are meant to be thinking specifically of epic at vv. 33–44, what reason do we have to suppose that the idea of a lyric triumph-song was ever in question in the first place?

It seems to me that we need a different explanation of what prompts the question of emulating Pindar and, consequently, of the relation between the two halves of the poem. The logical link between the two main topics is the epithet *maiore poeta plectro* ('poet of a grander plectrum,' 33), which contrasts Antonius as a poet with the 'slight' Horace (*paruus*, 31). The basis of the comparison, however, is not their relative fitness to fulfil a specific request for a specific kind of poem, but rather the character of their art in general. Antonius' position at the head of the triumph-song illustrates his 'grandness' just as the image of the Matine bee in 27–32 illustrates Horace's 'slightness'. The contrast between Horace and Antonius introduced in stanza 9 is thus parallel with the contrast between Horace and Pindar in the previous two stanzas. Antonius is compared to Horace, then, not in the first instance as a potential emulator of Pindar but rather as a superior model whom Horace cannot rival, like Pindar himself.

Important here is the distinction between *imitatio* and *aemulatio* as ways of following a literary model.[142] The difference is illustrated in the proem to book 3 of the *De rerum natura*, a dedicatory address to Lucretius' master Epicurus which exhibits many points of contact with our ode:

> te sequor, o Graiae gentis decus, inque tuis nunc
> ficta pedum pono pressis uestigia signis,
> non ita certandi cupidus quam propter amorem   5
> quod te imitari aueo; quid enim contendat hirundo
> cycnis, aut quidnam tremulis facere artubus haedi
> consimile in cursu possint et fortis equi uis?
> tu, pater, es rerum inuentor, tu patria nobis
> suppeditas praecepta, tuisque ex, inclute, chartis,   10

---

139 See Hardie 2015: 259, who argues that such a reading would require some additional marker of emphasis, such as *tu* (as in 2.12.9–10); cf. Thomas' paraphrase, which supplies the emphasis missing from the text: 'You'll be better at singing of Caesar (Thomas 2011: 103).'
140 Pasquali 1920: 780.
141 Harrison 1995: 118–22.
142 Thomas 2011: *ad loc.* glosses *aemulari* as 'a more combative term than *imitari*'.

> floriferis ut apes in saltibus omnia libant,
> omnia nos itidem depascimur aurea dicta,
> aurea, perpetua semper dignissima uita. (*DRN* 3.3–13)

> I follow you, O glory of the Greek race, and the prints that my feet make now I plant firmly in your footsteps, not so much out of a desire to compete as out of love, because I wish to imitate you; for how could a swallow contend with swans, or what could kids with their wobbly limbs do to match the vigorous gallop of a strong horse? You, father, are the discoverer of the world, you furnish me with fatherly instruction, and from your pages, O renowned one, just as bees in meadows teeming with blossoms drink of them all, I eat up all the golden sayings, golden and ever deserving of eternal life.

Footprints are an apt metaphor for the distinction Lucretius is drawing because they function as 'signs' (*signis*, 4) of two separate things: on the one hand they trace a path to a destination, while on the other hand they leave a recognisable mark, showing evidence that this particular person walked this way. Lucretius walks in Epicurus' footsteps not to obscure his marks and replace them with his own, but rather to use them as a guide on his own journey. The distinction is not between competition and imitation *per se*, but between two modes of 'following' an *exemplum* (*sequor*, 3), one which is content to 'merely' imitate and another which has the ulterior motive of overtaking and usurping.[143] Cicero makes a similar point when he defines *aemulatio* as a form of envy, noting that while the word can be used positively of the imitation of virtue (*imitatio uirtutis*), it places the emphasis on the desire implicit in acts of imitation to possess qualities belonging to others.[144]

Quintilian brings out another aspect of this distinction when he observes that one can never match a model by imitation alone, since imitation only reproduces, and the copy is by nature inferior to the model (*Inst.* 10.2.10–11). When, a little earlier in the same book (10.1.61), he cites *c.* 4.2.1–4 as saying that Pindar is *nemini imitabilem*, the implication is therefore that his talent is so transcendent that those who strive to follow in his footsteps fail to produce even pale imitations of the master. To attempt to go beyond mere imitation and pit oneself against

---

[143] Cf. Plin. *Epist.* 7.30.5, where the distinction is between *aemulari* on the one hand and *imitari et sequi* on the other (Thomas 2011: 105).
[144] Aemulatio autem dupliciter illa quidem dicitur, ut et in laude et in uitio nomen hoc sit; nam et imitatio uirtutis aemulatio dicitur — sed ea nihil hoc loco utimur; est enim laudis — et est aemulatio aegritudo, si eo, quod concupierit, alius potiatur, ipse careat (Cic. Tusc. 4.8.17).

Pindar as a rival is the height of hubris, and this is exactly what Horace is referring to when he speaks of *Pindarum quisquis studet aemulari*.¹⁴⁵ To imitate is to copy a likeness, to become 'another Pindar', whereas to emulate is to usurp an identity: the *next* Pindar. *Aemulatio* in this sense presupposes imitation, insofar as imitating a literary model traditionally implies a claim to a legacy,¹⁴⁶ but the point of our Lucretian passage is precisely that imitation can also be an end in itself in the case of a truly exemplary model.¹⁴⁷

Recognising a distinction between 'pure' or 'innocent' imitation and *aemulatio* can help provide new answers to the question posed by Pasquali which has guided scholarship on this poem ever since: 'Why does Horace Pindarise at the same moment that he advises against emulating Pindar?'¹⁴⁸ Pasquali and many others after him have noted that the synopsis of Pindaric poetry that fills vv. 5–24 is an occasion for Horace to do some Pindarising of his own, recasting both the content and the style of the Theban poet in his own recognisable idiom, all the while subtly highlighting points of continuity between the Pindaric corpus and his own past lyric output.¹⁴⁹ Harrison and Davis see this part of the poem as ironically undercutting the claims of the opening stanza and exposing them as false modesty,¹⁵⁰ but if we recognise that the topic of the stanza is not literary imitation *in toto* but *aemulatio* in particular, we can see something subtler at work here than bare self-contradiction.

4.7 The name of Icarus

The point is made by way of the myth of Daedalus and Icarus. This story already appears in Horace at *c*. 1.3.34–35 as an example of humankind's inveterate desire to overstep the bounds of nature: 'Daedalus experienced the open air on wings

---

145 The word *studet* already implies jealous striving. We may detect bilingual wordplay in the juxtaposition of *studet* and *aemulari*, both words which translate Greek ζηλόω.
146 For example, Ennius is dubbed an *alter Homerus* at *Epist*. 2.1.50, and Horace himself is styled 'Alcaeus' at *Epist*. 2.2.99. On exemplarity and identification see further Roller 2004.
147 Part of the difficulty is that *aemulari* can describe both the act of competing or entering into competition with someone (as in the English 'strive with', 'vie with') and the state of being in the position of competitor (as in the English verb 'rival'). Linguists would recognise these respectively as the *dynamic* and *stative* uses of the verb. On *imitatio* and *aemulatio*, and the related terms μίμησις and ζήλωσις, see further Russell 1979: 9–10.
148 'Come mai Orazio pindareggia proprio là dove sconsiglia dall'emulare Pindaro (Pasquali 1920: 782)?'
149 Harrison 1995: 110–15.
150 Harrison 1995: 115; Davis 1991: 134.

which do not belong to man (*expertus uacuum Daedalus aera | pennis non homini datis*).'¹⁵¹ This is in contrast with both the earlier version of the story in Hyginus' *Fabulae* and the two later renditions by Ovid, where Icarus causes his own death by flying too high (ignoring his father's instructions, as Ovid tells it):¹⁵² Horace places the blame fully on Daedalus for attempting to transpose onto humans the faculty of flight reserved for birds. While this moral is not stated overtly in *c.* 4.2.1–4, the future participle *daturus* (4) implies that falling is the inevitable outcome of flying 'on waxen wings of Daedalean make (2)', as though the failure of the artificial wings were a direct consequence of their artificiality.¹⁵³ Horace is not denying the feasibility of engineered flight *per se*; what is at issue here is rather the moral implications of usurping birds' natural place in the sky. However skilful his *imitation* of birds might be, Daedalus must nevertheless fail in the attempt to *become* bird, to transform the sky into a habitable environment.¹⁵⁴

The word for what Daedalus does with birds is *aemulatio* rather than mere *imitatio*, not only a replication but a theft of identity.¹⁵⁵ The theme of identity enters the scene with the word *nomina* in v. 4.¹⁵⁶ When Icarus' wings failed him, he gave his name to the Icarian Sea in which he drowned.¹⁵⁷ From Horace we learn that the poet who tries to match the sublime heights of the 'Dircaean swan' (25) likewise stakes his 'name' at the risk of being engulfed by the great name of Pindar. The conceit turns on the dual function of names and naming discussed in the

---

151 The mythological flights of Phaethon and Bellerophon are used to generate a similar moral at *c.* 4.9.25–31.
152 Hyg. *Fab.* 40; Ov. *A.A.* 2.19–98; *Met.* 8.183–235.
153 The idea of artifice is furthered by the striking description of the sea as 'glassy' (*uitreo*, 3), transforming it into a visually dazzling made object. Ovid introduces the theme of nature and artifice explicitly when he says that Daedalus' invention 'alters nature (*naturam [...] nouat*, *Met.* 8.189)' and aims to 'imitate real birds (*ut ueras imitetur auis*, 195).'
154 After all, while Daedalus may survive his own flight unscathed, he 'gives up his name' in another sense with the death of his only child. The imitation of birds succeeds, but the attempt to produce birdlike offspring fails.
155 For *aemulatio* as the appropriation of another's identity, see e.g. *Epist.* 1.19.12–16.
156 For the poetic plural, cf. 3.27.75–76 (of Europa lending her name to the eponymous continent). Thomas 2011: *ad loc.* provides numerous parallels where the plural *nomina* is used of the transference of a name from a person to a place. One shade of significance in the plural here is that it hints at the continued life of the name beyond the death of its original bearer. *Nomen* appears with thematic prevalence in *Odes* 4 also at 4.70–72, 6.30, 8.18–19, 9.46–47, and 15.13–14.
157 Ovid's two versions of the story (*A.A.* 2.19–98 and *Met.* 8.183–235) expand on the Horatian conceit of the sea robbing Icarus of both his life and his name with characteristic energy; see P. Hardie 2002: 246–47. The conceit also appears at *Tr.* 1.1.89–90 and 3.4a.21–24, on which see P. Hardie 2002: 294–96.

previous chapter. It was noted there that a name can be used both to mark identity and to measure reputation. In both cases, the act of naming serves to set the one named apart from the anonymous masses. The image of Icarus' name falling into the sea equates anonymity with the ultimate loss of self that comes in death.[158] The elemental opposite of this watery abyss is the sky, and in stanza 6 we see that Pindar's funeral laments can 'scorn black Orcus' by lifting up their subjects to the stars (*uiris animumque moresque | aureos educit in astra nigroque | inuidet Orco*, 22–24).[159] Icarus' dying gift of his *own* name is thus an ironic inversion of the encomiastic power of Pindar's poetry.

Pindaric praise, Horace tells us, has the power both to award its honorand with 'a prize greater than a hundred statues (*centum potiore signis | munere donat*, 19–20)' and to win the prize of the Apolline bay-wreath for the poet himself (*laurea donandus Apollinari*, 9). The emulator of Pindar thus competes with him on two fronts, as both *laudator* and *laudandus*. The awarding of a prize is like the use of a name: in nominating an individual as the winner, one sets that individual apart from the crowd, and thereafter the prizewinner has the victory 'to her name', as the expression goes. The anonymous multitude from which the victor is distinguished by Pindaric praise is signified obliquely by the 'one hundred statues (*centum signis*)' of v. 19, which replicate their subject's likeness in great number, but cannot match the singular power of the name.[160]

The reciprocality of the roles of *laudator* and *laudandus* likewise extends to the potency of their names. Pindar's power to manipulate names and naming is conceptually linked to his own name, that is, to his identity as the *lyricorum princeps*, in Quintilian's words, which is the equivalent of the *nomen poetae* which Horace claims to have received from Apollo at *c.* 4.6.30. The attempt to *become* Pindar through *aemulatio* is thus necessarily an attempt to reappropriate both

---

158 Cf. Pin. *O.* 1.82–84, with Kurke 2013: 26–27. The nameless masses of the dead make a memorable appearance in 4.9.13–28, where Horace acknowledges the countless precursors of figures made famous by Homeric epic who have vanished into oblivion.

159 The association of Pindaric praise with the sky and verticality is helped by *palma caelestis* (17), the repeated 'fall' of the enemies of the gods (*cecidere*, 14; *cecidit*, 15), and by the image of a cascading mountain stream which gains momentum from its altitude (5–8). Note also the contrast between the blackness of the underworld (*nigro*, 23) and the light of the stars, reflecting the 'golden character (*aureos* [...] *mores*, 22–23)' of the *laudandus*. The idea that poetic praise can lift one's name to the heavens is memorably expressed in Verg. *Ecl.* 9.27–29.

160 With this cf. Paullus Maximus from the previous poem, a man associated with both the number one hundred (*centum puer artium*, 4.1.15) and the production of commemorative scuplture to celebrate his victory over an *aemulus* (16–20).

Pindar's name and his power over names; but it is precisely the sense of inalienable self-identity conveyed by the use of Pindar's name in the text that proves the futility of the effort. Taking to the skies to rob Pindar of his name, the Icarus-poet ends up forfeiting his own, and this loss of *nomen* is iconised by the suppression of Icarus' name in the text, crowded out by the three names of Daedalus, Iullus Antonius, and, in emphatic initial position, Pindar himself (repeated at the end of the next stanza, v. 8).[161]

All this is to say that *aemulatio* is figured in this poem as an act of what we might call onomastic violence, that is, violence against the individuating power of the name. Horace shows us another side of the onomastic violence of *aemulatio* in *c*. 2.20, where Icarus also appears as a negative *exemplum*. Here Horace shows himself actually committing the Daedalean sin of transforming into a bird, boasting that he will rise above envy and escape even mortality by virtue of his poetic fame:

> non usitata nec tenui ferar
> penna biformis per liquidum aethera
>   uates, neque in terris morabor
>   longius, inuidiaque maior
> urbis relinquam. non ego pauperum   5
> sanguis parentum, non ego quem uocas,
>   dilecte Maecenas, obibo
>   nec Stygia cohibebor unda. (2.20.1–8)

On wings neither common nor feeble I will soar through the liquid air, a hybrid poet; I will linger on earth no more and leave the cities behind, greater than envy. I will not die, not I, the offspring of poor parents, not I whom you call upon, dear Maecenas, nor will I be mired in the Stygian flood.

The phrase *inuidia maior* (4), 'greater than envy' (a translation of Callimachus' κρέσσονα βασκανίης, *Ep*. 21.4 Pf.), is complemented in v. 13 by the parallel expression *Daedaleo notior Icaro*, 'more renowned than Daedalus' Icarus.'[162] Taken

---

161 The erasure of Icarus' name in Horace echoes Vergil's account at *Aen*. 6.30–33 that grief prevented Daedalus from depicting his son on the doors of the temple at Cumae (which also serves as a *praeteritio* in its own right, excusing Vergil from recounting the story of Icarus' fall). Thomas 2011: *ad* 1–4 and Fedeli and Ciccarelli 2008: 124 discuss the anagrammatic presence of Pindar's name in vv. 1–3.

162 Some MSS read *ocior*, which is attractive because the resultant hiatus would be a plausible incentive for scribal correction to a consonant-initial adjective. Bentley's *tutior* is unnecessary; the claim to immortality in vv. 1–8 already implies that Horace will not share Icarus' fate even if he repeats his fatal mistake.

together, these two passages hint at the idea that, in taking avian form, Horace is competing with Icarus himself. Horace's winged ascent is simultaneously a flight from death and a triumph over envy, and the conceit of surpassing Icarus is relevant to both: by taking to the skies, Horace challenges the claim to fame that made Icarus a mythic *exemplum* in the first place, and if he survives, as he assures us he will, he will replace Icarus as the *exemplum* of the possibilities of human aviation. Icarus will no longer be Icarus, and that name will lose its meaning. In order to usurp Icarus' name and identity, Horace must himself become *biformis*, two forms in one: the miraculous growth by which Horace becomes 'greater than envy' is also an expansion beyond the confines of the mundane individuality represented by the name given him at birth.

When Horace comes to compare himself directly with Pindar in *c.* 4.2.25–32, I argue, he does so in such a way as to absolve himself of the intent to do to Pindar the same violence he does to Icarus in *c.* 2.20; that is, however much he may imitate Pindar, he will not *Pindarum aemulari*, i.e. claim Pindar's name for himself. The contrast between the soaring swan and the hard-working bee recalls the appearance of the same two creatures in the passage from Lucretius cited above, the former illustrating Epicurus' natural superiority (6–7) and the latter embodying Lucretius' own activity as imitator, taking up the golden nectar produced by his master as both sustenance and raw material for his own work (10–13). The passage works out an implicit contrast between the industrious bees who diligently work for the food nature provides for them and the swallows and goat-kids who try to race swans and horses, and Horace's own swan-bee comparison can be seen as a condensed version of this same scheme, held together this time by words of size and quantity (*multa*, 25; *plurimum*, 30; *paruus*, 31; *maiore*, 33).

The focus of the comparison here is on movement and mobility as a gauge of a creature's mastery over its environment. The swan harnesses the immense power of the wind (*multa* [...] *aura*, 25) to ascend into the clouds in a pure unfettered verticality. By contrast, the small frame of the bee (*paruus*, 31) is dwarfed by the magnitude of its surrounding world and the labour that it demands (*plurimum* in v. 30 attaching by zeugma to both *laborem* and *nemus*),[163] which keeps the bee hovering close to the ground and meandering along a circuitous path (*circa*, 30). The overt point is that the bee's 'mode and manner (*more modoque*, 28)' of living is completely unlike that of the swan, but the implication that Horace is likewise completely unlike Pindar is belied, as many have noticed, by the fact that the

---

163 See my translation above.

description of the Matine bee is itself a direct imitation of Pindar *Pythian* 10.53–54.[164]

This apparent discrepancy can be resolved if we consider Horace's Matine bee as a cousin of the Lucretian bee that feeds on Epicurean nectar: this, too, is an *imitative* animal. The image of flitting through groves in search of thyme also recalls *Epist.* 1.3.21, where Horace enquires into his addressee's literary projects with the question 'What thyme-beds are you busily hovering about (*quae circumuolitas agilis thyma*)?'[165] The context here, which includes the topics of the challenge of imitating Pindar (9–14) and the danger of overzealous imitation (15–20), strongly suggests that the expected answer to the question is the name of a literary model. The bee makes yet another appearance in *Epist.* 1.19, also a poem deeply concerned with imitation:[166] in vv. 22–23, the innovative poet who attracts his own imitators is imaged as the king of the swarm,[167] and in vv. 44–45 an anonymous critic accuses Horace of fancying himself the only one to 'drip poetic honey (*manare poetica mella*, 44).'[168]

Some have argued that the Matine bee symbolises a 'Callimachean' preference for *ars*/τέχνη over *ingenium*/μανία, noting that the bee as an archetypal craftsman begs comparison with the waxworker Daedalus,[169] but this overlooks an important aspect of the swan/bee contrast which is self-evident in the Lucretian model. By asking how a swallow could ever compare with a swan, or a kid with a horse, Lucretius appeals to the absolute laws of nature to illustrate his fundamental incomparability with Epicurus. It is precisely these natural laws which Daedalus' engineered wings contravene. Unlike the human who flies on waxen wings, the bee's craft and power of flight are both given to it by nature, and this same nature restricts it to a humbler way of life than the swan. The upshot of the

---

[164] 'The choicest of praise-songs flits like a bee from one discourse to another (ἐγκωμίων γὰρ ἄωτος ὕμνων | ἐπ' ἄλλοτ' ἄλλον ὧτε μέλισσα θύνει λόγον).' See Harrison 1995: 114–15.
[165] The poem also treats the topic of imitating Pindar (9–14) and the danger of imitation tipping over into plagiarism, expressed by allusion to a beast fable involving birds (15–20).
[166] o imitatores, seruum pecus, ut mihi saepe | bilem, saepe iocum uestri mouere tumultus (19–20)!
[167] *qui sibi fidet,* | *dux reget examen*. That this is a swarm of bees in particular may be confirmed by the parallel with Verg. G. 4.21: *cum prima noui ducent examina reges*.
[168] In Mart. 11.42, *thyma* is used of the 'subjects' (*lemmata*) from which poetic 'honey' (*mella*) is made.
[169] Putnam 1986: 56; Fraenkel 1957: 435; Freis 1983: 28–30. Acosta-Hughes and Stephens 2012: 43–57 show that the Callimachean discourse on τέχνη is much more subtly dialectical than a simple rebuttal to Plato, and I would argue that the Augustan poets' take on the question of *ars* and *ingenium* is similarly layered and polyvalent.

swan/bee comparison is not simply that Horace's poetry does not stem from natural ability, but rather that he has found a way of flying and honey-making which is in perfect accordance with his own nature and does not pretend to the poetic heights which are reserved by nature for the Pindars of the world.[170]

Horace refers to the commonality between himself and the Matine bee as a *more modoque* (28), a 'mode and manner.' The two words are near-synonyms here, but they complement each other with their subtle differences. *Mos*, like Greek ἦθος, denotes behaviours that become characteristic by virtue of their repetition: 'custom' or 'habit'.[171] The word can refer either to the repeated behaviours themselves or — especially in the plural, as in v. 22 of this poem — to the 'character' of which those behaviours are characteristic. Both are relevant here: Horace is like the bee both in the way in which he goes about his work and in the character of that work itself. *Operosa* in v. 31 accordingly describes both the poet's creative process and the highly-wrought quality of the product. The same might be said for *paruus* (31) if we allow that the work of a bee-poet, like the intricate patterns of beehives, would be graced by minute detail indicative of the painstaking labour that went into it.[172]

This is where the different connotations of *modus* come into play. Unlike *mos*, *modus* can mean something close to 'style' or 'idiom', as in the phrase *dicendi modus*.[173] The word also has two specialised meanings deriving from the root sense of 'measure' which appear throughout the *Odes*: it can refer to one of Horace's favourite moral themes, 'moderation',[174] and can also denote a number of related concepts in music, prosody, and versification, including 'rhythm', 'metre', 'melody/harmony', and 'musical mode'.[175] In two places in book 4 (*cc.* 6.43 and 11.34), the plural *modi* is used in the context of teaching a composition for

---

170 Plato *Ion* 534a-b uses the image of the poet as a honeybee to illustrate the argument that poetry is governed by μανία ('divine inspiration') rather than τέχνη ('professional skill'). Lucretius' claim to be dependent on the precepts of Epicurus has more than a little in common with Socrates' discourse on the genesis of poetic creation (however much the theory might diverge), but Horace's worker bee by contrast seems more like an honest tradesman than Plato's 'light and winged and sacred thing' (κοῦφον γὰρ χρῆμα ποιητής ἐστι καὶ πτηνὸν καὶ ἱερόν, 534a).
171 *OLD, mōs* def. 1.
172 Cf. Fitzgerald 2016b: 111–13, who also sees Horace as recognising a deeper commonality between himself and the bee on stylistic grounds, emphasising the quality of *uarietas/poikilia* that he finds embodied in the creature.
173 Cf. *c.* 3.15.17.
174 *OLD, modus* def. 6; cc. 1.16.2, 1.24.1, 1.36.11, 2.6.7, 3.15.2; see also (*im*)*modicus*: 1.13.10, 1.18.7, 1.20.1.
175 *OLD, modus* deff. 7, 8; cc. 2.1.40, 2.9.9, 2.12.4, 3.3.72, 3.9.10, 3.11.7, 3.30.14, 4.6.43, 4.11.34; *moderare*: 1.24.14; *modulari*: 1.32.5.

musical performance. Horace also uses it in the aforementioned *Epist.* 1.3 to describe a fellow poet's efforts to write Pindaric poetry in Latin: 'Is he endeavouring under the auspices of the Muse to adapt Theban strains to Latin strings (*fidibusne Latinis | Thebanos aptare modos studet auspice Musa*, 12–13)?'

In vv. 10–12 of the present ode, Horace notes the metrical virtuosity which makes adapting Pindar into his native tongue a daunting task: 'he unravels novel words in bold dithyrambs, carried along by unruly measures (*per audacis noua dithyrambos | uerba deuoluit numerisque fertur | lege solutis*).'[176] The fact that Horace links Pindar's *audacia* specifically to metre here encourages us to take *modo* in v. 28 similarly as highlighting some aspect of the musical dimension of his own work. Indeed, the work of the honeybee as described here has a rhythm of its own, a repetitive circular buzzing (heard in the drone of *mo-mo-* in *more modoque*) which contrasts sharply with the mounting swell of the swan's ascent.[177] The *mos* and *modus* of the bee-poet, then, combine two strata of the poetic craft in one: they represent both an attitude toward the selection of material — that of the unpretentious imitator — and a discernible 'style' that colours the verse itself.

If this is right, then we can expect the contribution Horace makes to Antonius' song in vv. 45–52 to exemplify the style and manner of the bee-poet. Thomas thinks otherwise, arguing that 'such un-Callimachean behaviour' as Horace exhibits in cheering along with the crowd 'is counter to the aesthetics of 27–32, and of the Horatian outlook in general,' and concludes that 'it is hard to take these stanzas with complete seriousness.'[178] But if the characteristic virtue of the honeybee is that it stays within its modest sphere, toiling away dutifully at its allotted task, then Horace adheres to this example perfectly by resigning himself to merely contributing his own part to a collective cry which is greater than what any one voice can produce. In vv. 45–46, Horace tells us that he will add the 'better part' of his voice (*meae [...] uocis [...] bona pars*, 45–46)' without being certain that his own voice will even be heard above the din (*si quid loquar audiendum*, 45). This recalls the collective toil of the bee, indicated by *plurimum* (30): whether we attach the adjective to *laborem* (29), *nemus* (30), or both, we are reminded of how bees rely on their own vast numbers to cope with the vastness of their surrounding world.

The evocative contrast which closes the poem — between Antonius' sumptuous sacrifice of twenty head of cattle and Horace's meagre offering of a single

---

[176] For more on this poem's metrical commentary, see Phillips 2014 and Morgan 2010: 224–37.
[177] The bee's circularity (*circa*, 30) also contrasts with the processional forward motion of Antonius' song, implied in *procedis* (49).
[178] Thomas 2011: *ad* 45–52.

calf — bears out the same ethos as the unassuming bee. The *recusatio* interpretation makes this contrast far too black-and-white, reducing it to an emblem of the opposition between Antonius' 'epic' or 'Pindaric' excess and Horace's 'Callimachean' restraint.[179] Conversely, the relevant Callimachean-Vergilian intertexts clearly stipulate 'fat sacrifice but slender Muse',[180] and Horace complies with this by ensuring that his calf will be well-fed on 'rich pasturage' (*largis* [...] *herbis*, 55).[181] Each man simply gives in proportion to his means. The focus of the comparison, I suggest, is instead on the care which Horace devotes to his own offering despite the fact that it will inevitably be overshadowed by Antonius' ten bulls and ten cows. Horace has set aside this young bullock specifically for this purpose, separating it from its mother and the rest of the herd (*relicta | matre*, 54–55) and granting it a special plot of pastureland to graze on. Accordingly he describes the calf as 'growing ripe for my vow' (*iuuenescit* [...] | *in mea uota*, 55–56); that is, the payment of Horace's vow is the climactic stage of the calf's adolescence.

This act of sequestering, of marking out for sacrifice, is performed within the frame of the poem by the visual description of the animal in the final stanza (vv. 57–60). *Imitatus* in v. 57 brings the calf into the visible realm by way of analogy, likening its budding horns to the slender crescent of the new moon. It also harks back to the initial theme of *aemulatio*, introducing *imitatio* alongside it as its negative image. The contrast hinges on the difference between the way the Pindaric emulator associates himself with Pindar and the way the calf associates itself with the moon. We saw above that the fatal error of Pindaric *aemulatio* is the element of artifice, the attempt to overstep the bounds of one's nature. By contrast, although the calf is the subject of *imitatus*, its 'imitation' of the moon's horns cannot be ascribed to its agency. Rather, the participle *imitatus* is the predicate of the verb *iuuenescit*, which is to say that the calf's imitation of the moon is a function of the natural process of its organic growth.

The point is not only that the calf's moonlike horns are a spontaneous and artless work of art.[182] The incohative suffix of *iuuenescit* emphasises that the calf's growth is an ongoing development, while in vv. 57–58 we are reminded that the celestial body which the calf's horns resemble is also in a constant state of flux; the comparandum is not just the new moon, but 'the fiery arc of the moon as it restores its third rising' (*curuatos* [...] *ignis* | *tertium lunae referentis ortum*). By

---

179 Thomas 2011: *ad* 53–60; Harrison 1995: 125–27, 2007: 206; Davis 1991: 142–43.
180 τὸ μὲν θύος ὅττι πάχιστον | θρέψαι, τὴν Μοῦσαν δ' [...] λεπταλέην (Call. *Aet.* fr. 1.23–24); *pastorem* [...] *pinguis | pascere oportet ouis, deductum dicere carmen* (Verg. *Ecl.* 6.4–5).
181 Putnam 1986: 61.
182 Putnam 1986: 61–62.

calling to mind the moon's changing appearance on each successive night, Horace hints at the fact that aging will transform the calf in tandem with that which it imitates. Not only does the calf grow *like* the moon; it grows *with* the moon, a living simile. Through the quasi-artistic figuration of the moon in its horns, the calf practises a mode of imitation which is innocent of what I have called the onomastic violence of *aemulatio*. As an emergent product of nature, the calf's *imitatio* of the moon does not infringe upon the identity of its object as poetic *aemulatio* does.[183]

The identity or individuality of the calf is signalled by the white mark on its brow which sets it apart from the rest of the herd (vv. 59–60).[184] Its snow-coloured spot is set off by a field of tawny fur in the same way that the new moon appears bright against the night sky. This recalls the simile of *c*. 1.12.46–48, which, as discussed in the previous chapter, likens the supreme brilliance of Caesar's comet to the moon's unrivalled luminosity among the stars. Thus, in its own small way, the calf eludes the doom of anonymity from which Pindar's poetry delivers its honorands. As if to accentuate this, the rising of the moon which the calf's horns betoken reimagines the skyward ascent of the eulogised youth in vv. 22–24, whose 'golden character' Pindar 'lifts up to the stars, scorning black Orcus' (*moresque | aureos educit in astra nigroque | inuidet Orco*); the golden hue of the calf's coat answers to the figurative gold of the youth's reputation, and the snowy white of its distinctive mark shares in Pindar's repudiation of the black oblivion of the underworld.[185]

The image of rising also harks back to the vertiginous climb of the emulator with which the poem began. But whereas the Icarus-poet ends by giving up his name to the sea, Horace's gift of the lone calf implies no claim to outdo the offerings of any other, least of all Antonius' exorbitant display. Indeed, the mention in vv. 51–52 of gifts of incense given by the citizenry as a whole reminds us that even the private sacrifices of Horace and Antonius also form part of the public celebration in which all of Rome shares. The collectivisation of the Roman people that the *ludus* effects is balanced by the absolute singularity of the person of Augustus, expressed in vv. 37–40: 'None greater or better than him have the fates and the kind gods granted the earth, nor will again, even if time comes back

---

183 The imitative bent of the calf, like that of the bee, is complemented by the fact that its description closely imitates other poetry: Moschus' bull (Mosch. *Id.* 2.84–88; Fedeli and Ciccarelli 2008: 173–74), Diomedes' horse (Hom. *Il.* 23.454–55; Putnam 2016), and Aratus' description of the new moon on its third day (*Phaenomena* 783–87; Klooster 2013b).
184 Davis 1991: 143.
185 The verb which describes the 'drawing' of the mark on the calf (*duxit* 59) also recalls *educit* (23), which describes how Pindar 'lifts up' (lit. 'carries away') those he eulogises; cf. *reducit* (17).

around to the ancient gold' (*quo nihil maius meliusue terris | fata donauere bonique diui | nec dabunt, quamuis redeant in aurum | tempora priscum*).

This portrayal of Augustus as a gift from heaven which can be given only once inverts the fantasy in *c.* 4.5 of the *princeps* as a dying-and-rising sun god, and this divergent perspective on the permanency of Augustus explains the different approach of the refrain with which Horace honours him in vv. 45–52 as compared with the prayer of *c.* 4.5.37–40. As argued above, the closing stanza of *c.* 4.5 exhorts the Roman people to pray for the continuation of the *pax Augusta* with a ritual constancy that keeps pace with the unbroken rhythm of the rising and setting sun. In *c.* 4.2, by contrast, the 'long holidays for Hesperia' prayed for in 4.5.37–38 are nowhere in sight; the time-frame is restricted to the 'happy days' (*laetos* [...] *dies*, 41) immediately following Augustus' homecoming. Horace's salute *o sol pulcher, o laudande* (46–47) proclaims this a singular and momentous event by combining in a single act of address both the solar figure of the returning general and the dawn which marks the occasion of his return.[186]

The production of this cry of greeting is envisioned in v. 46 as the 'adding' (*accedet*) of the 'better part' of Horace's voice (lit. the 'good part', *bona pars*) to that of the crowd. *Bona* here repeats the epithet applied in v. 38 to the 'kind gods' who gave the gift of Augustus to the world (and cf. *diuis* [...] *benignis*, 51–52).[187] Horace's gift of the 'better part' of himself thus answers to — and, in a sense, reciprocates — the celestial gift that is Caesar's homecoming.[188] This consummates the motif of gift-giving and trophies which runs through the ode, beginning with Icarus' fatal gift of his own name in stanza 1.[189] Pindar, as we learn in the poem's first half, is renowned for earning the honour of Apollo's laurel (*laurea donandus*

---

186 While *laudande* grammatically modifies *sol*, the interjection of the second *o* leaves the adjective unattached, allowing us to project it onto Augustus by enallage. For the identification with the sun, cf. vv. 9–12 of the 'ithyphallic' hymn to Demetrios Poliorketes: 'His demeanour is solemn; his friends are all around him and he is in their midst, as though his friends were stars and he the sun' (σεμνόν τι φαίνεθ', οἱ φίλοι πάντες κύκλῳ, | ἐν μέσοισι δ' αὐτός, | ὅμοιος ὥσπερ οἱ φίλοι μὲν ἀστέρες, | ἥλιος δ' ἐκεῖνος). The adjective *pulcher* is used with *dies* of a happy or blessed day twice in the *Odes*, at 1.36.10 and 4.4.39. At *c.* 4.14.5–6, the sun's rays mark out the domain within which Augustus can be rightly addressed as 'greatest of princes' (*o, qua sol habitabilis | illustrat oras, maxime principum*, 4.14.5–6).
187 In *c.* 4.5, Augustus shares the quality of being *bonus* with the gods who begat him (vv. 1, 5, 37).
188 The expression *meae uocis bona pars* implies a divisibility of the self which echoes the much bolder sentiment of *c.* 3.30.6–7: *non omnis moriar multaque pars mei | uitabit Libitinam*. In Ov. *Met.* 15.875–79, this immortal *pars melior* is equated with the poet's *nomen*.
189 Words of giving: *daturus* (3), *donandus* (9), *munere donat* (20), *donauere* (38), *dabunt* (39), *dabimus* (51).

Apollinari, 9) and for his power to award a prize 'greater than a hundred statues' (*centum potiore signis | munere donat*, 19–20). Augustus is already destined to win a garland of his own to match Pindar's (35–36), and Horace supplements this honour with the sobriquet *laudande* (47) — nominally of the sun but attaching by extension to the man of the hour — which mirrors Pindar's *donandus* (9) in both form and prosody. In both contexts, the gerundive has an almost superlative force: it is not simply that Pindar deserves a laurel wreath and Augustus deserves praise, but rather that each man is *the one* who deserves the honour Horace accords to him. With the epithet *laudande*, Horace not only gives praise to Augustus, but also marks him out as a singular and irreplaceable object of praise, just as the award of the Apolline laurel wreath excludes all others from sharing in the distinction.

The supreme image of the supreme individuality embodied by both Pindar and Augustus is the sun. Here we may be reminded of Varro's etymological exposition of the word *sol*: 'because the sun is the *sole* god that shines bright enough to make it day (*quod solus ita lucet, ut ex eo deo dies sit, L.L.* 6.58).' The sun defies emulation; its rays melted the wax on the emulous Icarus' wings and plunged him into the sea. But the sun admits of *imitation*. Just as the spot on the calf's brow imitates the moon, the moon stands as a pale imitation of the sun's light in the sky, compensating for its periodic absences.[190] This is why, in order to approach the inalienable singularity of Augustus, it will not do for Horace to elevate his own individual standing as a poet by comparing himself with a Pindar or even with a Iullus Antonius. Instead, he must render himself divisible in voice, and sacrifice the better part of himself to the collective voice-body of the chorus.

---

190 For the idea of the moon imitating the sun, see e.g. Manilius 3.197: *Phoeben imitantem lumina fratris*.

5 Conclusion

This book began with Catullus *c.* 4 and what was termed the problem of presence in Hellenistic and Roman poetry. I defined this as the question of the reader's involvement in the worlds inhabited by poems. The conceptual framework I developed to explore this problem, structured around the fiction of occasion, did not so much offer a solution to it as to try to broaden its horizons and add layers of complexity. One of the goals here was to intertwine the theory and practice of literary reading as completely and as self-consciously as possible. The result of this was that the 'problem' with which we started duplicated itself and took on new forms from one chapter to the next. This antinomy — the problem of the problem of presence — is anticipated by the formula 'problem of presence' itself: in accordance with Gumbrecht's opposition of meaning and presence, to align presence with a problem that can be definitively solved already shifts it over into hermeneutics, and therefore into the realm of meaning.

In light of this, the best a conclusion can hope to do is to retrace the steps of the journey and give a sense of what has been gained along the way. To this end, I would like to outline a few of the larger-scale objectives to which this project contributes. These points are raised both in retrospect, to reflect on the central claims and arguments of this book, and as challenges aimed at inspiring future trajectories of research.

1. *Broadening the spectrum of 'fiction' and 'fictionality.'* It has been one of the contentions of this book that fiction and fictionality remain undertheorised in the study of classical literature. This is partly a question of genre. On the one hand, the close association of 'fiction' with the modern novel leads classicists to reserve discussion of fictionality for texts that remind them of this form of literature, among them the works of Ovid, Lucian, Theocritus, and the ancient novelists.[1] On the other hand, the neo-Aristotelian tripartite division of poetry into epic, dramatic, and lyric *mimesis* still wields considerable influence. We can see this influence at work for instance in the concept of 'mimetic poetry', a label for lyric which has borrowed some techniques from drama. We need a theory of fiction and fictionality for classical literature that does more than reaffirm old generic boundaries.

---

[1] See e.g. P. Hardie 2002; Ní Mheallaigh 2014; Payne 2007; Paschalis, Panayotakis, and Schmeling 2009; Winkler 1985.

Richard Walsh's revisionist approach to fictionality offers a promising starting point.² His work represents, among other things, an effort to reconceptualise fictionality in positive rather than negative terms, i.e. to focus on what fictionality *does* instead of how it diverges from the norms of 'factual' discourse. I have tried to reflect this positive slant on fictionality by invoking the imagination, a term which has fallen somewhat out of favour in our discipline. A framework for thinking about the literary imagination in a direct and unapologetic way is offered by Elaine Scarry's *Dreaming by the book*.³

2. *Moving beyond orality and literacy.* Most of the central problems addressed in this book are questions which entered the scholarly conversation under the influence of oral theory, and consequently oral theory has been considered an indispensable tool for dealing with these problems. The readings in this book can be seen from one perspective as an exercise in trying to pursue the same lines of enquiry without falling back on the oral/written binary. This came into focus most clearly with the readings of 'festival poetry' in chapters 1 and 2; the contention there was that when a poet adopts the stance of a 'master of ceremonies' directing some kind of ritual-centered performance, it is not useful to label this self-presentation as 'oral' or 'pseudo-oral'. Cultural studies is already heading in a positive direction here: a consensus is developing that recognises spoken and written language as always-already overlapping and mutually imbricated.⁴ My aim was to show one possible way for specifically *literary* theory to catch up with this new outlook.

3. *Foregrounding presence as an alternative to meaning.* Gumbrecht's concept of 'presence effects' as a neglected domain of aesthetic experience, obscured by the long reign of 'meaning', informs all the ideas pursued in this book. However, Gumbrecht's work does not offer a method to be absorbed and applied, let alone a 'theory' of literature. What it does offer is more in the vein of an ethos or an orientation, one which I suggest could prove invaluable for the study of Hellenistic and Roman poetry.⁵

For one thing, an orientation towards presence, specifically Gumbrecht's materialistic conception of presence, could provide us with a new vocabulary for talking about 'performance' in Hellenistic and Roman poetry without defining it in terms of orality vs. literacy.⁶ Oral theory claims performance exclusively for the

---

2 Walsh 2007.
3 Scarry 1999.
4 See e.g. Scodel 2014.
5 Recent uses of Gumbrecht in classical studies include Gurd 2007 and Stephens 2015b: 68.
6 See Lowrie 2010a on the troubling slipperiness of the term 'performance'.

'oral' camp, associating it with the liveness, immanence, and context-specificity which belongs only to the spoken word. This gives rise to the problematic view that texts which exhibit features of 'performance' can only do so to the extent that they obfuscate or disavow their textual nature. 'Performance' becomes a transcendent realm to which texts are elevated when they are 'brought to life' in recitation or on the stage.

A non-oralist conception of poetic performance, by contrast, would recognise points of continuity between different forms of textual reception and not hierarchise them. William Egginton sketches the theoretical underpinnings of such an approach that might be carried over into our field.[7] I have tried to bring something of this into the discussion of the choral voice in *Odes* IV. Whereas the Derridean paradigm, taken up by Lowrie, would find meaning in the gaps between the choral fantasy and the textual reality, I try to dispense with the hermeneutics of suspicion and emphasise the productive aspects of fantasy.

4. *Privileging the experience of reading.* This is intimately linked with the concept of 'presence'. The main strength of the perspective of experience is that it allows us to take a step back from the teleological aspects of interpretation. Meanings are typically conceptualised as products, something that we get *out* of texts and take *away* from our experience with them. Even if we adopt a reader-reception approach and foreground the reader's process of meaning-making, we still find ourselves assigning a fixed order and shape to reading, with the meaning(s) at the end of the process. Susan Sontag addressed this problem by declaring provocatively that '[in] place of a hermeneutics we need an erotics of art.'[8]

I propose that a turn towards phenomenology can help us begin to answer this challenge. To me, this means foregrounding first-person experience and backgrounding 'objective reality'. I have attempted throughout to employ the concept of 'space' in a way that is allied to these aims. It is worth quoting Merleau-Ponty on the subject again: '[space] is not the milieu (real or logical) in which things are laid out, but rather the means by which the position of things becomes possible.'[9] I found this conception of space congenial because it allowed me to speak of the 'spaces' of poems as inviting exploration, not because these spaces contain something meaningful or valuable to be extracted, but simply because they offer themselves up as places to to be in. This in turn allowed me to begin reorienting my thought away from the objects of the activity of literary reading

---

[7] Egginton 2007.
[8] Sontag 1966: 7.
[9] Merleau-Ponty 2012: 253.

and towards its *qualia*, in other words, what it is like to take part in the world of this poem.

This project is far from having actually realised this goal of a phenomenological turn. The goal I had in mind instead was simply to point a way to potential futures. I would now like to direct fuller attention to the future by outlining some of the areas of research that ultimately fell outside the scope of this project but were always in its sights. Building on the foundation of this book would require addressing these points more fully than I have so far been able to do.

1. *Other genres and forms of literature.* It served the immediate aims of this project to focus on verse texts that are not, or not entirely, story-driven. This left a large proportion of Hellenistic and Roman literature out of the picture, including drama, epic, and all prose. The ideas and concepts explored however are far from being applicable only to 'lyric' or 'melic', or only to verse. The orientation towards presence, and the focus on the experience of reading, makes more sense as a holistic approach than one tailored for certain text-types. I would also argue that the fiction of occasion is a similarly versatile concept. Works of oratory can obviously have occasions in the same way that poems can, and epic poems can incorporate situations of address similar to those of Horace's *Odes*. One possible avenue might be to trace the 'path of song' trope — linked to the fiction of occasion in chapter 2, but also traditionally associated with epic — through multiple genres.

2. *Cognitive poetics.* My readings have made sporadic and sometimes speculative use of concepts derived from fields that belong to the movement in the humanities and social sciences towards embodied cognition, especially cognitive linguistics, cognitive narratology, and the developing subdiscipline of cognitive poetics. The eclectic approach to methodology I adopted meant that cognitive science was always peripheral rather than central to my process, but I believe that a method more grounded in this discipline would be well placed to take the conversation begun here in a positive direction. One of the central aims of a cognitive poetics that this book has decidedly not reflected is a turn towards empirical research. However, privileging the experience of reading obliges us to exploit the data of experience, and modern cognitive science has developed powerful methods of producing those data. What an empirically-supported cognitive poetics would look like in the context of Hellenistic and Roman poetry, I cannot say, but I hope I have shown that such a possibility would be worth exploring.

3. *The persona and the poet's voice.* The problem of the 'lyric "I"', the first-person voice of non-narrative poetry, is so deeply bound up with the topic of this book that it could almost have taken up a chapter of its own. What it offers instead is a guide to a new way of approaching old problems that have filled volumes on

the 'lyric "I"', a guide which may be used as a prolegomenon to this immense and difficult area of study. In chapters 3 and 4, I experiment with a conception of 'voice' as a material presence which I suggest could be expanded to a method for thinking about what we mean when we talk about 'the poet's voice' or 'the first-person voice'. The first step, I propose, is the task of resituating the (poetic) voice in the body, a process which has been helped along by Steven Connor and also by Shane Butler in his recent monograph.[10]

Another important step, which I have not found the space to discuss in full here, is to completely rethink the concept of the 'poetic persona' which still has some currency in our field. I touched on this briefly in chapters 1 and 2 in connexion to the 'master of ceremonies' stance in Callimachus' *Hymn to Apollo*, Propertius 4.6 and Bion's *Adonis*. I proposed there that the 'speaker' in these poems should be identified with the poet rather than with some other fictional person. This proposal demands further elaboration and argumentation in a follow-up study. The groundwork for such a study, however, is already sketched out in chapter 3, which critiques the 'dramatic monologue' approach to Horace's *Odes*. As Jonathan Culler argues extensively, the idea of the poetic persona owes a great deal to the dramatic monologue theory of lyric.[11] Understanding space in Horatian lyric as dynamic and processual rather than statically pre-existing requires that we modify our conception of the voice that speaks within that space as well.

4. *Rhythm*. In chapters 2 and 4 in particular, I tried to use the idea of rhythm in a novel way. The thinking here was that talking about occasion is a way of situating poems in some kind of temporal order, and that it might be useful to consider the temporality of poems and occasions in connexion with the internal temporality of metre and cadence. The result was that I ended up using the term 'rhythm' to describe an interface between these two temporal systems. There is no vocabulary in place to map this kind of dynamic. What we would need is a way of talking about the 'sound effects' produced by metrical and prosodic patterning which does not subordinate these to 'meaning'. The programmatics for such a project are set out by Amittai Aviram, but bringing these ideas to bear on classical quantitative verse-forms is another matter.[12]

If these two blocks of four points each do not perhaps add up to a single unified project, they do at least point in the same general direction: toward a new way of thinking about Hellenistic and Roman poetry, which appreciates it for the experiences it makes possible and the presences it produces. I can only hope that

---

[10] Connor 2015, 2000; Butler 2015.
[11] Culler 2015.
[12] Aviram 1994.

the readings I have offered appear to the reader to point in this direction as well. Close-reading studies of this kind are always faced with the challenge of balancing the individual readings with the broader thesis into which they are made to fit, and often the reader's interest will be skewed decidedly towards one or the other. All I can reasonably hope to have accomplished is to compensate for this by making the poems of my corpus talk to each other in a cogent and productive way.

Bibliography

Abrahams, N. and N. Rand (1986) 'Psychoanalytic esthetics: time, rhythm, and the unconscious', *Diacritics* 16.3: 2–14.
Acosta-Hughes, B. (2002) *Polyeideia: the* Iambi *of Callimachus and the archaic iambic tradition* (Berkeley).
Acosta-Hughes, B. and S.A. Stephens (2012) *Callimachus in context: from Plato to the Augustan poets* (Cambridge).
Albert, W. (1988) *Das mimetische Gedicht in der Antike: Geschichte und Typologie von den Anfängen bis in die augusteische Zeit* (Frankfurt am Main).
Alexiou, M. (2002) [1974] *The ritual lament in Greek tradition*, trans. D. Yatromanolakis and P. Roilos (Oxford).
Ancona, R. (1994) *Time and the erotic in Horace's* Odes (Durham, NC).
Anderson, B. (2006) [1983] *Imagined communities: reflections on the origin and spread of nationalism*, rev. ed. (London).
Attridge, D. (2019) *The experience of poetry: from Homer's listeners to Shakespeare's readers* (Oxford).
Aviram, A.F. (1994) *Telling rhythm: body and meaning in poetry* (Ann Arbor, MI).
Bakker, E.J. (2005) *Pointing at the past: from formula to performance in Homeric poetics* (Washington, DC).
Barber, D. (2014) 'Presence and the future tense in Horace's *Odes*', *CJ* 109.3: 333–61.
Barchiesi, A. (1996) 'Poetry, praise, and patronage: Simonides in book 4 of Horace's *Odes*', *CA* 15.1: 5–47.
Barchiesi, A. (2007) '*Carmina*: *Odes* and *Carmen Saeculare*', in S.J. Harrison ed., *The Cambridge companion to Horace* (Cambridge) 144–61.
Barchiesi, A. (2009) 'Rituals in ink: Horace on the Greek lyric tradition', in Lowrie 2009b: 418–40, reprinted from M. Depew and D. Obbink eds. (2000) *Matrices of genre: authors, canons, and society* (Cambridge, MA) 167–82.
Bassi, K. (1989) 'The poetics of exclusion in Callimachus' *Hymn to Apollo*', *TAPA* 119: 219–31.
Becker, A. (2010) 'Listening to lyric: accent and ictus in the Latin Sapphic stanza', *CW* 103.2: 159–82.
Bell, C. (1992) *Ritual theory, ritual practice* (Oxford).
Best, S. and S. Marcus (2009) 'Surface reading: an introduction', *Representations* 108.1: 1–21.
Bettini, M. (2008) 'Weighty words, suspect speech: *fari* in Roman culture', *Arethusa* 41: 313–75.
Bing, P. (1988) *The well-read Muse: present and past in Callimachus and the Hellenistic poets*, Hypomnemata 90 (Göttingen).
Bing, P. (1993a) 'Impersonation of voice in Callimachus' *Hymn to Apollo*', *TAPA* 123: 181–98.
Bing, P. (1993b) 'The *bios*-tradition and poets' lives in Hellenistic poetry', in M. Ostwald, R.M. Rosen, J. Farrell eds., *Nomodeiktes: Greek studies in honor of Martin Ostwald* (Michigan) 619–32.
Bing, P. (1995) '*Ergänzungsspiel* in the epigrams of Callimachus', *A&A* 41: 115–31.
Bing, P. and J.S. Bruss eds. (2007) *Brill's companion to Hellenistic epigram* (Leiden).
Bradley, M. (2013) 'Colour as a synaesthetic experience in antiquity', in S. Butler and A. Purves eds., *Synaesthesia and the ancient senses* (Durham) 127–40.
Bradshaw, A.T. von S. (1970) 'Horace, *Odes* 4.1', *CQ* 20.1: 142–53.
Breed, B.W. (2000) 'Silenus and the *imago vocis* in *Eclogue* 6', *HSCP* 100: 327–39.

Breed, B.W. (2004) 'Tua, Caesar, aetas: Horace Ode 4.15 and the Augustan age', AJP 125: 245–53.
Breed, B.W. (2006) Pastoral inscriptions: reading and writing Virgil's Eclogues (London).
Bühler, K. (1934) Sprachtheorie: die Darstellungsfunktion der Sprache (Jena).
Budelmann, F. and T. Phillips eds. (2018) Textual events: performance and the lyric in early Greece (Oxford).
Bulloch, A.W. (1984) 'The future of a Hellenistic illusion. Some observations on Callimachus and religion', MH 41: 209–30.
Bulloch, A.W. (1985) Callimachus: the fifth hymn (Cambridge 1985).
Bulloch, A.W. (2010) 'Hymns and encomia', in Clauss and Cuypers 2010: 166–80.
Bundy, E.L. (1972) 'The quarrel between Kallimachos and Apollonios': part I: 'the epilogue of Kallimachos' hymn to Apollo,' California Studies in Classical Philology 5: 39–94.
Bundy, E.L. (1986) [1962] Studia pindarica (Berkeley).
Burnett, A.P. (1983) Three archaic poets: Archilochus, Alcaeus, Sappho (London).
Butler, S. (2015) The ancient phonograph (New York).
Cairns, F. (1984) 'Propertius and the battle of Actium (4.6)', in A.J. Woodman and D.A. West eds., Poetry and politics in the age of Augustus (Cambridge) 129–68.
Calame, C. (2011a) 'The Homeric Hymns as poetic offerings: musical and ritual relationships with the gods', in Faulkner 2011: 334–57.
Calame, C. (1974) 'Réflexions sur les genres littéraires en Grèce archaïque', QUCC 17: 113–28.
Calame, C. (1995a) The craft of poetic speech in ancient Greece, trans J. Orion (New York).
Calame, C. (1995b) 'From choral poetry to tragic stasimon: the enactment of women's song', Arion 3: 136–54.
Calame, C. (2005) 'Legendary narration and poetic procedure in Callimachus' Hymn to Apollo', in Masks of authority: fiction and pragmatics in ancient Greek poetics (New York) 70–87.
Calame, C. (2011b) 'Enunciative fiction and poetic performance. Choral voices in Bacchylides' Epinicians', in Athanassaki and Bowie 2011: 115–38.
Cameron, A. (1995) Callimachus and his critics (Princeton).
Cameron, H.D. (1989) 'Horace's Soracte ode (Carm. 1.9)', Arethusa 22: 147–59.
Caracciolo, M. (2011) 'The reader's virtual body: narrative space and its reconstruction', StoryWorlds 3: 117–38.
Carey, C. (1981) A commentary on five odes of Pindar: Pythian 2, Pythian 9, Nemean 1, Nemean 7, Isthmian 8 (New York).
Carey, C. (1989) 'The performance of the victory ode', AJP 110: 545–65.
Carey, C. (2009) 'Genre, occasion and performance', in F. Budelmann ed., The Cambridge companion to Greek lyric (Cambridge) 21–38.
Carson, A. (1986) Eros the bittersweet: an essay (Princeton, NJ).
Catlow, L. (1976) 'Fact, imagination, and memory in Horace: Odes 1.9', G&R 23.1: 74–81.
Cheshire, K. (2008) 'Kicking ΦΘΟΝΟΣ: Apollo and his chorus in Callimachus' Hymn 2', CP 103: 354–73.
Ciccarelli, I. and P. Fedeli eds. (2008) Q. Horatii Flacci carmina liber IV (Florence).
Citroni, M. (1995) Poesia e lettori in Roma antica. Forme della comunicazione letteraria (Rome).
Citroni, M. (2009) 'Occasion and levels of address in Horatian lyric', in Lowrie 2009b: 72–105 = (1983) 'Occasione e piani di destinazione nella lirica di Orazio', MD 10/11: 133–214.
Clauss, J.J. and M. Cuypers eds. (2010) A companion to Hellenistic literature (London).
Clay, J.S. (1989) 'Ode 1.9: Horace's September song', CW 83.2: 102–05.
Commager, S. (2009) 'The function of wine in Horace's Odes', in Lowrie 2009b: 33–49 = (1957) TAPA 88: 68–80.

Connor, S. (2000) *Dumbstruck: a cultural history of ventriloquism* (Oxford).
Connor, S. (2015) 'Choralities', transcript, *Voices and noises*, 27 March, viewed 9/3/2017, <http://stevenconnor.com/choralities.html>.
Courtney, E. (1997) 'Catullus' yacht (or was it?)', *CJ* 92: 113–22.
Culler, J. (2015) *Theory of the lyric* (Cambridge, MA).
Cunningham, M.P. (1957) '*Enarratio* of Horace *Odes* 1.9', *CP* 52.2: 98–102.
Cuypers, M.P. (2005) 'Interactive particles and narrative voices in Homer and Apollonius Rhodius', *Caeculus* 6: 35–69.
Dällenbach, L. (1989) *The mirror in the text* (Chicago).
D'Alessio, G.-B. (2004) 'Past present and future past: temporal deixis in Greek archaic lyric', *Arethusa* 37: 267–94.
D'Alessio, G.-B. (2018) 'Fiction and pragmatics in ancient Greek lyric: the case of Sappho', in Budelmann and Phillips 2018: 31–62.
Davis, G. (1991) *Polyhymnia: the rhetoric of Horatian lyric discourse* (Berkeley).
Davis, G. (2002) '*Ait phaselus*: the caricature of stylistic genre (*genus dicendi*) in Catullus *Carm.* 4', *MD* 48: 111–43.
Debrohun, J.B. (2003) Roman Propertius and the reinvention of elegy (Ann Arbor, MI).
Depew, M. (1993) 'Mimesis and aetiology', in Harder-Regtuit-Wakker 1993: 57–77.
Depew, M. (2000) 'Enacted and represented dedications: genre and Greek hymn', in Depew and Obbink 2000: 59–80.
Depew, M. and D. Obbink eds. (2000) *Matrices of genre: authors, canons, and society* (Cambridge, MA).
Detienne, M. (1994) [1977] *The gardens of Adonis: spices in Greek mythology*, trans. J. Lloyd (Princeton, NJ).
Du Quesnay, I.M. le M. (1995) 'Horace, *Odes* 4.5: *Pro Reditu Imperatoris Caesaris Divi Filii Augusti*', in S.J. Harrison ed., *Homage to Horace: a bimillenary celebration* (Oxford) 128–87.
Edmunds, L. (1992) *From a Sabine jar: reading Horace, Odes 1.9* (London).
Egginton, W. (2007) 'Performance and presence: analysis of a modern aporia', *Journal of literary theory* 1.1: 3–18.
Eisenhut, W. (1956) 'Die Einleitungsverse der Elegie IV 6 des Properz', *Hermes* 84.1: 121–8.
Estevez, V.A. (1981) 'ἀπώλετο καλὸς Ἄδωνις: a description of Bion's refrain', *Maia* 33: 35–42.
Erbse, H. (1955) 'Zum Apollonhymnos des Kallimachos', *Hermes* 83: 411–428.
Falivene, M.R. (1990) 'La mimesi in Callimaco: Inni II, IV, V, e VI', *QUCC* 36: 103–28.
Fantuzzi, M. (1985) *Bionis smyrnaei* Adonidis epitaphium, *Arca* 18 (Liverpool).
Fantuzzi, M. (2010) 'Sung poetry: the case of inscribed paeans', in Clauss and Cuypers 2010: 181–97.
Fantuzzi, M. (2011) 'Speaking with authority: polyphony in Callimachus' *Hymns*', in B. Acosta-Hughes et al. eds., *Brill's companion to Callimachus* (Leiden) 429–53.
Fantuzzi, M. and R.L. Hunter (2004) *Tradition and innovation in Hellenistic poetry* (Cambridge).
Fauconnier, G. and M. Turner (2002) *The way we think: conceptual blending and the mind's hidden complexities* (New York).
Faulkner, A. ed. (2011) *The Homeric hymns: interpretative essays* (Oxford).
Feeney, D.C. (2012) 'Representation and the materiality of the book in the polymetrics', in I.M. le M. Du Quesnay and A.J. Woodman eds., *Catullus: poems, books, readers* (Cambridge) 29–47.
Feeney, D.C. (1998) *Literature and religion at Rome: cultures, contexts, and beliefs* (Cambridge).

Feeney, D.C. (2009) 'Horace and the Greek lyric poets', in Lowrie 2009b: 202–31, reprinted from N. Rudd ed. (1993) *Horace 2000: a celebration* (London) 41–63.
Fitzgerald, W. (1995) *Catullan provocations: lyric poetry and the drama of position* (Berkeley).
Fitzgerald, W. (2010) 'Listening, ancient and modern', *Journal of the royal musical association* 135: 25–37.
Fitzgerald, W. (2016a) 'Resonance: the sonic environment of Vergil's *Eclogues*', *Dictynna* 13.
Fitzgerald, W. (2016b) *Variety: the life of a Roman concept* (Chicago).
Fleischmann, S. (1990) *Tense and narrativity: from medieval performance to modern fiction* (Austin, TX).
Fludernik, M. (1996) *Towards a 'natural' narratology* (New York).
Fludernik, M. (2003) 'Scene shift, metalepsis, and the metaleptic mode', *Style* 37: 382–400.
Ford, A. (1994) *Homer: the poetry of the past* (Ithaca, NY).
Fordyce, C.J. (1961) *Catullus: a commentary* (Oxford).
Foster, M. (2015) 'The double chorus of Horace *Odes* 4.1: a paeanic performance *in morem salium*', *AJP* 136.4: 607–32.
Foster, M. (2016) '*Poeta loquens*: poetic voices in Pindar's *Paean* 6 and Horace's *Odes* 4.6', in N.W. Slater ed., *Voice and voices in antiquity* (Leiden) 149–65.
Fraenkel, E. (1957) *Horace* (Oxford).
Fraser, P.M. (1972) *Ptolemaic Alexandria*, 3 vols. (Oxford).
Freis, R. (1983) 'The catalogue of Pindaric genres in Horace *Ode* 4.2', *CA* 2.1: 27–36.
Freudenburg, K. (2010) '*Horatius anceps*: persona and self-revelation in satire and song', in G. Davis ed., *A companion to Horace* (London) 271–90.
Friedländer, P. (1931) 'Vorklassisch und nachklassisch', in W. Jaeger ed., *Das Problem des Klassischen und die Antike* (Leipzig) 33–46.
Frye, N. (1985) 'Approaching the lyric', in C. Hošek and P. Parker eds., *Lyric poetry: beyond New Criticism* (Ithaca, NY) 31–37.
Furley, W.D. and J.M. Bremer eds. (2001) *Greek hymns: selected cult songs from the Archaic to the Hellenistic period*, 2 vols. (Tübingen).
Gadamer, H.-G. (2013) [1989] *Truth and method*, transs. D. Weinsheimer and D.G. Marshall (London).
Galbraith, M. (1995) 'Deictic shift theory and the poetics of involvement in narrative', in J.F. Duchan et al. eds., *Deixis in narrative: a cognitive science perspective* (Hillsdale, NJ) 19–59.
García, J.F. (2002) 'Symbolic action in the Homeric Hymns: the theme of recognition', *CA* 21 (2002) 5–39.
Genette, G. (1980) [1972] *Narrative discourse: an essay in method*, trans. J.E. Lewin (Ithaca, NY).
Giannisi, P. (2006) *Récits des voies: chant et cheminement en Grèce archaïque* (Grenoble).
Glare, P.G.W. (1968) *Oxford Latin dictionary* (Oxford).
Goffman, E. (1974) *Frame analysis: an essay on the organization of experience* (Boston).
Goldhill, S. (1991) *The poet's voice: essays on poetics and Greek literature* (Cambridge).
Gramps, A. (forthcoming) 'Three waterborne epigrams: Archimelus, Callimachus, Catullus', in U. Eigler ed., *Die Materialität des Textes zwischen Lebenswelt und Lesewelt* (Berlin).
Greene, R. (1991) *Post-Petrarchism: origins and innovations of the Western lyric sequence* (Princeton, NJ).
Grethlein, J. (2015) 'Aesthetic experiences, ancient and modern', *NLH* 46.2: 309–33.
Grethlein, J. and A. Rengakos eds. (2009) *Narratology and interpretation* (Göttingen).

Griffin, J. (2002) 'Look your last on lyric: Horace, *Odes* 4.15', in T.P. Wiseman ed., *Classics in progress: essays on ancient Greece and Rome* (Oxford) 311–32.
Günther, H.-C. (2006) 'The fourth book', in H.-C. Günther ed., *Brill's companion to Propertius* (Leiden) 353–95.
Günther, H.-C. (2013) 'The first collection of odes: *Carmina* I-III', in H.-C. Günther ed., *Brill's companion to Horace* (Leiden) 211–406.
Gumbrect, H.U. (2003) *The powers of philology: dynamics of textual scholarship* (Chicago).
Gumbrect, H.U. (2004) *Production of presence: what meaning cannot convey* (Stanford, CA).
Gurd, S.A. (2007) 'Meaning and material presence: four epigrams on Timomachus's unfinished *Medea*', *TAPA* 137: 305–31.
Gutzwiller, K.J. (1991) *Theocritus' pastoral analogies: the formation of a genre* (Madison, WI).
Gutzwiller, K.J. (2002) 'Art's echo: the tradition of Hellenistic ecphrastic epigram', in Harder-Regtuit-Wakker 2002: 85–112.
Habinek, T.A. (1985) 'The marriageability of Maximus: Horace, *Ode* 4.1.13–20', *AJP* 107.3: 407–16.
Harder, M.A. (2012) 'Callimachus', in I.J.F. de Jong ed., *Space in ancient Greek literature* (Leiden) 77–98.
Harder, M.A. (1992) 'Insubstantial voices: some observations on the hymns of Callimachus', *CQ* 42: 384–94.
Harder, M.A., R.F. Regtuit, G.C. Wakker eds. (1993) *Callimachus* (Leiden).
Harder, M.A., R.F. Regtuit, G.C. Wakker eds. (1998) *Genre in Hellenistic poetry* (Groningen).
Harder, M.A., R.F. Regtuit, G.C. Wakker eds. (2002) *Hellenistic epigrams* (Leiden).
Harder, M.A., R.F. Regtuit, G.C. Wakker eds. (2004) *Callimachus II* (Groningen).
Hardie, A. (1983) *Statius and the* Silvae: *poetry, patrons and epideixis in the Greco-Roman world* (Liverpool).
Hardie, A. (1998) 'Horace, the paean and Roman *choreia* (*Odes* 4.6)', *PLLS* 8: 251–93.
Hardie, A. (2002) 'The Pindaric sources of Horace *Odes* 1.12', *HSCP* 101: 371–404.
Hardie, A. (2015) 'A dithyramb for Augustus: Horace, *Odes* 4.2', *CQ* 65.1: 253–85.
Hardie, P.R. (1993) '*Vt pictura poesis*? Horace and the visual arts', in N. Rudd ed., *Horace 2000: a celebration* (London) 120–39.
Hardie, P.R. (2002) *Ovid's poetics of illusion* (Cambridge).
Hardie, P.R. (2012) *Rumour and renown: representations of fama in Western literature* (Cambridge).
Harris, R.K. (2000) *Rethinking writing* (London).
Harrison, S.J. (1995) 'Horace, Pindar, Iullus Antonius, and Augustus: *Odes* 4.2', in S.J. Harrison ed., *Homage to Horace: a bimillenary celebration* (Oxford) 108–27.
Harrison, S.J. (2007) *Generic enrichment in Vergil and Horace* (Oxford).
Havelock, E.A. (1963) *Preface to Plato* (Harvard).
Heinze, R. (2009) 'The Horatian ode', in Lowrie 2009b: 11–32 = (1923) 'Die horazische Ode', *Neue Jahrbücher für das klassische Altertum* 51: 153–68.
Henderson, J. (1997) *Figuring out Roman nobility: Juvenal's eighth Satire* (Exeter).
Heyworth, S.J. ed. (1994) 'Some allusions to Callimachus in Latin poetry', *MD* 33: 51–79.
Heyworth, S.J. ed. (2007a) *Sexti Properti elegi* (Oxford).
Heyworth, S.J. ed. (2007b) *Cynthia: a companion to the text of Propertius* (Oxford).
Hollander, J. (1981) *The figure of echo: a mode of allusion in Milton and after* (Berkeley, CA).
Hollander, J. (1985) 'Breaking into song: some notes on refrain', in C. Hošek and P. Parker eds., *Lyric poetry: beyond New Criticism* (Ithaca, NY) 73–89.

Hills, P.D. (2001) 'Ennius, Suetonius and the genesis of Horace, *Odes* 4', *CQ* 51.2: 613–16.
Holzberg, N. (2009) *Horaz: Dichter und Werk* (Munich).
Hopkinson, N. (1984) *Callimachus: hymn to Demeter* (Cambridge).
Hunter, R.L. (1992) 'Writing the god: form and meaning in Callimachus' *Hymn to Athena*', *MD* 29: 9–34.
Hutchinson, G.O. (2006) *Propertius: elegies book IV* (Cambridge).
Jahn, M. (1999) 'More aspects of focalization: refinements and applications', *GRAAT: Revue des Groupes de Recherches Anglo-Américaines de L'Université François Rabelais de Tours* 21: 85–110.
Janan, M. (2001) *The politics of desire: Propertius IV* (Berkeley, CA).
Johnson, M. (1987) *The body in the mind: the bodily basis of meaning, imagination, and reason* (Chicago).
Johnson, M. and G. Lakoff (1980) *Metaphors we live by* (Chicago).
Johnson, M. and G. Lakoff (1999) *Philosophy in the flesh: the embodied mind and its challenge to Western thought* (New York).
Johnson, T.S. (2004) *A symposion of praise: Horace returns to lyric in* Odes *IV* (Madison, WI).
Johnson, T.S. (2011) *Horace's iambic criticism: casting blame (iambikē poiēsis)* (Leiden).
Jong, I.J.F. de (2009) 'Metalepsis in ancient Greek literature', in Grethlein and Rengakos 2009: 87–116.
Keith, A.M. (2008) *Propertius: poet of love and leisure* (Bristol).
Kiessling, A. and R. Heinze eds. (1930) *Q. Horatius Flaccus, Oden und Epoden* (Berlin).
Klooster, J. (2013a) 'Apostrophe in Homer, Apollonius and Callimachus', in U.E. Eisen and P. von Möllendorff eds., *Über die Grenze: Metalepse in Text- und Bildmedien des Altertums* (Berlin) 151–73,
Klooster, J. (2013b) 'Horace, *carmen* 4.2.53–60: another look at the *vitulus*', *CQ* 63.1: 346–52.
Köhnken, A. (1981) 'Apollo's retort to Envy's criticism (two questions of relevance in Callimachus, *Hymn* 2, 105ff.)', *AJP* 102: 411–22.
Kurke, L. (2005) 'Choral lyric as "ritualization": poetic sacrifice and poetic *ego* in Pindar's sixth paian', *CA* 24.1: 81–130.
Kurke, L. (2013) *The traffic in praise: Pindar and the poetics of social economy*, 2nd ed. (Berkeley, CA).
La Penna, A. (1963) *Orazio e l'ideologia del principato* (Turin).
Lee, M.O. (1969) *Word, sound, and image in the odes of Horace* (Ann Arbor, MI).
Lefebvre, H. (1991) [1974] *The production of space*, trans. D. Nicholson-Smith (Oxford).
Levinson, S.C. (1983) *Pragmatics* (Cambridge).
Lewis, C.T. and C. Short (1969) [1879] *A Latin dictionary* (Oxford).
Linderski, J. (1986) 'The augural law', *ANRW* II.16.3: 2146–2312.
Lowrie, M. (2009a) *Writing, performance, and authority in Augustan Rome* (Oxford).
Lowrie, M. (2010a) 'Performance', in A. Barchiesi and W. Scheidel eds., *The Oxford handbook of Roman studies* (Oxford) 281–94.
Lowrie, M. (2010b) 'Horace: *Odes* 4', in G. Davis ed., *A companion to Horace* (London) 210–30.
Lowrie, M. ed. (2009b) *Horace:* Odes *and* Epodes (Oxford).
Lyne, R.O.A.M. (1995) *Horace: behind the public poetry* (New Haven, CT).
Lyons, J. (1977) *Semantics*, vol. 1 (Cambridge).
Mace, S.T. (1993) 'Amour, encore! The development of δηὖτε in archaic lyric', *GRBS* 34.4: 335–64.
MacKay, L.A. (1977) 'Horatiana: *Odes* 1.9 and 1.28', *CP* 72.4: 316–18.

Macleod, C.W. (1976) 'Propertius 4.1', *PLLS* 1: 141–53.
Macleod, C.W. (1979) 'Ethics and poetry in Horace's *Odes* (1.20; 2.3)', *G&R* 26: 21–29.
de Man, P. (1985) 'Lyrical voice in contemporary theory: Riffaterre and Jauss', in C. Hošek and P. Parker eds., *Lyric poetry: beyond New Criticism* (Ithaca, NY) 55–72.
Mayer, R. ed. (2012) *Horace, Odes, book I* (Cambridge).
McCarthy, K. (2019) *I, the poet: first-person form in Horace, Catullus, and Propertius* (Ithaca, NY).
McLuhan, M. (1964) *Understanding media: the extensions of man* (Chicago).
Merleau-Ponty, M. (2012) [1945] *Phenomenology of perception*, trans. D.A. Landes (Oxford).
ní Mheallaigh, K. (2014) *Reading fiction with Lucian: fakes, freaks and hyperreality* (Cambridge).
Miller, J.F. (2009) *Apollo, Augustus, and the poets* (Cambridge).
Morgan, L. (2010) Musa pedestris: *metre and meaning in Roman verse* (Oxford).
Morgan, K.A. (1993) 'Pindar the professional and the rhetoric of the κῶμος', *CP* 88: 1–15.
Moritz, L.A. (1976) 'Snow and spring: Horace's Soracte ode again', *G&R* 23.2: 169–76.
Morrison, A.D. (2007) *The narrator in Archaic Greek and Hellenistic poetry* (Cambridge).
Moskovit, L. (1977) 'Horace's Soracte ode as a poetic representation of an experience', *Studies in Philology* 74.2: 113–29.
Murray, O. (1985) 'Symposium and genre in the poetry of Horace', *JRS* 75: 39–50.
Nagy, G. (1994) 'Copies and models in Horace Odes 4.1 and 4.2', *CW* 87.5: 415–26.
Nagy, G. (1994–5) 'Genre and occasion', *Métis* 9–10: 11–25.
Nauta, R.R. (1994) 'Historicizing reading: the aesthetics of reception and Horace's "Soracte Ode"', in I.J.F. de Jong and J.P. Sullivan eds., *Modern critical theory and classical literature* (Brill) 207–30.
Newman, J.K. (1997) *Augustan Propertius: the recapitulation of a genre* (Berlin).
Nikolaev, A. (2012) 'Showing praise in Greek choral lyric and beyond', *AJP* 133: 543–72.
Nisbet, R.G.M. and M. Hubbard (1970) *A commentary on Horace: Odes, book I* (Oxford).
Norden, E. (1913) Agnostos theos: *Untersuchungen zur Formengeschichte religiöser Rede* (Leipzig).
Nünning, A. (2001) 'Mimesis des Erzählens: Prolegomena zu einer Wirkungsästhetik, Typologie und Funktionsgeschichte des Akts des Erzählens und der Metanarration', in J. Helbig ed., *Erzählen und Erzähltheorie im 20. Jahrhundert* (Heidelberg) 13–47.
Oliensis, E.S. (1998) *Horace and the rhetoric of authority* (Cambridge).
Ong, W.J. (1982) *Orality and literacy: the technologizing of the word* (London).
Page, D.L. ed. (1951) *Alcman: the* Partheneion (Oxford).
Paschalis, M. (2002) 'Constructing lyric space: Horace and the Alcaean song', in M. Paschalis ed., *Horace and Greek lyric poetry* (Crete) 71–84.
Paschalis, M. et al. eds. (2009) *Readers and writers in the ancient novel* (Groningen).
Payne, M. (2007) *Theocritus and the invention of fiction* (Cambridge).
Pasquali, G. (1920) *Orazio lirico, studi* (Florence).
Peponi, A.-E. (2004) 'Initiating the viewer: deixis and visual perception in Alcman's lyricdrama', *Arethusa* 37.3: 295–316.
Petrovic, I. (2011) 'Callimachus and contemporary religion: the *Hymn to Apollo*', in B. Acosta-Huges et al. eds., *Brill's companion to Callimachus* (Leiden) 264–85.
Pfeiffer, R. ed. (1985) *Callimachus*, 2 vols. (Oxford).
Pfeijffer, I.L. (1999) *First person futures in Pindar* (Stuttgart).

Pfeijffer, I.L. (1999) *Three Aeginetan odes of Pindar: a commentary on* Nemean *V,* Nemean *III, &* Pythian *VIII* (Leiden).
Pfister, M. (1988) *The theory and analysis of drama*, trans. J. Halliday (Cambridge).
Phillips, T. (2014) 'Between Pindar and Sappho: Horace *Odes* 4.2.9–12', *Mnemosyne* 67.3: 466–74.
Pillinger, H.E. (1969) 'Some Callimachean influences on Propertius, Book 4', *HSCP* 73: 171–99.
Porter, D.H. (1975) 'The recurrent motifs of Horace, *Carmina* IV', *HSCP* 79: 189–228.
Pöschl, V. (1966) 'Die Soracteode des Horaz (c.1,9)', *WS* 79: 365–83.
Pulleyn, S. (1997) *Prayer in Greek religion* (Oxford).
Purves, A.C. (2016) 'Feeling on the surface: touch and emotion in Fuseli and Homer', in S. Butler ed., *Deep classics: rethinking classical reception* (London) 67–85.
Purves, A.C. (2010) *Space and time in ancient Greek literature* (Cambridge).
Putnam, M.C.J. (1962) 'Catullus' journey (*carm.* 4)', *CP* 57: 10–19.
Putnam, M.C.J. (1969) 'Horace *c.* 1.20', *CJ* 64: 153–57.
Putnam, M.C.J. (1986) *Artifices of eternity: Horace's fourth book of Odes* (Ithaca, NY).
Putnam, M.C.J. (2016) '*Horatius felix*', in R.R. Caston and R.A. Kaster eds., *Hope, joy, and affection in the classical world* (Oxford) 111–22.
Quinn, K. ed. (1963) *Latin explorations: critical studies in Roman literature* (London).
Quinn, K. ed. (1969) *The Catullan revolution* (Michigan).
Quinn, K. ed. (1980) *Horace: the Odes* (London).
Race, W.H. (1992) 'How Greek poems begin', *YCS* 29:13–38.
Rappaport, R.A. (1999) *Ritual and religion in the making of humanity* (Cambridge).
Rawles, R. (2019) *Callimachus* (London).
Reed, J.D. (1997) *Bion of Smyrna: the fragments and the* Adonis (Cambridge).
Reed, J.D. (2006) 'Continuity and change in Greek bucolic between Theocritus and Vergil', in M. Fantuzzi and T. Papanghelis eds., *Brill's companion to Greek and Latin pastoral* (Leiden) 209–34.
Reitzenstein, R. (1906) *Hellenistische Wundererzählungen* (Leipzig).
Ricœur, P. (1988) *Time and narrative*, vol. 3, trans. K. Blamey and D. Pellauer (Chicago).
Rimell, V. (2015) *The closure of space in Roman poetics: empire's inward turn* (Cambridge).
Roller, M.B. (2004) 'Exemplarity in Roman culture: the cases of Horatius Cocles and Cloelia', *CP* 99.1: 1–56.
Rosenmeyer, T.G. (1969) *The green cabinet: Theocritus and the European pastoral lyric* (Berkeley, CA).
Rossi, L. (2009) 'Horace, a Greek lyrist without music', in Lowrie 2009b: 356–77 = (1998) 'Orazio, un lirico greco senza musica', *Seminari romani di cultura greca* 1: 163–81.
Rudd, N. (1960) 'Patterns in Horatian lyric', *AJP* 81.4: 373–92.
Rudd, N. (2004) *Horace: Odes and Epodes* (Harvard).
Russell, D.A. (1979) '*De imitatione*', in D. West and T. Woodman eds., *Creative imitation in Latin literature* (Cambridge) 1–16.
Rutherford, I. (2001) *Pindar's* paeans: *a reading of the fragments with a survey of the genre* (Oxford).
Scarry, E. (1999) *Dreaming by the book* (Princeton, NJ).
Schmidt, E.A. (2002) *Zeit und Form: Dichtungen des Horaz* (Heidelberg).
Scodel, R. ed. (2014) *Between orality and literacy: communication and adaptation in antiquity* (Leiden).
Shackleton-Bailey, D.R. ed. (1985) *Q. Horati Flacci opera* (Stuttgart).

Shields, M.G. (1958) '*Odes* 1.9: a study in imaginative unity', *Phoenix* 12.4: 166–73.
Short, W.M. (2008) 'Thinking places, placing thoughts: spatial metaphors of mental activity in Roman culture', *I quaderni del Ramo d'Oro on-line* 1: 106–29.
Short, W.M. (2016) 'Spatial metaphors of time in Roman culture', *CW* 109.3: 381–412.
Slater, W.J. (1969) 'Futures in Pindar', *CQ* 19: 86–94.
Sontag, S. (1966) 'Against interpretation', in *Against interpretation, and other essays* (New York) 4–14.
Sperber, D. and D. Wilson (1995) *Relevance: communication and cognition*, 2nd ed. (London).
Springer, C.P.E. (1988) 'Horace's Soracte ode: location, dislocation, and the reader', *CW* 82.1: 1–9.
Stanzel, F.K. (1986) *A theory of narrative*, trans. C. Goedsche (Cambridge).
Stephens, S.A. (2015a) *Callimachus: the hymns* (Oxford).
Stephens, S.A. (2015b) 'Callimachus and his narrators', in A. Faulker and O. Hodkinson eds., *Hymnic narrative and the narratology of Greek hymns* (Leiden) 49–68.
Stevens, W. (2006) [1954] *Collected poems* (London).
Stewart, G. (1990) *Reading voices: literature and the phonotext* (Berkeley).
Sterne, J. (2011) 'The theology of sound: a critique of orality', *Canadian Journal of Communication* 36: 207–25.
Sullivan, J.P. et al. (1981) 'Horace's Soracte Ode (C. I, 9)', in K. Stéphane ed., *Contemporary Literary Hermeneutics and Interpretation of Classical Texts* (Ottawa) 275–298.
Syndikus, H.P. (2001) *Die Lyrik des Horaz: eine Interpretation der Oden*, 2 vols. (Darmstadt).
Talmy, L. (2000) *Toward a cognitive semantics* (Cambridge, MA).
Tannen, D. (1982) 'The myth of orality and literacy', in W. Fawley ed., *Linguistics and literacy* (New York) 37–50.
Tarrant, R. (2020) *Horace's* Odes (Oxford).
Thomas, R.F. ed. (2011) *Horace:* Odes *book IV and* Carmen Saeculare (Cambridge).
Tucker, H.F. (1985) 'Dramatic monologue and the overhearing of lyric', in C. Hošek and P. Parker eds., *Lyric poetry: beyond New Criticism* (Ithaca, NY) 226–43.
Vamvouri Ruffy, M. (2004) *La fabrique du divin: les Hymnes de Callimaque à la lumière des Hymnes homériques et des Hymnes épigraphes* (Liège).
Vessey, D.W.T. (1985) 'From mountain to lovers' tryst: Horace's Soracte ode', 26–38.
Vestrheim, G. (2012) 'Voice and addressee in the mimetic hymns of Callimachus', *Symbolae Osloenses* 86: 21–73.
Walsh, G.B. (1990) 'Surprised by self: audible thought in Hellenistic poetry', *CP* 85.1: 1–21.
Walsh, R. (1997) 'Who is the narrator?', *Poetics today* 18.4: 495–513.
Walsh, R. (2007) *The rhetoric of fictionality: narrative theory and the idea of fiction* (Columbus, OH).
Webb, R. (2016) *Ekphrasis, imagination and persuasion in ancient rhetorical theory and practice* (New York).
Welch, T.S. (2005) *The elegiac cityscape: Propertius and the meaning of Roman monuments* (Cincinnati, OH).
Werth, P. (1994) 'Extended metaphor: a text world account', *Language & literature* 3.2: 79–103.
West, D.A. (1967) *Reading Horace* (Edinburgh).
West, D.A. (1995) *Horace Odes I*: Carpe Diem (Oxford).
Wickham, E.C. ed. (1975) *Q. Horati Flacci opera* (Oxford).
von Wilamowitz-Moellendorf, U. (1900) *Bion von Smyrna,* Adonis (Berlin).
Williams, F.J. (1978) *Callimachus,* Hymn to Apollo: *a commentary* (Oxford).

Williams, G.W. (1962) 'Poetry in the moral climate of Augustan Rome', *JRS* 52: 28–46.
Williams, G.W. (1968) *Tradition and originality in Roman poetry* (Oxford).
Wills, J. (1996) *Repetition in Latin poetry: figures of allusion* (Oxford).
Wimmel, W. (1965) '*Recusatio*-Form und Pindarode', *Philologus* 109: 83–103.
Winkler, J.J. (1985) Auctor *and* actor: *a narratological reading of Apuleius'* Golden Ass (Berkeley).
Wray, D. (2004) *Catullus and the poetics of Roman manhood* (Cambridge).
Yatromanolakis, D. (2004) 'Ritual poetics in archaic Lesbos: contextualizing genre in Sappho', in D. Yatromanolakis and P. Roilos eds., *Greek ritual poetics* (Washington, DC) 56–70.
Zarecki, J.P. (2010) 'A duet of praise: Horace, Vergil, and the subject of *canemus* in *Carm.* 4.15.32', *CJ* 105.3: 245–62.
Zorzetti, N. (1991) 'Poetry and ancient city: the case of Rome', *CJ* 86: 311–29.
Zwaan, R.A. (2004) 'The immersed experiencer: towards an embodied theory of language comprehension', in B.H. Ross ed., *The psychology of learning and motivation*, Vol. 44 (San Diego, CA) 35–63.

Index Rerum et Nominum

address, addressee ix–xii, 14–15, 20–22, 26, 33, 35, 55 n. 69, 57, 60, 64–65, 68–71, 74, 76–87, 92–93, 105, 107, 117–18, 122–23, 125, 136 n. 33, 145, 151, 155–58, 164–65, 185, 190

Aphrodite/Venus 29–30, 35, 60–75, 139–40, 143–53, 158–62

Apollo (Phoebus) 2–34, 35–57, 71 n. 114, 126–27, 134, 135 n. 29, 137 n. 38, 141, 146, 186

Augustus (Octavian, Caesar) 36–57, 112, 118, 120–24, 135–36, 138–40, 162–86

body, embodiment x, 44, 70–72, 81, 98, 108, 125, 133, 137–39, 156–58, 166, 190

deixis ix–xi, 4, 9, 19–20, 23, 26–27, 35, 40, 47, 55–56, 69, 85, 87, 98, 165

dramatic monologue 91–99, 191

Epicurus, Epicureanism 81, 102, 105, 173–74, 179–81

epiphany v, xvii, 10–12, 20–23, 26, 28–32, 35, 40, 51–53, 55 n. 67, 57, 122–24, 134–35, 149–51

–epiphanic effect 28–32, 40, 74

experience of reading v, xvi, 44, 65, 83, 94, 98, 105–07, 189–90

experiential frames 1, 13–24, 30, 55, 70–71, 83, 138

fictionality xiii, xv, 3–5, 14–18, 20–24, 27–30, 33–34, 44, 68–69, 76–78, 85–86, 93–99, 187–88

mimetic (poetry) v, x, xvii, 1–35, 40, 57–58, 60 n. 84, 67–68, 74, 95–96, 132, 187

names and naming 112, 176–79
–onomastic violence 178, 184

narratology v, 1, 18–20, 190

oral performance, orality v, xvi, 4, 24–32, 35, 64–65, 76–77, 188

performativity, speech act 5, 15–17, 29, 78–79, 82–84, 106–08, 119, 122–23, 132, 139, 145, 158, 166–67

persona 2 n. 6, 68, 74–75, 190–91

Pindar 12 n. 38, 16–17, 54, 60 n. 84, 112–13, 139 n. 45, 159 n. 116, 168–86

presence v–vi, ix–xviii, 1, 23, 29–30, 57, 76–126, 134–43, 149, 151, 167–68, 187–89

repetition v, 43, 58–65, 136–68, 181

ritual 4, 13 n. 39, 15, 28 n. 82, 37–42, 47–49, 54, 58, 67–69, 74, 84 n. 20, 137–39, 144–47, 162, 166, 185, 188

sense-suggestion 24, 30–32, 35, 40–41, 89, 106

space (theories of) xvii, 9, 33–34, 40–41, 71–74, 94–99, 189–91
–space of inclusion xvii, 8–13, 19, 23, 26, 30, 41, 82, 107, 134

Venus *see Aphrodite/Venus*

voice xiii–xiv, 4, 8, 12, 19, 58, 61, 81–84, 107–08, 112, 115, 117–18, 120–42, 156–58, 161–62, 166, 168–69, 171–72, 182, 185–86, 189–91

Index Locorum

Alcman
PMG 1   23–24

Apollonius Rhodius
Argonautica   71 n. 115

Aristophanes
Lysistrata   58 n. 74, 68 n. 107

Asclepiades
AP 12.135   156 n. 106

Augustus
Res Gestae
34.16–21   50–51

Bion of Smyrna
fr. 10   73
Lament for Adonis
1–2   58–60
2   73 n. 119
3   152 n. 93
3–5   62–63, 69–71
5   64 n. 91
5–6   60–61
6   58 n. 77, 73 n. 119
7   67
7–11   65
12–13   61 n. 85
15   58 n. 77, 60, 73 n. 119
16   61 n. 85
18–19   68 n. 104
21–23   65
24   66–67, 72
25–28   65–66
28   60
31–38   68 n. 104
32   58
32–40   61
34   58 n. 77
35–38   72–74
37   60
40–46   61 n. 85
42–43   64 n. 91
45   64 n. 91
42–53   61 n. 86
46–50   64
50   58 n. 77
50–51   61 n. 85, 64 n. 91
54–55   67
57   58 n. 77, 64 n. 91
59   71, 73
62   73 n. 119
62–63   64–65
63   60
64–65   61 n. 85
64–66   66
67   58 n. 77, 60
68   66
71   61 n. 85
77–78   61 n. 85, 66
80   73 n. 119
85   58 n. 77
86   60, 73 n. 119
87–95   68 n. 104
88–89   61 n. 85
90   58
94   58
97–98   62, 67
98   61 n. 85

Callimachus
Aetia
fr. 1   183 n. 180
Epigrams
21   178
42   154 n. 100
44   156 n. 106
Hymn to Athena   115
Hymn to Zeus
8   14
14   42 n. 21
Hymn to Apollo
1–5   21–22, 23 n. 73
1–21   3–7, 9–11
4   3, 14, 20–24, 29–31
5   24
7   16 n. 47

206 — Index Locorum

8	16, 18
11	16
12–13	16 n. 47
13	15
16	15, 17–18
17	14, 16 n. 47, 18
25	10–11, 16 n. 47
25–7	14
28–31	8, 12
29	16 n. 47
30	16 n. 47, 18
31–36	53
32–35	22
34–35	30–31
47	11 n. 34
69–71	15
80	10–11, 15
97	18
97–105	11–13
102–3	10
113	15, 16 n. 47
Hymn to Artemis	111
fr. 227.1 Pf.	10 n. 33, 134–35

Catullus

4	ix–xv
11	46 n. 38
51	155–56
61	31
62	153 n. 97

Cicero
Brutus 75 — 130
De Divinatione
2.62.128–40 — 160 n. 121, 161 n. 125
Tusculan Disputations
4.7 — 130
4.8.17 — 174 n. 144

Ennius
Annales — 50 n. 55, 143 n. 62

Euripides
Iphigenia at Aulis
1211–15 — 116 n. 111

Hesiod
Theogony
894–96 — 114–15
Works and Days
659 — 42 n. 21

Homer
Homeric Hymn 3 to Apollo — 16–17, 135 n. 31
Homeric Hymn 4 to Hermes — 42 n. 21
Iliad

1.8	111
2.484–87	118 n. 114
12.243	51 n. 59
15.365	55 n. 69
18.56	119 n. 118
22.199–201	159 n. 118
23.454–55	184 n. 183

Horace
Sermones
2.1.57–60 — 145 n. 73
Epodes
9.5 — 150 n. 86
11.7–10 — 156 n. 106
Odes

1.1.29–34	142 n. 60
1.2	122, 123 n. 131, 167 n. 130
1.3.8	154 n. 100
1.3.34–35	175–76
1.6	142 n. 59, 172
1.7.8–9	171 n. 134
1.9	85–108, 117, 143
1.12	108–24
1.12.3–4	80
1.12.46–48	184
1.13	155–58
1.19	143, 148
1.20	78–84, 108, 111, 113, 117, 143
1.27	85 n. 22, 93 n. 52
1.30	143, 151–52
1.33	154 n. 99
1.34	149
1.36.10	185 n. 186
1.36.12	153 n. 97

1.37.1–4	153 n. 97	4.14.5–6	185 n. 186
2.1	142 n. 59	4.14.34–40	146–47
2.4.22–24	146, 149	4.14.43	123 n. 130
2.5.20–24	142 n. 61	4.15	125–31, 137–42, 150 n. 86
2.8	145 n. 71		
2.11	85 n. 22	4.15.13–14	176 n. 156
2.12	172–73	4.15.30	161 n. 126
2.14.22	85 n. 22, 86 n. 25	Carmen Saeculare	52 n. 62, 131–35, 146, 153 n. 97
2.17.5	154 n. 100		
2.20	178–79	Epistles	
3.3	142 n. 59	1.1.4	146
3.4	149	1.1.80	119 n. 119
3.4.25–28	142 n. 60	1.3.12–13	182
3.5.1–4	122–123	1.3.21	180
3.13	93 n. 52	1.7.25–28	149 n. 83
3.15.17	181 n. 173	1.14.33	149 n. 83
3.19	85 n. 22	1.19	180
3.25	142 n. 59, 149	1.19.12–16	176 n. 155
3.27.75–76	176 n. 156	1.20.26–28	146 n. 76
3.30.4–5	147–48	2.1.15	123 n. 130, 136
3.30.6–7	185 n. 188	2.1.132–38	135–37
4.1	125–26, 142–62, 177 n. 160	2.2.99	175 n. 146
4.2	125–26, 159 n. 116, 162, 168–86	**Hyginus** *Fabulae* 40	176 n. 152
4.2.33–52	164		
4.3	136 n. 36, 169	**Ibycus**	
4.4	136 n. 36	fr. 286 PMG	143 n. 64
4.4.39	185 n. 186		
4.4.70–72	176 n. 156	**Livy**	
4.5	125–26, 136 n. 36, 162–68, 185	*Ab Vrbe Condita* 1.6	51 n. 58
4.6	125–26, 131–32, 134	1.44	146 n. 75
4.6.30	176 n. 156, 177	3.24	146 n. 75
4.6.43	181–82	7.2.3–8	137 n. 38
4.7.13–16	136 n. 36, 167 n. 129		
4.8.18–19	176 n. 156	**Lucian**	
4.9.29	151 n. 89	*Syria Dea*	58 n. 74, 68 n. 107
4.9.46–47	176 n. 156		
4.10	160 n. 120	**Lucretius**	
4.11.13–20	147 n. 78	*De Rerum Natura*	
4.11.21–36	154 n. 99	1.1–61	139 n. 47
4.11.25–31	176 n. 151	3.3–13	173–74, 180
4.11.34	181–82	4.549–71	81 n. 14
4.13	93, 145 n. 71, 148–49, 154 n. 101	4.568–71	82 n. 16
		4.570–93	73 n. 118
4.14.1–6	136 n. 36	4.603–11	81 n. 14

Manilius
Astronomica
3.197 — 186 n. 190

Martial
10.38.9 — 146 n. 76
11.42 — 180 n. 168

Moschus
Idyll 2.84–88 — 184 n. 183
[Moschus]
Lament for Bion — 59 n. 80, 74

Ovid
Ars Amatoria
2.19–98 — 176 nn. 152, 157
Remedia Amoris
703–06 — 135 n. 29
Metamorphoses
8.183–235 — 176 nn. 152–53, 157
15.622 — 136 n. 33
15.875–79 — 185 n. 188
Fasti
1.609–10 — 51 n. 56
Tristia
1.1.89–90 — 176 n. 157
2.53–54 — 123 n. 130
3.4a.21–24 — 176 n. 157
4.10.77–78 — 146 n. 76
Ex Ponto
1.2.105 — 123 n. 130, 136 n. 33

Pindar
Nemean
3.10–12 — 112–13
Olympian 1
11 — 42 n. 21
82–84 — 177 n. 158
2.1–2 — 112–13
5.19 — 137 n. 38
9.47 — 42 n. 21
14.21–24 — 81
Pythian
10.53–54 — 179–80
fr. 146 — 115

Plato
Ion
534a–b — 181 n. 170
Phaedrus
258e–269c — 104 n. 91
Republic
398e — 137 n. 38

Pliny Minor
Epistles
7.30.5 — 174 n. 143

Plutarch
Alcibiades — 58 n. 74, 68 n. 107
Nicias — 58 n. 74, 68 n. 107

Propertius
2.10 — 49
2.21 — 49
2.31 — 53 n. 65
3.1 — 49
3.4 — 49
3.17 — 46 n. 37
4.1.1–2 — 47 n. 43
4.1.47 — 49
4.1.56–70 — 49
4.1.67 — 50
4.1.73–74 — 127 n. 5
4.2 — 45
4.4 — 45, 50 n. 52
4.6.1 — 48
4.6.1–14 — 37–44
4.6.10 — 113
4.6.11–14 — 48, 50
4.6.15 — 47 n. 42
4.6.15–18 — 45–47
4.6.17–18 — 56–57
4.6.19 — 48, 55–56
4.6.19–24 — 47–48
4.6.20–21 — 48
4.6.23 — 50 n. 54
4.6.27 — 47 n. 42
4.6.27–28 — 56
4.6.29 — 50 n. 54
4.6.31–36 — 53
4.6.38 — 50 n. 54
4.6.41–44 — 51

4.6.47–50	53 n. 63	*Idyll* 2	62 n. 88
4.6.56	50 n. 54	*Idyll* 15	58 n. 74, 62 n. 88, 68 n. 107
4.6.57–60	51–52		
4.6.59	50 n. 54	*Idyll* 18	62 n. 88
4.6.67–68	46 n. 36, 55–57		
4.6.69–76	53–55	**Tibullus**	
4.6.76	57 n. 73	1.3.59–64	153 n. 97
4.6.81	50 n. 54	2.1	31–32
4.6.85–86	42–44	2.5.1–4	127 n. 5
4.7	149 n. 84		
4.9	45, 50 n. 52	**Varro**	
4.10	45, 50 n. 52	*De Lingua Latina*	
		5.85	153 n. 96
Quintilian		6.58	186
Institutio Oratoria			
1.8.1	157 n. 114	**Vergil**	
1.10.31	129 n. 14	*Eclogues*	
6.2.32	120 n. 124	1.41	123 n. 130
10.1.61	159 n. 116, 171–72, 174–75	1.82–83	62 n. 88
		4.1	141
10.2.10–11	174	6.1–8	141
		6.4–5	183 n. 180
Sappho		6.82–86	81 n. 14
fr. 1	143–45, 148, 152, 161	6.84	81 n. 13
fr. 2	29–30, 150–51	6.85–86	62 n. 88
fr. 31	155–56	9.27–29	177 n. 159
fr. 140a	69	9.51–55	62 n. 88
		10.77	62 n. 88
Sophocles		*Georgics*	
Philoctetes 828	70	1.10	136 n. 33
		4.21	180 n. 167
Suetonius		4.523–27	58 n. 76
Vita Augusti	46 n. 36, 50–51	*Aeneid*	
Vita Horati	143 n. 62	4.74–89	160 n. 122
		6.30–33	178 n. 161
Theocritus		6.865–66	120
Idyll 1		10.185–93	158 n. 115
7–8	66 n. 96		
64–142	59–60	**[Vergil]**	
144–45	62 n. 88	*Ciris* 245	136 n. 33

www.ingramcontent.com/pod-product-compliance
Lightning Source LLC
Chambersburg PA
CBHW020230170426
43201CB00007B/377